Unlocking Speaking and Listening

Speaking and listening are key elements of the primary English National Curriculum; they are also fundamental to children's language development and learning. The need for teachers to develop children's talk in its own right and also to use talk as a means of learning is central to effective primary practice, yet it is an area in which teachers often have little confidence.

Now in a fully revised and updated edition, *Unlocking Speaking and Listening* aims to address a recognized need by tackling key issues surrounding speaking and listening with rigour, depth and a strong focus on research.

The contributors offer creative and practical advice on teaching speaking and listening from the early years through Key Stages 1 and 2. Areas covered are interrelated and include:

- Drama and storytelling
- Working with EAL children
- Gifted and talented pupils
- Special educational needs
- Using ICT.

With contributions from experts in the field, this book is a vital resource to help both trainee and practising primary teachers understand and promote the importance of speaking and listening as an effective tool for learning across the primary curriculum.

Deborah Jones is a Reader in Education and Course Leader for the Doctorate of Education at Brunel University.

Pamela Hodson is Principal Lecturer and Head of Primary English at Kingston University.

Unlocking Speaking and Listening

Second edition

Edited by Deborah Jones
and Pamela Hodson

LONDON AND NEW YORK

First published 2006
by David Fulton Publishers

This second edition published 2012
by Routledge
2 Park Square, Milton Park, Abingdon, Oxon OX14 4RN

Simultaneously published in the USA and Canada
by Routledge
711 Third Avenue, New York, NY 10017

Routledge is an imprint of the Taylor & Francis Group, an informa business

British Library Cataloguing in Publication Data
A catalogue record for this book is available from the British Library

Library of Congress Cataloging in Publication Data
Unlocking speaking and listening / edited by Deborah Jones and Pamela Hodson. — 2nd ed.
     p. cm.
Includes bibliographical references and index.
1. English language—Study and teaching (Elementary)—Great Britain.   2. English
language—Spoken English—Great Britain.   I. Jones, Deborah.   II. Hodson, Pam.
LB1576.U56 2012
372.6'044—dc22

                                                                              2011015280

ISBN: 978-0-415-60316-4 (hbk)
ISBN: 978-0-415-60317-1 (pbk)
ISBN: 978-0-203-80223-6 (ebk)

Typeset in Bembo
by RefineCatch Limited, Bungay, Suffolk

Contents

Illustrations

Notes on Contributors

Elizabeth Briten is a Senior Lecturer at Kingston University, where she is Subject Leader for Primary Science teaching across both BA and PGCE programmes. She has extensive experience of both primary teaching and lecturing within the Higher Education setting. Her research interests include the development of science knowledge for teaching.

Alastair K. Daniel is a Senior Lecturer and course leader for Literacy and Language in Education at London Metropolitan University. Alastair spent his years in the classroom as a specialist in Drama and Dance. Following nearly eight years of teaching in London and Kent, Alastair combined professional storytelling in schools with teaching in Higher Education where he developed a specialism in oracy and narrative in education. As a storyteller he has significant experience working with children from Foundation Stage to Key Stage 5, and in particular with students for whom English is an additional language. At Kingston University, Alastair taught undergraduate and post-graduate courses in English and Drama. He has also been involved in a range of CPD work and has been a visiting lecturer at universities in both England and Belgium.

Yota Dimitriadi is a lecturer in ICT at Reading University. She was formerly a Senior Lecturer at Kingston University and a research associate for the Special Educational Needs Joint Initiative for Training (SENJIT). Her past experience includes working as a secondary English teacher before moving to the British Dyslexia Association. Her research interests have focused on the use of technology for children with SEN and for whom English is an additional language.

Robert Fisher taught for more than 20 years in schools in the UK, Africa and Hong Kong and was head of a primary school in Richmond. He has published more than 30 books on education, including *Teaching Children to Think, Teaching Children to Learn, Teaching Thinking*, the *Stories for Thinking* series and *Creative Dialogue* (Routledge 2010). His books have been translated into 13 languages. He was awarded a PhD for research into philosophy for children, was Professor of Education at Brunel University and is a keynote speaker and consultant on teaching thinking, dialogic learning and creativity. He cultivates his own creativity through art, sculpture, poetry, music and tango, has a website at www.teachingthinking.net and blogs featuring his art and poetry.

Nicola Grove started her career as an English teacher, then became a speech and language therapist, specialising in augmentative and alternative communication. Her doctoral research was on the development of sign language in children with learning disabilities and her career has combined work in special schools and resource centres and university lecturing. She began using poetry and story in special schools in the 1980s, and worked with teachers to explore strategies for making literature accessible. The results contributed to a book, *Ways into Literature*, which won the NASEN/TES award in 1999. She began researching the use of oral storytelling with children and adults with learning disabilities in 2001, and in 2004 set up the first inclusive storytelling course, with funding from the National Lottery. Nicola now works as Director of Openstorytellers, the only professional group of storytellers with learning disabilities, and as a freelance trainer and consultant.

Pamela Hodson is a principal lecturer at Kingston University where she is subject leader for primary English. Formerly at Brunel University, she was also Head of the English department in a comprehensive school in Richmond upon Thames. She worked for three years as an advisory teacher on the LINC (Language in the National Curriculum) Project and is co-author, with Deborah Jones, of *Teaching Children to Write*. Her research interests focus on the development of student teachers' subject knowledge in language and literacy.

Sarah Jackson-Stevens is a Senior Lecturer in Primary Mathematics at Kingston University. Having taught in primary schools in Somerset, she returned to London in 2002 to work in Higher Education. Sarah's interests include promoting high quality talk in mathematics through effective guided group work; developing assessment methods in primary mathematics and exploring links between mathematics and music.

Colleen Johnson worked in theatre in education before going into secondary and then primary school teaching. She lectured in English and drama on ITT, PGCE and Master's level programmes in Primary and Secondary education at Brunel University and more recently, St Mary's University College. She continues to work as an education consultant, specialising in drama, voice production and lecturing skills.

Deborah Jones is a Reader in Education at Brunel University, where she leads the Doctor of Education Programme. Other teaching includes BA, MA and CPD in a range of institutions. She started her career as a primary teacher and has worked on the LINC project. Her research interests include literacy and gender in education. Recent publications include *Metacognitive Approaches to Developing Oracy* and *Men in the Lives of Young Children* (Routledge).

Ruth Lewis was a senior manager for the Hounslow Language Support Service. Her expertise in teaching children for whom English is an Additional Language, has been developed over many years and in different Local Authorities. She has produced several books and teaching materials and has also provided training in this area for teachers in the UK and abroad.

Geeta Ludhra is a lecturer at Brunel University where she teaches on the Primary PGCert. English and Professional Practice programmes. Her background is in primary teaching and she has taught in diverse settings in West London. She has worked as a leading literacy teacher and additional posts of responsibility have included deputy headship. Her research interests include supporting the language needs of bilingual learners and the importance of the heritage language in maintaining a sense of cultural identity. She is interested in the role of talk within the primary and secondary curriculum with a particular focus on critical reflection through talk and drama. She is currently studying for her doctorate, exploring the identities and voices of South-Asian adolescents in the UK secondary school context.

Yasmin Mukadam is a lecturer in early years education at Kingston University, teaching on Early Years Professional Status (EYPS) programmes. She is a qualified Early Years Practitioner who has developed and implemented training provision for the early years' workforce as a local authority training co-ordinator. Her research interests are the impact of higher education on practitioners' pedagogical practice and the role of mentoring as a support mechanism.

Paty Paliokosta is a Senior Lecturer in Inclusive Education and is involved in undergraduate and postgraduate programmes, including Master's, Doctorate and EYPS at Kingston University. She has worked for a number of years at inner city local authorities mainly as Inclusion Manager and LA Inclusion Adviser. Among other initiatives, she has been involved in the implementation and evaluation of speaking and listening approaches and interventions. She completed her PhD in Inclusive Education and her teaching and research interests include transition issues for vulnerable groups and multi-professionalism in integrated working.

Hilma Rask taught in London primary schools for a number of years, and also taught English as a Foreign Language to adults in both Finland and England. As an advisory teacher, she established and managed the work of a primary language support team in Richmond upon Thames. She spent nine years as a lecturer in Primary Education at Brunel University. Her special interests include international and comparative education, early years education and language and literacy. Hilma currently works as a freelance education consultant and researcher.

Lalitha Sivalingam is the Programme Leader for the EYPS pathway at Kingston University. She has Qualified Teacher Status from the Institute of Education in Singapore and was the owner/manager of her own nursery for 14 years. In addition, she has worked as an assessor and internal verifier for the Children's Workforce Development Council. Her research interests focus on the impact of higher education on practitioners' pedagogical practice and the role of professionals in raising the quality of early years' education and childcare.

Nicola Treby is a senior lecturer in science education at Kingston University, where she teaches cross-phase on both the primary BA and secondary PGCE courses. Prior to teaching at Kingston University, Nicola was an advanced skills teacher in Surrey. Her interests and experiences in school were varied, but focused mainly on improving teaching and learning in science education.

Mary Williams taught for 20 years as a primary school teacher, the last nine as headteacher of a nursery/infant school. She was subject leader for primary English at Brunel University where she taught on a range of undergraduate and postgraduate courses. She is co-editor of *Unlocking Literacy* and *Unlocking Creativity* with Bob Fisher and is editor of *Unlocking Writing* (David Fulton Publishers).

Acknowledgements

We would particularly like to thank the following children whose talk has provided the inspiration for producing this book: Evan, Cerys and Dylan Jones, Priti Patel, Andrew Turner, James Fox, Gemma Payne, Harriet and James Taylor, Robina Bibi, Joshua Nagle, Daniel Rosenberg, Jack Barney and Sophie and James Cobley.

We would also like to thank the students of Brunel and Kingston University who have worked with us as co-researchers and provided fresh insights into developing speaking and listening in the classroom context. We are also indebted to the support given by Joanna Newman in presenting the manuscript.

Introduction

Deborah Jones and Pamela Hodson

In the five years since the publication of the first edition of this book, the primary curriculum in the UK has undergone extensive review. The content of what constitutes the 'English' curriculum has remained at the forefront of debate and controversy and, tantalisingly, the key role of speaking and listening has re-emerged only to be succeeded by a political focus on the teaching of early reading and phonics in particular. The National Strategies are no longer in existence and it is against a background of some uncertainty about the content of the future primary curriculum that this book has been written. This second edition of the book, therefore, seeks to reaffirm the central role that talk plays in children's learning and celebrate the enormous potential that a focus on speaking and listening presents to teachers for innovative and creative teaching.

Although the title of the book adheres to the phrase 'speaking and listening', the term that has been in common usage since the advent of the first National Curriculum in 1990, the book aims to embrace a much wider view of children's spoken language development by exploring features of communication which involve every aspect of ourselves and our identities. Readers will note that throughout the book the term 'oracy' is also used, which unites the skills of speaking and listening, and acknowledges their interrelatedness. The book assumes a view that children possess a great deal of implicit knowledge about language and so it is crucial that teachers start from an understanding of what children already know and can achieve in spoken language.

Based on a sociolinguistic perspective (Halliday 1978), the book adopts a view that engaging in spoken language involves a series of choices in relation to the purpose, the context and the audience for the talk. In this way, children should be engaged in activities which allow them to explore a range and variety of spoken modes of language and to discuss the appropriate choice of language in different contexts. The book also explores the key role that talk plays in children's learning and the central role of the teacher in supporting children's spoken language development based on a sociocultural perspective (Vygotsky 1978).

It is evident that many teachers, though convinced of the value of Speaking and Listening, still remain insecure about how to use talk effectively within the teaching and learning process. The structure of this book aims to present teachers with a rationale for talk, together with appropriate strategies for engaging children in a range of subject areas, also reflecting the varying needs of different groups of children. The experience of working on the LINC project (Language in the Curriculum, 1989–1992) convinced the editors that teachers' practice can only be enhanced when underpinned by sound subject knowledge and a rigorous theoretical base. This book therefore, aims to provide practical strategies for planning, teaching and assessing Speaking and Listening. Throughout, this is supported by theory and research which will enhance teachers' subject knowledge.

Overview of the book

In Chapter 1, Pamela Hodson explores the current educational context for developing children's spoken language and discusses recent research and initiatives which have placed a strong emphasis on the role that talk plays in learning. She adopts the view that talk is essentially a social act requiring children to make choices about the language that they use. The chapter addresses aspects of the knowledge about language that teachers need in order to support children's progress in this key area. Themes which resonate throughout the book are identified in this chapter: the need to promote a positive ethos where speaking and listening is embraced and celebrated in a whole school context; the central role of the teacher in modelling spoken language and the need to plan explicitly for using talk in the classroom.

Chapter 2 highlights the need for embedding the planning, teaching and assessment of Speaking and Listening into the everyday routines of the primary classroom. Deborah Jones demonstrates an awareness of the complexity of assessing Speaking and Listening and acknowledges that teachers find this a challenging area. The chapter therefore presents practical strategies for promoting children's development and shows how evidence of progression in Speaking and Listening can be harnessed and recorded. This is particularly important in the current context where the overriding political discourse focuses on underachievement in children. The chapter identifies that teachers' judgements need to be based on sound observational evidence of children's speaking and listening in a range of contexts.

Chapter 3 focuses on Speaking and Listening in the Foundation Stage of education. Hilma Rask and Paty Paliokosta emphasise the critical role of the teacher as both active listener and an expert companion in dialogue with children. They draw on observations from classroom experience to highlight how purposeful Speaking and Listening can support children's learning in an early years setting. They argue that teachers and practitioners gain insights into children's learning when they reflect upon what babies, toddlers and young children actually say and do during their play activities. Finally, they emphasise that in the light of such reflection, appropriate action should be taken to further enrich language learning provision for young children.

Alastair K. Daniel explores the essential role of the teacher as a principal classroom storyteller. In Chapter 4, he sets out to show that by experiencing imaginative storytelling, children are not only inspired to become creative and confident storytellers in their own right, but can also become active and comprehending listeners. This chapter is concerned with identifying the essential elements of effective storytelling and how to develop teachers' confidence and skills across the curriculum.

In Chapter 5, Colleen Johnson discusses how drama can create a myriad of contexts in which children are able to experience diversity in spoken language. Such experiences, she argues, can help develop children's skills in speaking and active listening, through paired, group and whole class work. The range of talk generated in drama is extensive and may encompass speaking *as* a character or planning *for* a scene, dialogue *in* performance or *responding to* performance, whole class discussions both *in* role and *out of* role. Such experiences, aided by effective teacher questioning, can stimulate children's critical reflection upon the ways in which talk enhances their learning. She identifies the fact that teachers may feel they lack confidence in this area and therefore her chapter provides practical strategies for the non-specialist which can be incorporated within lessons such as literacy and personal, social, and moral education.

Chapter 6 considers the key role of Speaking and Listening as it relates to gifted and talented children. Drawing on findings from a DfES-funded project, 'Nurturing Young Talent', Mary Williams identifies how higher-ability pupils need to be motivated through challenging activities that promote deep levels of thinking. She emphasises the inter-relationship of speaking, listening, reading and writing to show how children's potential in oracy can be utilised to the full. Practical ways of challenging and stimulating higher-ability pupils are suggested.

Robert Fisher advocates an approach called Philosophy for Children which emphasises the development of children's critical thinking through questioning and dialogue in the classroom context. In Chapter 7, therefore, he focuses on a special form of 'talking to think' which not only helps children's communication skills but also develops habits of intelligent behaviour. The chapter shows how philosophical discussion with children can be used to develop intelligence, together with dialogic and thinking skills. It describes practical ways to create a community of enquiry in the classroom and shows how philosophical discussion not only benefits speaking and listening and thinking skills but also provides a powerful model for social and democratic values. Finally, it draws upon research which shows that the positive effects of philosophical discussion can extend across the curriculum.

Chapter 8 outlines principles and strategies to support bilingual language development. In so doing, it raises important questions about the complexities of bilingualism as being more than just an understanding of two languages. Bilingualism is seen as an important achievement that needs to be recognised and nurtured by society, schools and teachers. The chapter encourages the reader to look at bilingual talk within the broader contexts of power, culture and identity. Geeta Ludhra draws on her deputy headship work as part of the National EAL Pilot Project (2004–2006) and Ruth Lewis draws on her experiences of working in the Hounslow Language Service.

In Chapter 9, Nicola Grove considers the challenges facing teachers in supporting SEN children in Speaking and Listening. Adopting an interactionist perspective, she addresses these issues within the wider concept of communication and presents practical strategies for inclusive practice in mainstream classrooms. Using a case study approach, she illustrates a range of special educational needs and advocates a pedagogical approach which supports all children and recognises the interaction between context, communication and the learner. Practical examples are provided of how individual children's performance may be affected by underlying difficulties, learning and conversational demands, and also the environment.

Chapter 10 explores the use of talk for learning in science and mathematics. A variety of areas are discussed, including the notion of exploratory talk and its role in developing children's scientific and mathematical knowledge and understanding. The role of the teacher in planning for talk is also considered, including incorporating ways of eliciting children's prior knowledge through constructive dialogue. Additionally, this chapter suggests some of the strategies and approaches that can be used, such as guided group work, as well as the choice and management of resources in stimulating high quality talk in science and mathematics. These key areas are illuminated by references to case studies, based on classroom-based enquiry and the experience of teachers working towards qualified teacher status.

The role and potential of technology in supporting children's Speaking and Listening development are discussed in the final chapter. Dimitriadi, Hodson and Ludhra draw upon a range of case studies where technology (from the use of the humble tape recorder to technologies such as digital video, voice-activated software and programmable toys) is used to extend children's exploratory talk. The book therefore, concludes with a focus on the new technologies and points the way forward for future contexts for developing children's speaking and listening.

Bibliography

Halliday, M.A.K. (1978) *Language and Social Semiotic: The Social Interpretation of Language and Meaning*, Oxford: Heinemann Educational.

Vygotsky, L.S. (1978) *Mind in Society: The Development of Higher Psychological Processes*. Cambridge, MA: Harvard University Press.

1

Listening to Children's Voices: Unlocking Speaking and Listening in the Primary Classroom

Pamela Hodson

> Talking in school is very important – you need to be able to ask questions, get along with your friends and talk about your feelings. We also talk when we're doing investigations in science, such as discussing which melts the fastest – ice or chocolate. And the best thing is – we get to eat the chocolate!
>
> (Gemma, aged 9)

This quotation demonstrates how children can readily identify some of the different kinds of talk that occur in the classroom, whether for social purposes and the establishment of relationships or for learning and communication. In Gemma's school, the development of children's spoken language is considered key to underpinning their learning in all areas of the curriculum and is valued by teachers and children alike. This reflects the emphasis embedded in the first English National Curriculum (DES 1990) where the inclusion of speaking and listening as a separate profile component demonstrated a conviction that children's speaking and listening skills were central to their overall language development. It is evident that children are empowered by having a voice in the classroom but initiatives such as the Literacy and Numeracy strategies have not always fostered this approach and have had an impact on classroom practice. Indeed, Robin Alexander (2005) has gone as far to suggest that these strategies have actually promoted low level classroom interactions which are cognitively unchallenging.[1] Recently, there has been a re-emergence of interest in the role of talk in the primary context from both political and educational spheres. With the demise of the Literacy and Numeracy strategies and their focus on a narrow view of literacy (reading and writing), it would seem appropriate to reappraise the potential that using and developing children's talk presents in the primary context.

This chapter will aim to explore the current educational context for developing children's spoken language and will discuss recent research and initiatives which have placed a strong emphasis on the role that talk plays in learning and the key role of the teacher. It will adopt a view that talk is essentially a social act that occurs in a range of contexts which require children to make choices about the language that they use according to the purpose of their talk and who they are talking to. It will also discuss aspects of the knowledge about language that teachers need in order to support children's progress in this key area. The teaching of speaking and listening has always been a richly controversial and much debated field and it also brings to the fore complex and challenging issues, not least in reappraising how children learn in the classroom. The latter part of this chapter will, therefore, consider some of the practical strategies that can be employed to promote effective talk.

Current context

The primary curriculum has, as a whole, been the subject of extensive review and scrutiny in recent times and while the teaching of early reading has been at the forefront in both the political and public domain, the importance of developing children's spoken language has received significant attention. However, the view of the child embedded in recent government reports is not a positive one. The Bercow Report (DfES 2008) and the Independent Review of the Primary Curriculum (DCFS 2009) focus on children's underachievement in their spoken language, using emotive phrases such as 'word poverty' to describe the language of children from 'unfavourable background conditions' (ibid.: 3.10). This contrasts strongly with the discourse of the first English National Curriculum (Cox 1989) in which children's capacity in language and implicit knowledge were to be celebrated and developed in a range of contexts. A recent Ofsted Report (DfE 2011) high-lights the importance of an emphasis on speaking and listening from an early age which appears to be inexorably linked to the teaching of reading, writing and spelling through systematic [synthetic] phonics. Fundamentally, there appears to be a view of children's talk as the servant to literacy development. It does have to be acknowledged that there is an increasing body of research which demonstrates that children do not enter into mainstream schooling from an even playing field and that the quality of the language experienced at home does have an impact on their future academic attainment. Hart and Risley's research in America (2003) indicated that children from higher-income homes will be exposed to 45 million words compared to only 13 million words for a child from a low-income family. It also showed that low-income children were less likely to engage in extended conversations.

In this context, it is perhaps useful to consider Gordon Wells' reflections on what children know about language from a very early age:

In abstract, these rules state that a yes/no interrogative sentence can be formed from its associated declarative sentence by taking the first auxiliary verb group in the main clause and permuting it with the subject noun phrase of the same main clause . . . and then permuting it as before. This is apparently what every young child who can ask a question knows!

(Wells 2009: xvii)[2]

This highlights the fact that all children have a great deal of implicit knowledge about language and underlines the need for teachers to carry out rigorous observations of a child's spoken language in a range of contexts in order to be able to assess what a child can do. It also presents a strong rationale for the foregrounding of speaking and listening and for teachers to use and exploit the potential of talk in primary classrooms.

In parallel with the government's report on primary education, an independent review (the Cambridge Review 2009)[3] was carried out by Robin Alexander *et al.* which critiqued government policy and the narrow view of language presented in the term 'speaking and listening' and highlighted the significance of the term 'oracy' coined by Wilkinson[4] (MacLure *et al.* 1988) in the 1960s which united the skills of speaking and listening. The Cambridge Review also focused on the fundamental role that language plays in learning and the key role that the teacher plays, advocating an approach called dialogic teaching. This approach is discussed later in the chapter and underpins the chapter on talk in science and mathematics.

Recent research and initiatives

Background

National initiatives for the development of speaking and listening are not new. In 1987, the National Oracy Project was established to enhance the role of speaking and listening in the learning process by improving children's performance across the curriculum and encouraging active learning. The late 1980s and early 1990s proved to be an extremely rich era in teaching where the profile of speaking and listening was high and debate was fierce. In addition to the National Oracy Project, the LINC Project (Language in the National Curriculum, 1989–1992) was designed to support teachers' knowledge and understanding of language in order to implement the effective introduction of the National Curriculum. Unlike the National Literacy Strategy, the LINC project did not set out to give teachers guidance on how to teach, but rather sought to enhance teachers' knowledge about language in its widest sense to enable them to implement the recommendations of the English National Curriculum (DES 1990). The project proved to be highly controversial with government and politicians, but successful with many teachers.

Influences from both of these projects can be seen in guidance which appeared on speaking and listening in 2003. This was developed as a result of a partnership between the QCA and the National Literacy Strategy in response to a perceived need to support teachers and to raise the profile of speaking and listening in the primary classroom (DfES 2003b). As the guidance highlights, its aim was to complement the Strategy's objectives for reading and writing and reflect the

National Curriculum programmes of study for speaking and listening both in English and across the curriculum (QCA 2003). This guidance on speaking and listening needs to be set in the context of *Excellence and Enjoyment: A Strategy for Primary Schools* (DfEE 2003a) which appeared in the same year and advocated a more flexible approach to teaching literacy. It suggested that schools should be adapting the Strategy to meet their own particular needs, highlighting the non-statutory nature of both the Literacy and Numeracy Strategies.[5] In essence, there appeared to be a clear mandate for schools to take ownership of the teaching of the curriculum and adapt it in a more creative fashion.

However, schools' and teachers' responses to implementing the guidance could best be described as tentative and the materials did not receive the same attention as those which had focused on the teaching of reading and writing. This was followed by the Rose Report (DfES 2006) and although it primarily focused on the teaching of early reading, it did emphasise the need to develop children's speaking and listening skills from the early years. Along with reading and writing, the report recognised that speaking and listening are central to children's intellectual, social and emotional development. The gradual re-emergence of the importance of talk was confirmed in the National Strategy's reworked guidance (PNS Framework for Literacy 2006) which mirrored more closely the National Curriculum (1999) and identified 12 inter-related strands for teaching literacy, with speaking, listening, group discussion and interaction at the fore. In the same year, Ofsted's (2006) survey of speaking and listening in schools recognised that in order to improve provision for speaking and listening, teachers' understanding of the nature of talk needed to be enhanced; the use of drama techniques should be extended and speaking and listening (including standard English) should be taught directly. It also identified that assessment should be improved; an area which teachers, because of the transitory nature of talk, have always found challenging.

Current initiatives

Much of the recent research into speaking and listening (Alexander 2004; Mercer and Littleton 2007) has explored the role that talk plays in children's learning and is based on Vygotsky's (1978) concept of the zone of proximal development and the notion that the gap that exists between children's knowledge and their ability to solve problems independently can be reached with the support of a more capable peer. This is also linked to Bruner's (1978) theory of scaffolding and the key role that the adult plays in supporting a child's thought and language development. Underpinning Alexander's (2004) 'Talk for Learning' Project is a focus on the need to exploit the potential of talk to improve teaching and learning in the classroom. The work of Mercer *et al.* (2007) at Cambridge University in the 'Thinking Together' Project[6] encourages teachers to use a dialogue-based approach to thinking and learning and explores the use of talk in a variety of subject areas including Maths, ICT and Science. In Scotland, the HMIE Project 'Talking for Scotland' (HMIE 2005) has produced professional development materials to enhance teachers' understanding of the nature of talking and listening. The National Strategy's (n.d.)

initiative 'Every Child a Talker' again focuses on the need to help practitioners and parents to provide a supportive and stimulating environment to encourage children's spoken language in the early years of their development. It is evident that much recent research, therefore, plays a strong emphasis on teachers' knowledge and understanding of the nature of language and the key role they play in the classroom. In the following, aspects of what that understanding might entail are addressed with some suggestions for practice in the classroom.

The teacher's role

Barnes identifies the crucial role that teachers play in managing the social relations in the classroom (Barnes 2009, in Mercer and Hodgkinson 2009). For many teachers, this management of the social relations may seem to be undermined when they give some of the control to children. However, there are clear implications for the crucial role that a teacher plays in building a bridge between the child's current knowledge and helping them towards progressively more advanced levels of competence (Vygotsky 1978). This makes significant demands on the teacher's knowledge and understanding of each individual child's competence in speaking and listening and highlights the need for effective assessment and rigorous planning in order to provide the child with appropriate scaffolding. As the expert role model for spoken language, teachers also need to present an appropriate model for spoken standard English in the classroom and to present opportunities for children to use and explore appropriate contexts for using standard English. This is an integral part of the National Curriculum (2000) programmes of study for speaking and listening and the objectives for speaking and listening.

Standard English

The view adopted by the Working Group for National Curriculum English (1989) that standard English is a social dialect associated with particular uses especially in areas of power, proved to be highly unpopular among people who wanted it to be viewed as the 'correct' way to talk. The Group stated that standard English was not inherently superior to all other forms of English and highlighted research which demonstrated that all other dialects were rule-governed and systematic, not deviant forms of standard English. For teachers, it is vital to respect the child's home dialect but it is certainly true to say, that not having the ability to use standard English will exclude adults from areas of power, such as government, law, education, commerce and the media. For children, they need to be made aware that standard English can be spoken with any accent (regional newsreaders provide ready-made evidence of this) and that its use is not confined to speakers who may use an accent such as 'Received pronunciation' or BBC English as it is sometimes known.

The explicit study of standard English provides a rich resource for language study in the classroom and is most effective when explored in context. Many children, from an early age, demonstrate the ability to change their language according to whom they are with and why they are speaking. Observations of children's self-corrections in whole class teaching demonstrate this.

He didn't do anything!

A Year 4 class was discussing the actions of the characters in the story they were reading. Anna responded to her teacher's question by stating emphatically, 'He didn't do nothing wrong'. After a moment's pause, she re-stated carefully, 'He didn't do *anything* wrong', with a deliberate emphasis on the 'anything' to underscore her knowledge. In this context, the teacher had allowed time for Anna's self-correction before intervening or re-modelling her response, providing the opportunity for the child to demonstrate her growing proficiency in using language appropriately in a given context. This knowledge can be exploited and developed further through role-play, formal debates and presentations in the classroom where the appropriate use of standard English can provide both the focus for use and reflection on language usage.

As standard English is the form of language most commonly used in writing, the need to develop children's competence in this area is unquestionable. However, in standard English, there are differences of style, particularly in the continuum between formal and informal language and differences between standard English spoken in different parts of the wider-speaking English world. Most children, used to exposure of films and TV series from America and Australia, can readily identify different word usages; the BBC website http://www.bbc.co.uk/voices provides an extensive resource of regional accents and dialects.

Types of talk in the classroom

Teachers also need to reflect on the kind of speaking and listening that they promote in the classroom. It is evident that there is a significant difference between spoken discourse in the classroom and that in the community outside the school walls. Two main kinds of talk which occur in classroom contexts can be identified (Barnes 2009, in Mercer and Hodgkinson 2009): presentational talk, which typifies much of the talk that children are required to do, and exploratory talk. In essence, a lot of classroom practice is typified by the IRF (Initiation, Response, Feedback) or IRE (Initiation, Response, Evaluation) sequence where the teacher initiates talk with a question, children respond, and through the teacher's feedback, the teacher controls the language and meaning and signals what is to be viewed as relevant knowledge within the classroom. This kind of sequence is characteristic of many of the teacher–pupil interchanges which take place during whole class teaching in the Literacy Hour, both in shared reading or writing and the plenary. Research into classroom interactions by Alexander (Carter 2003) highlights the fact that the exchanges between teachers and children tend to be brief rather than sustained; closed questions predominate and children are very much focused on giving the right answer. There is little speculative talk and the 'child's answer marks the end of an exchange and the teacher's feedback formally closes it'. He recommends a move towards dialogic teaching and identifies four conditions which underpin this approach to teaching.

- *collective*: pupils and teachers address learning tasks together, whether as a group or as a class, rather than in isolation;

- *reciprocal*: pupils and teachers listen to each other, share ideas and consider alternative viewpoints;

- *cumulative*: pupils and teachers build on their own and each other's ideas and chain them into coherent lines of thinking and enquiry;

- *supportive*: pupils articulate their ideas freely, without fear of embarrassment over 'wrong' answers, and they help each other to reach common understandings.

In contrast, the community outside the classroom presents a rich and varied picture of language use, evolving language styles and of different communication practices. For many children whose mother tongue is not English, they are extremely adept at switching between two or more languages, depending who they are with. Although it is not always possible to replicate these practices in the classroom, teachers also need to take account of the children's linguistic repertoires outside of the school and find ways to celebrate it in the classroom.

Whole-school approach to speaking and listening

It would be true to say that no teacher can operate in isolation, no matter how deep their conviction of the central role of talk in children's learning. If this approach is not reflected and supported by the whole school in which they have to operate, then it will be very difficult. For teachers, the research and recent initiatives present considerable challenges, not least in generating a change in a classroom ethos which, since the inception of the Literacy Strategy, has focused largely on teacher-led and teacher-controlled discussion and in promoting a whole-school ethos where speaking and listening is valued. In addition, speaking and listening is an extremely complex and controversial topic. Many teachers face pressure from parents and the media to promote a more traditional view of learning, where a quiet classroom is perceived as the most effective for successful teaching and learning.

However, in Iver Village School in Buckinghamshire, the role of speaking and listening in children's learning is crucial to their whole-school approach to talk. Stemming from a conviction that children's oral development is critical for their social, literacy and cognitive growth, speaking and listening had already been identified as key to raising standards in all areas of the curriculum. The whole school were involved in a process of reviewing the curriculum and the following areas were addressed:

- identifying opportunities for speaking and listening in each unit of work;

- using staff meetings and outside agencies to inform teachers' understanding of speaking and listening;

- introducing speaking and listening first into literacy lessons and then into all subjects.

Key to the success of the work at the school was a process of review, innovation and evaluation which involved all of the staff. In order to embed speaking and listening, the staff focused on adopting strategies such as using the interactive whiteboard to support 'oral starters' at the beginning of a literacy lesson, where teachers used sentences such as 'Tell me why . . .' to promote detailed responses from the children. Oral storytelling, performance poetry and formal presentations were integrated into the schemes of work. In order to support the development of children's critical engagement and discursive skills around concepts, the teachers devised a series of questions related to particular subject areas which would then become an intrinsic part of the topics (Table 1.1). The work undertaken at this school underlines the complexity of the teaching of speaking and listening and highlights the importance of the role of the teacher.

TABLE 1.1 Questions to embed critical engagement and discussion

LITERACY	NUMERACY	HISTORY
Topic: Spoken and Written Language	**Topic: Subtraction**	**Topic: The Tudors**
▪ There is no difference between spoken and written language ▪ Punctuation can replace pauses and gestures ▪ You have to use whole sentences when you speak, but not when you write ▪ Punctuation can replace pauses and gestures ▪ You can't write down everything you say	▪ You can 'count on' to subtract ▪ Subtracting two odd numbers always makes an even number ▪ Another way to subtract is to say, 'Find the quotient.' ▪ Knowing my number bonds to ten helps me subtract.	▪ Tudor people didn't know anything about the rest of the world ▪ Henry VIII wasn't interested in religion ▪ Henry VIII was allowed to have six wives because he was king ▪ What plates were made of tells us if they belonged to rich or poor people
Topic: Vocabulary Extension	**Topic: Multiplication**	**Topic: Invaders and Settlers**
▪ Technical words are nothing to do with non-fiction writing ▪ If I write 'He's gone round the bend,' I don't mean that he's gone out of sight ▪ Some words only have one opposite, while others have more than one ▪ Onomatopoeia means words which echo sounds	▪ If I want to multiply by 6, I can multiply by 3, then double ▪ For some calculations, I halve the smaller number and double the other ▪ Quotient is the opposite of product ▪ To make a number square, multiply it by itself	▪ Invaders only came to Britain by invitation ▪ What happened is more important than when it happened ▪ Nothing is left from the Roman, Viking or Anglo-Saxon invasions

Source: Devised by Chris Smith and Jane Balgobin, Iver Village Junior School. www.speakingthoughts.co.uk

A climate for talk – raising the profile of speaking and listening

A whole-school approach which values talk needs to be mirrored in a classroom ethos where positive achievements in speaking and listening are valued and celebrated. The transitory and ephemeral nature of speech makes this difficult, but teachers can raise the profile of speaking and listening by making it the end product of an extended scheme of work (a debate which identifies arguments for and against a key question) or a role – play which demonstrates children's understanding of a text they are reading. Talk can also form the basis for discussion and analysis:

- Who do you feel most comfortable speaking and listening with?
- When do you feel most comfortable speaking and listening?
- Where do you feel most comfortable speaking and listening?
- What do you like discussing?
- Why?

Talk diaries can raise the profile of speaking and listening for children. The first two hours of Rosie's (aged 11) diary, looked like this (Table 1.2).

TABLE 1.2 Talk diary

WHO	WHEN	WHERE	TYPES OF LANGUAGE
Brother	Before school	At home	Questions – asking where clothes are Responding to questions, 'Yes, I've done my homework'
Friend/Mum	On the way to school	Mobile phone in the car	Asking friend to bring computer game to school Listening to mum Arguing with brother
Friends	Before school	Playground	Discussing Arguing Negotiating – how long can I have the game for? Organising – to meet at break-time
Teacher	Beginning of school	Classroom	Answering my name

A talk diary such as this also recognises children's speaking and listening outside of the classroom/ school context and presents opportunities to discuss and contextualise language in its social context. Children, with the support of the teacher, can then begin to identify and discuss the kind of language they are using.

Whole-class teaching

Whole-class teaching provides the teacher with opportunities to model standard English in appropriate contexts and also to demonstrate the tentative and speculative nature of talk. Teachers' questions also play a key role in scaffolding children's learning, particularly in making progressively greater cognitive demands of the children through the use of higher order questions. When time is given for thought, reflection and support from talk partners, this context also provides a ready audience for children to give structured and extended contributions and to listen to and respond to the contributions made by other children in the classroom. Children's oral responses, moreover, provide opportunities for a teacher to assess a child's understanding and learning in a medium other than writing.

Group work

Children are used to sitting in groups as part of the organisational structure of the Literacy Hour and although teachers may no longer use this structure in its original form, many aspects such as group activities and plenaries still prevail. However, observational evidence shows that in general, children are working as individuals in those groups and are not engaged in genuine collaboration on tasks which require exploratory talk. Teachers also need to consider carefully how they organise children for speaking and listening activities. Placing children in mixed ability groups can provide children with opportunities to interact with children who may be more linguistically competent. Gender is also another significant consideration and, depending on the nature of the task, it may be appropriate to organise children in single sex groups. Children should also be given the opportunity for some autonomy on how groups are organised; this in itself can provide an interesting area for debate!

The plenary

The plenary offers time for opportunities for children's extended speaking and reflective listening. It also provides the teacher with the opportunity to assess children's understanding of texts through talk, as an alternative mode of assessment to writing. Children are often able to make positive, supportive comments about each other's work, but find it more difficult to be critical. By scaffolding their critical responses with language which articulates a speculative, considered approach, teachers can empower children to offer supportive criticism without being unduly challenging to their peers. This scaffolding can take the form of prompt sentences which support children's responses:

- I think what we have learned from this investigation is . . .
- We think that we still need to consider . . .
- I think there are good reasons for believing . . .[7]

Good speakers and listeners

Children as young as six can provide thoughtful responses, demonstrating that they do in fact have a great deal of implicit understanding of the nature of talk and the role of the critical friend. The focus for this discussion was based on art:

'So what do you think makes a good speaker?'

'My friend Aysha is a good speaker. When we're painting, she helps me. She says, "Why don't you use this colour here?" or "That bit's really good." It's nice to be told your work's good.'

Children should also be part of the process for valuing speaking and listening in the classroom: discussions of what makes a good speaker and a good listener can provide the basis for establishing shared and agreed ground rules for effective speaking and listening that can then be displayed on the classroom wall. This also serves to enhance and make explicit the place of speaking and listening in the classroom.

Different audiences

Providing different audiences is also a valuable way of raising the profile of speaking and listening – inviting other classes, teachers and parents to observe children engaged in a purposeful activity can fulfil a variety of functions, not least, demonstrating that talk is a valued part of classroom practice. Both the media and internet resources offer the opportunity to extend children's encounters with different speakers beyond the classroom. If children's reading of literature were confined to texts written by the class teacher or their peers, 'their knowledge of language would be unnecessarily limited' (Hewitt 2003); the same must also be true of providing a limited number of role models for speaking and listening. Therefore, in providing both audiences and appropriate role models for spoken language, teachers need to exploit opportunities beyond the classroom.

Integrating speaking and listening, reading and writing

At Key Stage 3, a document entitled 'Introducing the Grammar of Talk' (QCA 2004) discusses and identifies what kind of shared language can be used to describe talk itself. While this may not be wholly appropriate to children in primary schools, it is important that children are made aware of the differences between speech and writing and that speech is not simply a substandard form of writing. In this document, Carter (ibid.)[1] discusses the need for teachers to be sensitive to the fact that talk is a different mode of language which requires a different grammar to describe how it is used. The discussion questions on spoken and written language formulated by teachers at Iver School already identified can form the basis for this kind of investigation.

The National Curriculum (English 2000) stresses the interrelatedness of the four modes of language: speaking, listening reading and writing. Research into effective practice in writing (Frater 2002) also demonstrates that children make successful progress in their writing development when opportunities for speaking and listening are an integral part of work on reading and writing. Drama activities can create the context for exploring literature by encouraging the expression of hypothesis and opinion (see Johnson's Chapter 5 in this volume on drama). In addition, children can be actively involved in making meaning from literary texts through the appropriate and selective use of DARTs (Directed Activities Related to Texts) activities (Lunzer and Gardner 1979). These activities are not new; they were developed in the 1970s in response to research into reading which showed that children did a great deal of copying from texts, rather than actually gleaning information from their reading.

The directed activities related to text are:

- Cloze – omitting key words in a text.
- Sequencing – providing opportunities for children to restructure texts.
- Prediction.

Teachers frequently make use of the latter strategy by stopping reading at a critical point in a narrative and asking children to predict or hypothesise what could happen next. Sequencing activities can work equally well with fiction and non-fiction texts, requiring children to read and re-read parts of text in order to make meaning from the whole. Cloze activities provide interactive learning experiences where children can discuss, negotiate, speculate and justify word choices. In all DARTs activities, it is important to reassure children that they are not seeking the 'right' answer – but are searching for an appropriate answer. This close reading and discussion of texts can scaffold children's understanding when responding in the written form.

Some final reflections

This chapter began by highlighting the fact that children know a great deal implicitly about talk and explores some of the ways in which teachers can seek to extend and develop this key area of language. In a recently observed lesson where Year 5 children were exploring the richness of different accents and dialects, one child observed, 'You know the more you think about language, you realise it's a bit like a code – you need to know what to say and when and how you say it. And it's fun to try to crack it!' It is evident that children can be enthused and excited about talk. Both government policy and recent research and initiatives (Alexander 2004; Mercer and Littleton 2007) have recognised the crucial role that talk plays in children's learning and have highlighted the need for schools and teachers to evaluate their own practice. In addition, they should place, as Wilkinson suggests, speaking and listening at the heart of the primary curriculum – not just in literacy teaching but in all subjects.

Notes

1 Robin Alexander, writing in the *Education Weekly* of the *Guardian* on 19 April 2005. Available at: www.education.guardian.co.uk/egweekly/story/0..1462428.00.html.
2 See Wells (2009). This study follows the language and literacy development of a sample of children from their first words to the end of primary school. In this quotation, Wells reflects on the work of Chomsky and his theory that children's understanding of the syntax of language was not taught, but 'were latent in the structure of the mind' (ibid: xviii).
3 See http://www.primaryreview.org.uk.

4 The National Oracy Project was highly influential in informing the recommendations for the Speaking and Listening requirements of the English National Curriculum.

5 Excellence and Enjoyment (DfES 2003a) was intended to give more autonomy back to schools so that schools themselves decide which aspects of a subject that pupils will study in depth, how long to spend on each subject and how to arrange learning in the school day. It also identifies that one of the key ways to support literacy and numeracy is by reaffirming the place of speaking and listening both as a key foundation for literacy and also an essential aspect of all effective learning.

6 See Thinking Together Project, available at: http://www.thinkingtogether.educ.cam.ac.uk.

7 See Robert Fisher's Chapter 7 in this book, 'Talking to Think: Why Children Need Philosophical Discussion'.

Bibliography

Alexander, R.J. (2005) *Talk for Learning: The Second Year*, Northallerton: North Yorkshire County Council.

Alexander, R.J. et al. (2009) *Children, their World, their Education: Final Report and Recommendations of the Cambridge Primary Review*, Abingdon: Routledge.

Carter, R. (2003) *New Perspectives on Spoken English in the Classroom*, Suffolk: QCA Publications.

DCFS (2008) *Bercow Report: A Review of Services for Children and Young People (0–19) with Speech, Language and Communication Needs.* Available at: www.dcsf.gov.uk/bercowreview/docs/7771-DCSF-BERCOW.PDF (accessed September 2010).

DCFS (2009) *Independent Review of the Primary Curriculum.* Available at: http://publications.education.gov.uk/eOrderingDownload/Primary_curriculum-report.pdf (accessed September 2010).

DES (1990) *The National Curriculum, English*, London: HMSO.

DfEE (1998) *The National Literacy Strategy*, London: HMSO.

DfEE (1999) *The National Curriculum: Handbook for Primary Teachers in England*, London: HMSO.

DfEE (2000) *English in the National Curriculum*, London: HMSO.

DfES (2003a) *Excellence and Enjoyment: A Strategy for Primary Schools*, Nottingham: DfES.

DfES (2003b) *Speaking, Listening, Learning: Working with Children in Key Stages 1 and 2*, Nottingham: DfES.

DfES (2006) *Independent Review of the Teaching of Early Reading* (the Rose Report). Available at: http://www.standards.dfes.gov.uk/phonics/report.pdf (accessed September 2010).

Education Department of South Australia (2004a) *Oral Language Developmental Continuum*, Rigby: Heinemann.

Education Department of South Australia (2004b) *Oral Language Resource Book*, Rigby: Heinemann.

Fisher, R. and Williams, M. (eds) (2004) *Unlocking Creativity Teaching across the Curriculum*, London: David Fulton Publishers.

Frater, G. (2001) *Effective Practice in Writing at KS2*, London: The Basic Skills Agency.

Hart, B. and Risley, T. (2003) 'The early catastrophe', *Education Review*, 17(1): 110–18.

Hewitt, R. (2003) 'Is there a case for considering talk as part of the oral heritage and as a performance skill?' In *New Perspectives on Spoken English in the Classroom*, Suffolk: QCA Publications.

HMIE (2005) 'Talking for Scotland', CPD materials for teachers. Available at: http://www.hmie.gov.uk/.../Talking%20for%20Scotland%NEWpdf.

Lunzer, E. and Gardner, K. (1979) *The Effective Use of Reading*, London: Heinemann Educational.

MacLure, M., Phillips, A.M. and Wilkinson, T. (eds) (1988) *Oracy Matters: The Development of Talking and Listening in Education*, Buckingham: Open University Press.

Mercer, N. and Hodgkinson, S. (eds) (2009) *Exploring Talk in School: Inspired by the Work of Douglas Barnes*, London: Sage Publications.

Mercer, N. and Littleton, K. (2007) *Dialogue and the Development of Children's Thinking*, Abingdon: Routledge.

National Strategies (n.d.) *Every Child a Talker.* Available at: http://www.nationalstrategies. standards.dcsf.gov.uk/node/277287 (accessed 10 January 2011).

Ofsted (2011) *Removing Barriers to Literacy*, London: HMI.

QCA (2003) *New Perspectives on Spoken English in the Classroom*, Suffolk: QCA Publications.

QCA (2004) 'Introducing the grammar of talk', report, QCA / 04 / 1291, Suffolk: QCA Publications.

Vygotsky, L.S. (1978) *Mind in Society*, Cambridge, MA: Harvard University Press.

Wells, G. (2009) *The Meaning Makers*, 2nd edn, Portsmouth, NH: Heinemann.

Speaking and Listening: Planning and Assessment

Deborah Jones

When I talk, my thoughts click.

(Jess, age 8)

Introduction

There is a sense in which all of us are helped by articulating our thoughts. It is often within the process of explaining or describing what we think, that our thoughts 'click' into place and we understand what we already know. In other words, making our implicit thoughts explicit through talk is a powerful learning tool for both adults and children. It may be assumed that because talk is interwoven into the fabric of the classroom and daily life in general, that competency develops 'naturally' and without the need for explicit teaching. By contrast, this chapter will highlight the importance of rigorous planning for speaking and listening and in addition the need to plan in specific and regular opportunities for assessing this area.

At the most basic level, then, one of the ways teachers can assess what children know and understand is by listening to children talking, that is, assessment through talk. At another level, however, as teachers, we are engaged in developing children's talk and therefore need to assess the talk itself in a variety of contexts and for a range of purposes and audiences. So, the process of planning for and assessing speaking and listening, as part of the curriculum, is one which is multi-faceted; effective planning and assessment should provide a rich experience in terms of what it yields for both children and teachers.

Current context

A prevalent discourse in the current educational context focuses on children's underachievement (DCFS 2008). As such, any judgements made by teachers need to be informed by a clear understanding of how children's language develops. In addition, assessments should encompass focused observations of talk across a range of contexts and for different purposes and audiences. Assessing what children can do and highlighting their achievements should be part of an holistic approach to formative assessment which also informs their future learning.

National Curriculum assessment has undergone many changes since its introduction. Each year, handbooks of guidance (QCDA 2011) are published, laying down the statutory assessment requirements for each Key Stage.[1] Both summative assessment (measuring attainment after teaching and learning) and formative assessment (informing the teaching and learning processes) are required.

There have been several important influences on the way assessment is approached. As a result of extensive research, Black and Wiliam[2] found that formative assessment strategies raise standards of attainment and produced five key factors that improve learning through assessment:

- the provision of effective feedback to pupils;
- the active involvement of pupils in their own learning;
- adjusting teaching according to assessment results;
- recognizing the huge influence assessment has on pupil self-esteem and motivation;
- the need for pupils to be able to assess themselves and understand how to improve.

Other important factors for formative assessment were also noted:

- sharing learning goals with pupils;
- involving pupils in self assessment;
- providing feedback which enables pupils to recognize and take the next steps.

Based on this research, Clarke[3] has drawn out additional aspects of formative assessment as follows:

- focusing feedback around learning intentions;
- organizing appropriate target setting;
- raising children's self-esteem throughout.

In 2002, the Assessment Reform Group produced *Assessment for Learning: 10 Principles*.[4] An important distinction is made, 'Assessment for Learning' being defined as the process of classroom assessment to improve learning, whereas assessment of learning is defined as the measurement of what children can do. In 2008, the Assessment for Learning Strategy was launched, the DCSF aiming to support schools in developing pupil assessment and improving pupil progression. It promoted the 'Assessing Pupil Progress' (APP) approach, which aims to provide a structured approach to teacher assessment through building up detailed, personalized profiles of where pupils are in subjects and what they need to do to improve. In literacy, APP materials have been produced for Reading, Writing and Speaking and

Listening.[5] All these initiatives have impacted not only on how assessment is perceived, but also upon how assessment in schools is carried out.

Approaches to planning and assessing speaking and listening

Currently, within the English National Curriculum (2000), a teacher assessment level must be reported for all children at the end of Key Stage 1. At the end of Key Stage 2, children are required to undergo both standardized assessments and teacher assessments for Reading and Writing, but teacher assessment only for Speaking and Listening (QCDA 2011). Criteria for assessment may be found as level descriptions within the *English in the National Curriculum* (DfEE 1999). The Early Years Foundation Stage Profile is used to summarize each child's development and learning attainment at the end of the Early Years Foundation Stage. This is at the end of the reception year for most children. Subsequently, documentation, 'Speaking, Listening, Learning: Working with children in Key Stages 1 and 2' (DfES 2003)[6] was produced by the Primary National Strategy. It related Speaking and Listening to the programmes of study in the English National Curriculum and presented four strands: Speaking, Listening, Group discussion and interaction, and Drama. Teaching objectives were provided covering these four strands across the various terms and years. This package offered brief guidelines for the assessment of the four strands and included a generic record sheet for teacher use. Whereas some useful suggestions are made here, it states teachers, when assessing children, should be clear that 'it is not their accent or dialect that is being assessed, the length of their contribution, the opinion expressed or their confidence' (ibid.: 30). Herein lies the difficulty in reducing the richness and complexity of Speaking and Listening to a set of objectives. Aspects such as confidence, self-esteem, gender, dialects and languages spoken, are all crucial to any assessments we make in this area (further consideration will be given to this below).

At the heart of any effective approach to the assessment of speaking and listening are two main aspects. First, a set of clear criteria on which to base observations and second, the way in which these assessments enable the teacher to plan the next learning steps. One example of a particularly useful method which incorporates these aspects is to be found in the *First Steps* materials.[7] These include a Developmental Continuum of aspects of speaking and listening, which can be used to record children's development and see progression clearly. In addition, helpful teaching emphases are included which parallel the various stages of development and aim to move children on. This not only provides a clear framework but also a rigorous approach to formative assessment.

The principles of assessment

There are certain principles which must inform our assessment practice, whatever the curricular area. These will necessarily reflect our approach to teaching and learning, as assessment is inextricably linked to both of these.

First, assessment should be continuous. Any assessments undertaken should take place over a period of time, in part to give children the best possible chance of showing what they can do and also to build up a picture of progression and development over time.

Second, assessment should be curricular. Assessments need to be related to what children are currently learning and take place within a strong context of meaning unlike some forms of traditional assessment which are bolt-on activities, quite unrelated to classroom work.

Next, assessment should be consultative. Assessment is not something the adult does to the child; rather it is a supportive collaborative process, shared between a range of people. Input from children, parents/carers, teachers and other adults is all a useful part of practice.

Finally, assessment should be communicative. Feedback by teachers to children or between peers, whether oral or written should communicate clearly, as should assessment documentation. These should be adapted to the audience, for example, reports for parents need to be jargon-free. It is essential that shared understandings are established and maintained.

Planning for speaking and listening

Aspects of talk

When planning for talk, it is important to consider the nature of talk and in so doing to identify four discrete, but interdependent aspects of speaking and listening:

- *Social* – for developing relationships.
- *Communicative* – for transferring meaning.
- *Cultural* – when different meanings are adopted by different speech communities; among children these might be associated with popular culture.
- *Cognitive* – using talk as a means of learning.

As teachers, we can plan to develop any of these aspects, indeed, all these need to progress if a child is to become a well-rounded speaker. Children need to learn about the social elements of talk, the expression of feelings, the development of relationships and how additional aspects such as body language work with talk in order to develop such relationships and affect or sharpen our communication.

The use of drama or circle time can be crucial for extending children's understandings of these aspects (see Chapter 5) but the cognitive aspect is fundamental. In planning for effective speaking and listening opportunities then, we are also planning for effective learning. One way in which this can be done, is by focusing on exploratory talk. As the National Oracy Project points out:[8]

> Learning is the product of the interaction between the old and the new, the known and the not known . . . through talk it is possible to explore and clarify new meanings, review and revise old meanings, until there can be an accommodation between the two.
>
> (Baddeley 1992: 41)

Research by Mercer[9] highlights the value of this kind of exploratory talk but notes that observational research indicates very little of it occurs naturally in the classroom. However, research from Australia (Cormack and Wignall 1998)[10] shows that, despite fears from teachers that children would not be focused, when children were provided with structured opportunities to work with their peers, they were able to use speaking and listening to:

- interrogate their own understanding;
- aid recall;
- instruct others;
- work on ideas and propositions;
- problematize;
- argue a personal point of view;
- rehearse subject-specific language;
- progressively shape knowledge;
- generate ideas;
- 'sponsor' learning.

(Cormack and Wignall 1998)

The research also highlights that this effective use of speaking and listening for cognitive purposes was dependent on the clarity of the task (children knew what kind of talk was required) and an appropriate selection of topic which allowed children to build on their previous knowledge and understanding. These aspects can form the basis of an effective teacher checklist when planning for exploratory talk in the classroom (see Table 2.1).

TABLE 2.1 Planning for exploratory talk teacher checklist

ACTIVITY	
LEARNING INTENTION:	COMMENTS (HOW?)
Do the children know: • *What* to do? • *Why* they're doing it? Does the activity enable the children to: • Interrogate their own understanding? • Aid recall? • Instruct others? • Work on ideas and propositions? • Problematize? • Argue a personal point of view? • Rehearse subject-specific language? • Progressively shape knowledge? • Generate ideas? • 'Sponsor' learning?	

Audience and purpose

Many schools which have Speaking and Listening as a priority for development, have adopted a functional approach to language. This is based on functional linguistics (Halliday 1978) where the structure of the language we use and the structure of the social action are mutually determining. Put simply, we vary what we say and how we say it according to who we are with (the audience) and why we are speaking (the purpose). For children, development and progression in their speaking and listening skills are marked by an increasing confidence and competence in achieving these aims.

A preliminary analysis of the kinds of speaking and listening children engage in at the beginning of the school day could look like Table 2.2.

TABLE 2.2 Children's speaking and listening at the start of the school day

ACTIVITY	AUDIENCE	PURPOSE	SETTING
Arriving at school with parents/carers	Parents/carers	To say goodbye To reaffirm arrangements for after school Social and communicative	Playground
Meeting friends	Peers	To share information To re-establish relationships Social, communicative, cultural	Playground
Teacher greeting pupils	Teacher	To greet communicative	Classroom
Circle Time	Teacher/ teaching assistant	To listen to other children To give a sustained, individual account/anecdote/story communicative	Classroom

Again, observational evidence would seem to indicate that although children may implicitly be able to vary how they speak according to who they are with, the opportunities for extending their speaking and listening repertoire need careful planning. Table 2.3 may provide a useful checklist/planning sheet for the types of talk experience which are offered to children. Clearly to develop this area effectively, the aspects in Table 2.3 need to be routinely monitored.

TABLE 2.3 Planning for talk checklist: contexts planner

ACTIVITY	AUDIENCE (SIZE/ STATUS, ETC.)	PURPOSE	SETTING

Findings from the National Oracy Project highlight that 'the quality of children's talk is greatly affected by features not necessarily related to their oral ability'(Baddeley 1992: 76) As a result, it is not enough to note the teaching and assessment objectives alone, rather consideration of a wider range of factors needs to take place, see Table 2.4.

TABLE 2.4 Planning for talk checklist: wider factors

How will the following impact on individuals/groups?

Child/group _____

Gender	
Group size	
Personality	
Confidence	
Self-esteem	
Competency in additional languages	
Use of non-standard dialects	

If we are to gain a comprehensive picture of the child's abilities in this regard, then all these aspects need to be considered and it is part of the teacher's role to act in the light of any factors which may be impeding pupils' development and performance.

To reiterate, planning, teaching, learning and assessing are parts of a cycle. All elements are interdependent, therefore it is vital that teachers have observed and assessed children's speaking and listening development in order to plan for progression. It is important that planning for teaching and planning for assessment should happen together. Fundamentally, speaking and listening should be embedded in the curriculum and not be a 'bolt-on', decontextualized activity. Teachers need to identify areas of the curriculum where the activities and the children's learning would be aided by speaking and listening. It is important to consider all curriculum areas, not just English, as talk is integral to all subjects. Assessments of talk can be planned for during collaborative science investigations, for example (see Chapter 10 for a discussion of talk in scientific enquiry). In addition, teachers should identify where aspects of speaking and listening should have an explicit focus as part of the English curriculum. Some speaking and listening activities may need to be planned for over an extended period of time whereas others may constitute just a part of one lesson. All plans should do the following:

- identify assessment objectives which are clearly linked to teaching and learning objectives/intentions (WHAT);
- specify which children (individuals/groups) are to be assessed (WHO);
- indicate the method of assessment and recording mechanism (HOW);
- timing, that is, at which point assessment should take place and how long it should last (WHEN).

If assessment is to be effective, all these aspects must be considered.

Managing assessment

A key factor is that assessment opportunities must be identified and written in on all plans as part of the initial planning process. It is true to say that unless this happens assessment will become haphazard and difficult to manage. It needs to be built into the routines and structures of the classroom. Some teachers have found it useful to annotate their weekly plans with the symbol 'A' (for assessment) to indicate exactly when it will take place.

Assessing in whole-class time

It is notoriously difficult to assess when whole-class teaching because there are so many elements for the teacher to consider. However, with careful planning, certain aspects may usefully be focused upon. The use of targeted questions (Table 2.5), for example, can provide helpful insights into children's development in terms of their cognitive understanding and also with regard to their competence in speaking and listening. As part of the formative assessment cycle, teachers can employ different levels of questioning in order to further a child's understanding or to develop their competence. In these sessions it is usually only possible to direct questions towards and note responses of one or two children. Having an adult other than the teacher to observe and record can be invaluable.

TABLE 2.5 Targeted question sheet

Date: _____

Child: _____

Assessment objective: _____

QUESTION (INCL. TYPE)	CHILD RESPONSE	COMMENT

The following sheet can be used for focused assessments when working with small groups (Table 2.6). It should be noted that assessment of speaking and listening can take place in any curricular area, not just in literacy sessions.

TABLE 2.6 Small group assessment

SMALL GROUP S/L OBSERVATION SHEET 1

Date: _____

Assessment objective: _____

NAME OF CHILD	OBSERVATION AND DEVELOPMENT POINTS

Clearly activities designed to facilitate talk and collaboration will be best, for example, Directed Activities Related to Texts (DARTS) such as cloze procedure (see Chapter 1) provide ample opportunity for observing and recording an individual child's speaking and listening behaviour. Observation sheet 2 in Table 2.7 is ideal for use in this context and provides tangible snapshot evidence of the child's abilities.

Involving children in their own learning

At the heart of these initiatives is the realization that the most powerful learners are those who have control over their own learning, using self-assessment.

Why self-assessment?

Central to the notion of self-assessment is the belief that we learn best through interacting with others. More specifically, Vygotsky[11] describes the 'zone of proximal development', that is, the gap between what children can do on their own and what they can do with the help of a more competent individual. So, with assistance, children can reach a higher level of attainment than they could do alone. This involves the more competent adult (possibly a teacher, other adult or peer) interacting with children as a focused part of the teaching and learning process. Linked to this is the work of Sadler (1989)[12] who notes that formative assessment is dependent on two elements. First, the learner needs to understand the gap between a leaning goal and his or her current level and secondly there is a need for the learner to close this gap up. As Black *et al.* (2004: 14)[13] state, 'although the teacher can stimulate and guide this process, the learning has to be done by the student'. This is not just about implementing strategies, this is about defining beliefs about teaching, learning and assessing, and setting up a classroom culture where pedagogy is clearly linked to those beliefs.

In practice, this means that planning and assessment need to be shared with children so that they are 'let in' on the processes of teaching and learning. As a result, learning intentions will be communicated to children in a language they can

TABLE 2.7 Observation of an individual child's speaking and listening behaviour

---

SMALL GROUP S/L OBSERVATION SHEET

Look for signs of evaluative & reflective thinking and tick features observed, then complete s/l description and analysis.

questioning commenting repeating planning participating collaborating responding reinforcing suggesting . . . . arguing discussing hypothesizing requesting reasoning persuading conceding encouraging reflecting	**NAME:** **DATE:** **ACTIVITY:** **GROUP SIZE** **S/L DESCRIPTION AND ANALYSIS** **AREAS FOR DEVELOPMENT**	supporting asserting initiating . . . . describing narrating sequencing stating speculating negotiating justifying categorizing recalling comparing

Look for communication strategies:

eye contact	facial expression	physical contact
listening attentively	body language	gestures
bludgeoning	causing silences	awareness of audience

understand. Pupils need to know not only what activities they are required to do, but also why they need to do them and what the success criteria will be. These strategies will ensure that children are not learning in a vacuum. Rather they will be certain of what they are doing, why they are doing it, and how successful they are being in the process. By identifying and sharing these aspects, any feedback/discussion of learning between teacher and pupil will have a clear framework. It is important that teachers explain to children what assessment is and why it needs to be done, equally, that it is a shared process. Setting up the classroom environment then, where children are free to make mistakes without recrimination and where errors will be viewed as part of the learning process is essential. Risk-free environments are fundamental to dynamic teaching/learning/assessment contexts where children have shared control over their own learning.

In summary, then, steps to follow in order to establish a successful teaching/ learning/assessing context are as follows:

- Set up a risk-free environment where children's self-esteem is built up.
- Explain what assessment is and why it is important.
- Share learning intentions in a language children can understand. This should include what is to be done and why.
- Describe the success criteria.
- Enable children to evaluate their work in relation to the success criteria.
- Have shared feedback between teacher and child.
- Set targets together.
- Reflect on the learning throughout.

Self-assessment and talk

Self-assessment and talk is a particularly sensitive area. The ways in which we talk, the languages we speak or dialects we use are part of our identity and form a large part of who we are. As such, we can become very vulnerable when our talk is opened up for scrutiny. Children, in particular, need to know that assessment of their speaking and listening skills is part of a process designed to help them. They should know that formative assessment will enable them to express themselves more effectively, develop their repertoires of talk and expand their registers of talk, in ways which enable them to exercise control over situations. It is worth explaining to children that sometimes written assessments do not demonstrate real under- standing of their capabilities because these are always mediated through writing. Being part of the assessment process and learning to assess themselves can be an enormously positive experience for children, an experience which not only involves them in their own learning but also enhances their self-esteem. Making these aspects explicit to children and discussing the power of spoken language with them is a crucial part of the classroom where children are learning effectively not only about talk, but how to talk. In this area, more than any other, setting up a risk-free environment where self-esteem remains intact is of paramount importance. Children need to know that effective speakers and listeners can become powerful learners, teachers and citizens.

Peer assessment

Closely aligned to self-assessment is peer assessment where children can work through several of the stages above, together. When setting up a system for peer assessment, ground rules should be clearly decided upon and established as part of a democratic classroom process, for example:

- Respect each other.
- Respect each other's work.

- Be clear on the learning intentions.
- Read/examine the work carefully.
- Ask questions.
- Listen carefully to answers.
- Give feedback with your reasons.
- Discuss targets/ways forward together.
- Reflect.

When specifically focusing on talk, further ground rules may be as follows:

- Find out how many languages are spoken.
- Respect accents and dialects.
- Be sensitive if people lack confidence in talking.
- Give everyone a chance to talk.
- Make sure you understand what people mean.

Clearly, the above will need discussion and explanation, but all this will help establish a climate where children can come to understand that the way in which we speak actually forms part of our identity as human beings and as such is not to be ridiculed or denigrated. This, as emphasized, is a sensitive area which will need constant reinforcement.

Reflecting on talk (my own and others)

> I could hardly believe how children's own talk came on in leaps and bounds as a result of watching others talk and then discussing it – it was incredible!
>
> (Year 5 teacher)

In one classroom the teacher was developing a programme whereby children could observe and participate in the power of spoken language. This was a project which effectively combined both peer and self-assessment and relied heavily upon discussion and reflection as a means of developing understandings. Children watched a range of video extracts in which different speakers were having a variety of effects on different audiences in different contexts and used the grids in Table 2.8 to focus their observation and reflection. Contexts were on a continuum and ranged from the formal to the informal, for example, from the law court to the family setting. Watching others engaged in dialogue and making comments on it enabled the children to remove themselves from the situation to begin with, until they became more confident and felt able to comment on their own talk. Role play was an effective step in the process, where children were given situation cards and were asked to act them out. Usually they were given planning time when they used the grids in Table 2.8 to decide how to play their parts. These activities were set up with an observer, who then discussed the situation with the participants after, or even at

TABLE 2.8 Reflecting on talk: contexts, audiences, purposes

WHERE? _____

WHY? (purpose of talk) _____

WHO?	HOW? (pitch, volume, tone, accent, body language)
SPEAKER 1 _____	
SPEAKER 2 _____	

EFFECTS (what and why)

SPEAKER 1 ON SPEAKER 2
SPEAKER 2 ON SPEAKER 1

YOUR FEELINGS (what and why)

IF YOU WERE SPEAKER 1
IF YOU WERE SPEAKER 2

VERDICT

HOW EFFECTIVE WAS SPEAKER 1? WHY?
HOW EFFECTIVE WAS SPEAKER 2? WHY?

various freeze frame stages throughout. In this particular classroom the teacher initially modelled the role of the observer/questioner with the whole class in order to help children understand the nature of the activity. Different aspects were focused upon during the course of the project, for example, accent, body language, etc. and more were added in as the project developed.

As part of their ongoing work in the classroom, children regularly reflected on and monitored their roles as speakers and listeners when working as part of a group. Table 2.9 is an example of one very simple sheet they used to focus their reflections.

TABLE 2.9 Reflection: working in a group

	YES	NO	COMMENTS/REASONS
I listened to others			
I asked other people's opinions			
I waited for a turn to speak			
I managed to make my points			
I was the leader			
I was a supporter			
I helped others by explaining			
NEXT TIME . . . (How could I improve?)			

Written and oral reflections on talk, their own and those of other people, are a vital way of moving children on in their learning. It is often within reflection that children make explicit, for the first time, their developing understandings about the nature of talk, and about their abilities to use it effectively.

Some final reflections

Speaking and listening are fundamental to learning and teaching. Talk is both a means of learning and an aspect to be developed and refined in its own right. It is also a powerful tool for communicating thoughts, expressing feelings, exercising power and generally developing our identities as human beings. Within the classroom, both assessment of and through talk is vital. One teacher describes her own assessment learning curve:

> When I first assessed my children using oracy as the medium, not writing, not only did I realize how much I underestimated their knowledge and understanding, but they even looked different. Assessing through talk makes you focus on the child.
>
> (Year 2 teacher)

Assessing talk provides immediacy of access into the child's mind and a unique window into the learning process. For this reason alone it deserves both our consideration and commitment.

Notes

1 Handbooks of guidance for assessment are produced each year for each Key Stage, e.g. QCDA (2011) *Assessment and Reporting Arrangements* (DfE). They can be accessed at http:/www.qcda.gov.uk.ara.

2 Research on assessment and learning by Paul Black and Dylan Wiliam is recorded in the following document: Assessment Reform Group (1999).

3 S. Clarke (2004; 2008) underscores the importance of sharing specific learning intentions with children in a language which is accessible to them.

4 The document *Assessment for Learning: 10 Principles* is available for download at: http://www. assessment-reform-group.org-uk/publications.html.

5 *Assessing Pupils' Progress* may be accessed from the QCDA website at: http://www.qcda.gov. uk/resources/400.aspx.

6 Reference to assessment is made in DfES (2003).

7 Developmental continua for reading, writing and oracy are included in the *First Steps* materials (Raison 1996; Raison *et al.* 1996) and published by Longman.

8 NOP (Baddeley 1992) provides a clear rationale for talk in the classroom context, together with useful strategies for developing this area.

9 See Mercer (2000) and Mercer and Dawes (2009).

10 This research is part of the *Classroom Discourse Project*, undertaken in Australia in 1998. See Cormack and Wignall (1998).

11 More on the zone of proximal development can be found in Vygotsky (1978).

12 The theoretical position of Sadler has greatly informed understandings about assessment in education. An influential text is Sadler (1998).

13 Black *et al.* (2004) provide a useful expansion of previous booklets.

Bibliography

Assessment Reform Group (1999) *Assessment for Learning: Beyond the Black Box*, Cambridge: University of Cambridge, School of Education.

Baddeley, G. (ed.) (1992) *Learning Together through Talk: The National Oracy Project*, London: Hodder and Stoughton.

Black, P. *et al.* (2004) *Assessment for Learning*, Maidenhead: Open University Press.

Cormack, P. and Wignall, P. (1998) *Classroom Discourse Project*, Canberra; Department of Employment, Education, Training and Youth Affairs.

DCFS (2008) *Bercow Report: A Review of Services for Children and Young People (0-19) with Speech, Language and Communication Needs*. Available at: www.dcsf.gov.uk/bercowreview/docs/7771-DCSF-BERCOW.PDF (accessed September 2010).

DfEE (1999) *English in the National Curriculum*, London: HMSO.

DfES (2003) *Speaking, Listening, Learning: Working with Children in Key Stages 1 and 2*, Nottingham: DfES.

Halliday, M.A.K. (1978) *Language and Social Semiotic: The Social Interpretation of Language and Meaning*, London: Heinemann Educational.

Mercer, N. (2000) *Words and Minds: How We Use Language to Think Together*, London: Routledge.

Mercer, N. and Dawes, L. (2009) 'The value of exploratory talk', in N. Mercer, and S. Hodgkinson (eds) *Exploring Talk in School*, London: Sage.

QCDA (2011) *Assessment and Reporting Arrangements*. Available at: http:/www.qcda.gov.uk.ara.

Raison, G. (1996) *First Steps*, Harlow: Longman.

Raison, G. *et al.* (1996) *Oral Development Continuum*, Harlow: Longman.

Sadler, R. (1998) 'Formative assessment and the design of instructional systems', *Instructional Science*, 18:119–44.

Vygotsky, L.S. (1978) *Mind in Society: The Development of Higher Psychological Processes*, Cambridge, MA: Harvard University Press.

Further reading

Baddeley, G. (ed.) (1992) *Learning Together through Talk: The National Oracy Project*, London: Hodder and Stoughton.

Barnes, D., Blatchford, P. and Kutnick, P. (2009) *Group Work in Primary Classrooms*, Abingdon: Routledge.

Barrs, M. *et al.* (1988) *The Primary Language Record*, London: Record, CLPE.

Black, P. *et al.* (2004) *Assessment for Learning*, Maidenhead: Open University Press.

Black, P. and Wiliam, D. (2011) 'Assessment for Learning in the classroom', in J. Gardner (ed.) *Assessment for Learning: Practice, Theory and Policy*, London: Sage.

Clarke, S. (2004) *Unlocking Formative Assessment*, London: Hodder & Stoughton.

Clarke, S. (2008) *Active Learning through Formative Assessment*, London: Hodder & Stoughton.

DCFS (2008) *Bercow Report: A Review of Services for Children and Young People (0-19) with Speech, Language and Communication Needs*. Available at: www.dcsf.gov.uk/bercowreview/docs/7771-DCSF-BERCOW.PDF (accessed September 2010).

DCFS (2009) *Independent Review of the Primary Curriculum*. Available at: http://publications.education.gov.uk/eOrderingDownload/Primary_curriculum-report.pdf (accessed September 2010).

DfEE (1998) *National Literacy Strategy: Framework for Teaching*, London: HMSO.

DfEE (1999) *The National Curriculum: Handbook for Primary Teachers in England*, London: HMSO.

Drummond, M.J. (2007) *Assessing Children's Learning*, London: David Fulton.

Fisher, R. (2008) 'Dialogic teaching: developing thinking and metacognition through philosophical discussion', in D. Jones and R. Evans (eds) *Metacognitive Approaches to Developing Oracy: Developing Speaking and Listening with Young Children*, Abingdon: Routledge.

Hall, K. and Burke, W.M. (2008) *Making Formative Assessment Work: Effective Practice in the Primary Classroom*, Maidenhead: Open University Press.

Harrison, C. *et al.* (2008) *Inside the Primary Black Box (Inside the Black Box)*, London: King's College London.

Marshall, B. (2011) *Testing English: Formative and Summative Approaches to English Assessment*, London: Continuum.

Mercer, N. and Hodgkinson, S. (eds) (2009) *Exploring Talk in School*, London: Sage.

Myhill, D., Jones, S. and Hopper, R. (2006) *Talking, Listening and Learning: Effective Talk in the Primary Classroom*, Maidenhead: Open University Press.

Pollard, A. (2008) *Reflective Teaching: Evidence Informed Professional Practice*, London: Continuum.

QCA (1999) *Target Setting and Assessment in the National Literacy Strategy*, London: QCA.

QCDA (2011) *Assessment and Reporting Arrangements*, London: DfEE.

Raison, G. (1996) *First Steps*, Harlow: Longman.

Raison, G. *et al.* (1996) *Oral Development Continuum*, Harlow: Longman.

Torrance, H. and Pryor, J. (2002) *Investigating Formative Assessment*, Maidenhead: Open University Press.

Fostering Speaking and Listening in Early Years and Foundation Stage Settings

Hilma Rask and Paty Paliokosta with contributions from Lalitha Sivalingham and Yasmin Mukadam

The aim of this chapter is to explore the role that talking and listening play in developing and extending children's learning in the early stages of education. The importance of the practitioner or teacher as both an active listener and an expert companion in dialogue with children will be discussed. Reference will be made to adults working with children in early years' settings as *practitioners* and those working in schools as *teachers*. It will be argued that teachers and practitioners gain insights into children's learning when they reflect upon what babies, toddlers and young children actually say and do during their play activities. Finally, it will be emphasised that in the light of such reflection, appropriate action should be taken to further enrich language learning provision for the children in their care.

Throughout the chapter, vignettes from observations of children will be used to illustrate ways in which purposeful talking and listening can foster children's learning in early years settings. Effective strategies for developing and extending young children's speaking and listening skills will also be discussed in line with recommendations included in EYFS documentation (DCSF 2007), in Early Years Professional Status (EYPS) standards as well as in *Every Child a Talker: Guidance for Early Language Lead Practitioners* (DCSF 2008) and *Letters and Sounds: Principles and Practice of High Quality Phonics* (DCSF 2007).

A rationale for speaking and listening

One of the most important contributions to understanding how children learn has been proposed by Vygotsky's (1978) model of the zone of proximal development. His research suggested that learning takes place most effectively within a context of social interaction through the joint construction of meaning.[1] With the help of a more competent adult or peer, a child is able to move towards new learning (Vygotsky 1978). This idea also influenced the research of Jerome Bruner (1985) with his proposal that the more experienced adult or peer acts as a 'scaffold' for new learning. Vygotsky (1978) emphasised the vital links between thought and language. Bruner (1985) also aptly described language as, 'a tool of thought'. What is important for the teacher or practitioner in the light of this research is to consider the key role of the adult in providing the necessary scaffold for learning which extend children's knowledge, skills and understanding through talk and action. What the child can do in co-operation with a more experienced learner, such as the practitioner, enables the child to move towards new learning. Clearly, speaking and listening have a vital role in the process of learning and are dependent on a communication friendly environment. It has been recognised in the Early Years Foundation Stage that 'the practitioner is an equal part of the environment and the practitioner's actions can enhance the environment for the child' (DCSF 2008:40) in a setting where every child is recognised as 'unique and as a competent learner from birth who can be resilient, capable, confident and self-assured' (ibid.:40; EYFS principle: a unique child). This implies that the practitioner tunes in, responds and values all attempts at communication which may not have yet reached the developmental level of spoken language (ibid.). In this context, Early Years Practitioners are expected 'to listen to children, pay attention to what they say and value and respect their views' (EYPS Standard 27). This also applies to toddlers and children who use alternative means of communication, such as sign language or Makaton. In this context, it is actually more appropriate to talk about expressive and receptive communication rather than speaking and listening, so the terms will be used interchangeably in the text.

When looking at the importance of interactions between young children and their caregivers it is important to go further back to the very early stages of communication, to the so-called 'proto-conversations' found in main carer–infant social interactions; these should also be taken into account when interacting with babies and toddlers or children who have not yet reached the developmental stage of speech.

Practitioners need to be prepared to engage and empathise with the needs and feelings of babies and young children. The reason for this is that 'accurate responses to a baby's message, leading to satisfaction of her or his needs, are likely to strengthen a "secure attachment" between carer and child' (Johnson 2010: 19). The pattern of responses includes facial expression, posture, tone of voice, tempo of movement, physiological changes such as heart rate/body temperature and apparent action, along with strong feelings and emotions (Schore 2009, in Johnson 2010).

One aspect of communication, for example, that practitioners need to tune in to is humorous engagement and laughing with the child (Reddy and Trevarthen 2004); the practitioners' acknowledgement of the importance of expressive and receptive communication is fundamental. Such interactions should be valued as integral to building positive relationships in communication-friendly settings.

In addition to the social aspects of language development, babies, toddlers and young children have to learn the sound system within that language, that is, the phonology. Here the practitioner's role is to model the use of speech sounds when there are speech immaturities. This needs to take place in a language and sounds–rich environment that develops children's speaking and listening skills and phonological awareness. The *Letters and Sounds* publication (DCSF 2007), which was developed in line with the DCSF core criteria for phonics, promotes activities that are intended to be used as part of a broad and rich language curriculum that has speaking and listening at its centre. One of its key elements is that it links language with physical and practical experiences, and provides an environment rich in print. In this way children can make links between what they hear and what they read.

Children gradually start to grasp ways in which language is fitted together and structured: the syntax and grammar. A skilled practitioner needs to be responsive and model the appropriate forms, or extend children's utterances in the contexts they occur. In addition, children need to understand the 'semantics' or meaning of the language. Finally, they need to understand the ways in which language is used in particular contexts and settings, known as the pragmatics of language. For example, it is important for practitioners to talk to children before carrying out a physical care task (DCSF 2008) to make it more meaningful for them. The importance of the practitioner's tuning-in is again very important as by being responsive and explaining the physical task they are carrying out, they reduce anxiety and support receptive language development.

Language is also a means of learning and cognition and exposure to high quality teaching of speaking and listening has a direct impact on children's learning and their standards of achievement.[2] Throughout their schooling, pupils gain from being able to articulate their ideas with clarity and form the ability to listen with accuracy, demonstrating increasingly critical analysis. Through collaboration and group discussions pupils learn to take account of the views of others and to listen with attention. They learn to take turns, negotiate and to modify their views on a particular issue in the light of other spoken contributions.

In his longitudinal Bristol-based study, Wells (2009) documented the often complex dialogues which took place between children and their mothers because there were known shared contexts and reference points in their own familiar world. His research also indicated that listening to, reading, and talking about stories together at home in the early years of life brought significant benefits for future literacy learning at school. Such experiences challenged children towards an understanding of language out of direct context, for they learned to make meaning from words alone[3] (Wells 1986, 2009). This is an important piece of research with implications for practitioners working with young children. The importance of storytelling in all areas of development has been widely recognised (Cooper 2005). Daniel, in the following section, explores in depth the role of storytelling in speaking and listening. Its importance lies in a wide spectrum from using language to express and shape intention to making friends.

Drama also has an important place in the development of oral confidence and early literacy,[4] since this enables pupils to take on the roles of other characters, express feelings and explore issues (DfEE 1999). Story acting, i.e. dramatisation of stories that happen on the same day a story has been read, can be used as a transition activity and best serves young children's interests (Cooper 2005). The receptive and expressive language skills that young children use in the context of such activities can contribute to the development of their future literacy learning.

Listening to children talking: assessing speaking and listening skills

The guidance that was provided for the Foundation Stage curriculum offered the practitioner a valuable framework of progression through the use of the stepping stones,[5] which set out the development of listening and speaking skills. This provided the practitioner with the broad brush strokes with which to plan for individual needs, and to monitor development along the continuum of language learning. Also useful are the guidelines issued on the progression of speaking and listening skills for pupils new to learning English, as these provide additional guidance to be used in conjunction with the stepping stones when planning for the needs of bilingual pupils and assessing their progress over time (QCA 2000).

Effective assessment needs to be continuous, curricular, consultative and communicative (see Chapter 2). When routine and systematic record keeping procedures become embedded within the classroom, a valuable cumulative record of progress emerges over time. Many practitioners have found it useful to make use of 'PostIt notes' or self-adhesive label rolls which can easily be attached to a larger record sheet, as they recognise the need to seize the moment, to note down what children do and say during their play and activities. This helps in the cycle of planning, providing insights into children's learning processes and current levels of linguistic knowledge and understanding, which informs future planning.[6] For example, the practitioner might discover that a child needs more experience of the same activity to consolidate learning. She may need a new range of activities to further embed conceptual language learning, or she may need new challenges in another direction, having demonstrated full conceptual understanding through her talk and actions. Recording the stages of the child's linguistic ability (language for communication and thinking and the way they link sounds and letters) will enable children's development to be shared between parents and practitioners.

It is important that assessment procedures acknowledge parental contributions and that information is comprehensively shared with parents and carers. Young children themselves can make effective contributions to their own assessments. There are clear indicators that young children are able to do more than they are often invited to. For example, when making visual representations of children's block play for their own analysis, children sought to involve themselves in these activities and were keen to talk about their plans.[7]

Practitioners speaking and listening – a pedagogy of listening?

Listening is not the same as hearing. The listening practitioner has to attend to what the child actually does and says in particular contexts and interpret the underlying meaning of utterances. For example, children's spoken responses may reveal how well they understand a task or a new concept. It may reveal the exact nature of any misapprehensions. There is another aspect of listening, which is to recognise, from the tone of voice, when a child is asking for help, which is again in line with the aforementioned 'tuning-in'. A child may reach a level of frustration or despondency where adult support or intervention may be needed. So when we refer to 'listening', practitioners need to use not just their ears but all their senses to tune in to the thousand languages, symbols and codes children use to express themselves and communicate. Listening within this approach implies 'the active process through which teachers take notes or photographs, or collect other evidence of children's activity in order to learn what deeply interests them and what they understand' (Lewin-Benham 2008: 186). The notion of 'sustained shared thinking' is not a new one and is in line with Vygotsky's (1978), Bruner's (1985) and Lave's (1991) theories after a longitudinal project in Early Years (EPPE) by Sylva *et al.* (2006) that identified a correlation between successful early years settings and the promotion of opportunities for sustained shared thinking.

The next section will draw upon examples from the classroom, presented as illustrative vignettes which investigate aspects of speaking and listening in a range of early years settings.

Case Study 1 Communicating with babies during feeding time

During feeding time, the practitioner makes eye contact while feeding the baby. She talks about the food that is being offered and responds to the sounds that the baby makes to indicate his/her satisfaction or dissatisfaction. The practitioner uses exaggerated sounds and smiles and gives the baby time to respond. She also encourages the baby to respond by asking questions and answering questions repeating key words and sounds such as 'Hmm is it yummy? Yes, it is yummy!' She tunes in to the baby's responses when the baby indicates that she has had enough. The practitioner respects the baby's choice of having enough, smiles and says 'Well done, all gone now. Yummy food all gone! Yummy all gone!'

She then proceeds to clean the baby's face and talks through all her actions. 'Let's wipe you clean. All done now! You clever girl, all done now.' She playfully imitates what the baby does and directs the baby's attention to a musical toy.

When the practitioner was feeding the baby, she gave the baby her undivided attention. She made positive eye contact and smiled and made sounds to indicate her pleasure in engaging with the baby. She responded to the sounds made by the baby and encouraged this communication by smiling and repeating actions and words. According to Vygotsky (1978), children are sensitive and responsive to adults and other children who will enable them to make sense of what they have experienced. Froebel and Isaacs have suggested that children also need to be able to learn things and be given time and encouragement to make choices (Bruce, 1997). Imitating, repeating, echoing, listening and responding exposes babies to language opportunities and encourages communication. Use of facial expression, body language, gestures and vocalisations are ways in which babies and young children make themselves understood, long before language emerges.

Case Study 2 Circle discussion in the nursery

Gail, the teacher in charge of a multilingual nursery class, has asked the children to sit in a circle and joins them for a short discussion of their activities. Dennis, the child on her right says, 'I am next to you.' Baljit, the child on her left, responds with, 'And I am next to you too.' Gail smiles to them both and says, 'Yes, you are both next to me, and I am in the middle.' They all laugh and nod in agreement.

At first glance, this kind of talk sounds very ordinary but it is the kind of talk which good teachers or practitioners engage in constantly in early years' settings. Gail automatically and systematically acts as the experienced talker and listener, who can scaffold new learning (Bruner 1985). She takes her conversational cues from the language offered by the children and she adds on new elements to extend and expand linguistic and conceptual usage. Here, for example, she adds on the prepositional phrase 'in the middle', whilst acknowledging and valuing the children's use of the preposition 'next to'. She does this in a context which makes the meaning totally explicit, for Gail is an artful opportunist in guiding and extending children's talk through routine daily activities in the classroom. When Gail orchestrates activities in her busy multilingual nursery, she is constantly alert to what children say and do. Sometimes she rephrases the talk which children offer, in order to clarify and to make their meaning clear to others. She extends and elaborates through the use of her own carefully chosen vocabulary. Her use of the structural patterns of English is always appropriate to the needs of individuals and their current level of oral competence. She exploits real concrete experiences to make meaning clear and to establish exactly what the children know and understand.[8]

When Gail asks questions of her young audience, they are rarely of a closed nature where the answer is either right or wrong. Instead she opens up enquiry, invites speculation and early hypothesis through the use of genuine open-ended questions. For example, she asks two boys constructing a tall tower outdoors. 'I wonder what will happen if you add one more brick?' To a group of children who have discovered ants in the sand tray, she asks 'Why do you think the ants got into our sand tray?' and she listens with genuine interest to their somewhat unusual ideas. In such ways she provides rich early experiences of speaking and listening, in the context of purposeful planned learning activities (DfEE 2000). This draws on the notion of 'sustained shared thinking' which has been defined by Siraj-Blatchford et al. (2002: 6) as an episode in which: 'two or more individuals "work together" in an intellectual way to solve a problem, clarify a concept, evaluate an activity, extend a narrative etc. Both parties must contribute to the thinking and it must develop and extend.'

Case Study 3 The great big giant: drama and talk

Two small boys greeted the visitor at the door, excitedly calling out:

'Come on, come and see our giant. He's so big.'

'Yeah, we've got a giant over there, and he's friendly and all.'

The giant had moved in over the weekend. In his long stripy sweater and elephant sized trousers, he draped amiably over the tented storytelling and book area in the reception classroom. His arrival had provoked intense excitement, and the student teacher encouraged speculation through questions such as 'I wonder where he came from?' She asked what kind of books a giant might like to read, and invited the children to find some in their class book collection, which she had supplemented in advance. The children began to ask their own questions, such as where the giant would sleep in the classroom at night. They were encouraged to suggest ways in which to make the giant feel welcome and happy. They kept dramatising his reactions in suitable, transitional parts of the day.

This example illustrates the power of dramatic events such as the introduction of a large puppet, or an imaginary person visiting a classroom for a period of time as an additional stimulus for focused talk. For young children such events can provide a link between their imaginative play and the world of children's literature. Speaking and listening skills can be much enhanced and exploited through the provision of vivid visual and concrete experiences, and this can provide an additional gateway through to emerging literacy skills (DfEE 2000; DCSF, 2008).

Further suggestions to develop talk through drama and role play might include:

- a visit from a familiar folktale character, such as Little Red Riding Hood, Goldilocks or one of the three bears;

- puppet toys and a simple puppet theatre to hide behind for anonymity;

- a mystery bag found in the classroom full of, for example, food items from the story of the hungry caterpillar (Carle 1970);

- various items, such as, objects from a well-known story, strategically hidden around the classroom;

- the teacher or practitioner appearing dressed in the role of a story-character, ready to answer questions from the children about the story;

- large masks for children to re-enact a favourite story together in a role play area set aside in the room;

- the construction of simple buildings for role play purposes, such as a large castle or pirate ship, or vet's surgery.

Case Study 4 Making monsters together: inclusion in action

Caroline is leading a discussion with a large group of children in her classroom of 5-year-olds, as they prepare to make monsters out of junk materials. Michael, a child with severe hearing impairment, is taking part as an active member of the group, through the use of radio microphones. Caroline has made sure that Michael can see her face clearly and she takes care to articulate her speech distinctly when she speaks to all the children. This helps him to lip read and to gain clues from her facial expressions and gestures as she talks. This aids his comprehension. Michael likes to use a mixture of speech and signing when he communicates and he receives excellent additional support from his teaching assistant, who is herself deaf and an expert signer. In fact, many of Michael's friends in the classroom are starting to learn some signing as well and Caroline has joined a lunchtime class with other staff to improve her own signing. Michael enjoys the practical activity which follows on from the discussion, and with support, tells the class that his monster is 'big, cross and scary'.

This example illustrates the importance of enabling participation of all pupils in the classroom. It shows how effectively a child with special educational needs can be enabled to participate alongside his peers, because his needs have been appropriately identified and provided for in ways which support both his communicative skills as well as his self-esteem and social skills' (DfEE 2000; DCSF 2008). Michael's teacher has taken steps to increase her own knowledge and skills through learning basic signing. She has been keen to work in close partnership with her specialist teaching assistant and external specialist agencies.

Case Study 5 Making houses: observation and intervention in the role play area

The final year student in the reception class was being observed by a senior colleague who was acting as her mentor. The focus of the activities was based around the story of the three little pigs. The student teacher worked with a group of six children making books about the story, after a highly stimulating whole-class exploration of the text. She had asked her teaching assistant to support a second group of less experienced writers with a simpler sequencing task. The rest of the class were to be engaged with self-chosen activities relating to the story which had been arranged in the adjoining area.

The free choice activities had been carefully set up. The children had been challenged to construct different houses for the three little pigs using large sticks, bundles of straw and construction bricks. The children started the tasks with enthusiasm, but it was evident that as soon as they came up against a challenge which they were unable to resolve, they moved away from the activity and moved to a different task. Very soon the majority of children had moved to the nearby sand tray. Their play was becoming repetitive and much of the talk was now social chatter. The observer noticed that one boy stayed at the sticks for a sustained period of time and attempted to place the sticks together. He said aloud, to nobody in particular, 'This one is too short. It won't fit'. After several attempts he gave up and walked off.

The mentor, classroom assistant and student had a very useful discussion of the lesson and evaluated together what had gone really well, such as the whole-class story focus, and then discussed what could be improved. They decided that the construction tasks required more adult intervention through talk and observation, if the intended conceptual language learning was to take place. They identified that the problem was an organisational and management issue. The student decided to deploy the classroom assistant to work with children in the construction activities and see what happened to the children's talk and learning as a result of this. She would continue to work with a group on the bookmaking discussion task and would additionally manage the work of the second group undertaking the sequencing task. She arranged to change roles with her colleague half-way through the session, in order to monitor all the learning.

The next day there was a noticeable change in both the children's interest and engagement with the construction tasks and the quality of their talk as they worked alongside an interested adult. The skilled nursery nurse discussed the problem of joining the sticks together with the children and drew their attention to the range of joining materials such as raffia, string, masking tape and glue which had been provided. The children talked animatedly to her about their discoveries, as they tried out different ways of joining sticks and the straw bundles to make houses. Of particular note was the way in which most individuals began to use the conceptual mathematical vocabulary introduced and reinforced by the nursery nurse, such as 'much too short', 'not thick enough' and 'too long'. As arranged, the student teacher and the nursery nurse changed roles and the student continued the discussion with the children during the construction tasks. She noticed, for example, that a normally rather reserved girl offered complex sentences when she excitedly explained how she selected sticks of exactly the same length to use. This child revealed much greater knowledge and understanding of the process than had been anticipated by the teacher.

Talking about the session afterwards, both adults considered that this had been an invaluable opportunity to reflect on their approaches and decided to continue with this pattern of working. The student teacher commented that it was easy to think that the children would learn just because the play activities were well set up and inviting. 'But unless you actually listen to what they are saying and talk with them about it all, you don't really know what they have been learning and what they need to learn next. The trouble is you can't be everywhere at once, so you have to use your time really well.' This example also highlights the value of reflection on practice.[10] It illustrates how the student teacher was able to considerably improve the provision she had made for language and learning through reviewing the management and organisation of her planned curriculum.

Case Study 6 Playing with language: developing phonological awareness in the nursery through games, songs and rhymes

Penny, a nursery teacher in charge of a large inner city multilingual nursery, ensures that she provides time during the day for the children to build up a repertoire of familiar songs, nursery rhymes and jingles. The children respond to these routine shared times with increasing delight and are eager participants. Penny has noticed the particular benefits which bilingual children who are at a very early stage of learning English gain from these sessions. The more confident of these children join in with repeated chorus lines and phrases, while less confident children sometimes join in with actions and gestures. They also listen with increasing attention, especially when Penny uses additional visual aids for counting verses such as, 'five currant buns from the baker's shop'.

Penny is alert to the need to keep the sessions short, sharply focused, and above all, motivating and fun-filled. She uses a great variety of simple games to encourage the children to play with the sounds of the English language. For example, the children walk through puddles saying 'Splish, splash, splosh. I need a wash'. They shake imaginary jellies saying 'Wibble wobble, wibble wobble, jelly on a plate'. Penny has noticed that many children spontaneously try out their own rhyming sounds as they play together. It seems clear to her that children are experimenting with the sounds of language and that they find this to be much fun. For example, Penny noticed that two boys playing at the water tray were in endless giggles as over and over again, they repeated the phrase, 'Silly Billy', which they had heard from a parent helper.

Penny takes time to listen to individual responses during shared song and rhyme sessions, sometimes directing her nursery nurse colleague to lead the session while she notes and attends to individual responses and participation. This enables her to identify children who may be slow to respond, or do not listen with accuracy. These are children she identifies for additional small group focus. Penny has also run a parent workshop where she included a session on the use of familiar nursery rhymes, songs and jingles and made available a selection of tapes and games for home use. Several parents have mentioned that they are enjoying sharing these activities at home and that older and younger siblings have also joined in, as well as some grandparents.

She is aware of the value of developing early phonological awareness through the medium of language games, songs and rhymes. She knows that research evidence suggests a close correlation between good pre-school phonological knowledge and understanding and later success in reading, even taking account of different intelligence levels and social backgrounds of the children (Bradley and Bryant 1983). Penny has taken good account in her own practice of the research which identifies early sensitivity to onset and rhyme as a vital factor for later success in reading and writing, and she is aware that learning nursery rhymes benefits future literacy[11] (Goswami and Bryant 1992; Maclean *et al.* 1993). She takes every opportunity to provide the children in her care with time to play with language through activities which they enjoy and which develop early phonological skills and also actively encourages parents to spend time at home sharing nursery rhymes and jingles. This leads the children to experiment and reflect upon language together with their teacher or practitioner and other significant adults.

Some final reflections

It is important that the speaking and listening skills which are fostered in the early years and Foundation Stage of education have a continuing focus and status across the curriculum areas during the next stages of education (DfEE 2003). This final vignette, based upon the experiences of a young teacher, serves as an important lesson relating to speaking and listening and the power of words. It has raised wry smiles among a student teacher audience whenever it has been shared with them, and hopefully has encouraged students to reflect carefully upon the messages their own words would give to the children they were about to teach.

Maria plays at school: a lesson for her teacher

I looked around my multilingual classroom, taking what I had come to call my talking health check. This consisted of a short tracking observation of activities of targeted children. I noted the four children at the listening station, earphones on, animatedly joining in with the folktale story of 'The Gingerbread Man' as they followed the text in their own booklets. I noted the three girls seated together on a rug, retelling the same story together, using the figurines on a magnet board. Things were going well, I thought to myself. This is a classroom where speaking and listening are valued. It was then I noticed her: 4-year-old Maria, a Spanish mother tongue speaker, alone in the home corner. She appeared to be speaking in English, although her preferred language when playing alone was Spanish. I could not wait to hear what she was saying. I crept closer. Maria sat on a chair, clutching a capacious handbag. She was surrounded by an orderly array of assorted dolls and toy animals on a small rug. To my eternal shame, I heard her say, in the parrot perfect voice of her teacher 'Sit down children! I said, be quiet! Be quiet!' Maria was playing at schools.

Maria's message is a profound one. It serves to remind us of the need for continual critical reflection on what we espouse as educators and what we actually do and say as practitioners each day. Her message emphasises that children's voices can both inform the teacher, and direct future planning for teaching and learning. If Maria could be heard now, perhaps she would be saying these words, instead: 'Keep talking children. I am listening. I am attending, I am tuning in . . .'

Notes

1 A useful discussion on the contributions of Vygotsky and Bruner to understanding the language and learning process is offered in Sutherland (1992).

2 Although addressed to teachers of pupils in Key Stages 1 and 2, this booklet is essential reading for Foundation Stage practitioners, as it provides linkages with the next stage of learning. See DfEE (2003).

3 Although the focus of this study involved a sample of mothers talking with their children, the evidence base was wide and the findings of much significance. See Wells (1986).

4 Useful ideas for exploiting drama and story making are presented in Hendy (1996).

5 Practitioners find it useful to plan directly from the stepping stones level charts when planning for the full range of language and learning needs of the children. See DfEE (2000).

6 DfEE (2000) sets out a clear set of principles to guide practice and emphasises that children learn in different ways and at different rates.

7 An excellent account of research directed by Tina Bruce and the Froebel Blockplay Research Group, which explores children talking and learning together, is provided in Gura (1992).

8 Nutbrown (1996) argues a cogent case for respectful observations of children at play.

9 The Revised Code of Practice for Pupils with Special Educational Needs promotes inclusive education. See DfEE (2001).

10 The value of reflective practice is highlighted in TTA (2001) when mentors and newly qualified practitioners discuss how factual feedback statements and open-ended questioning encourage reflection.

11 Research undertaken by Maclean *et al.* (1987) found very strong connections between awareness of rhyme and knowledge of nursery rhymes, and how this has a positive impact on later literacy success.

Bibliography

Bradley, L. and Bryant, P.E. (1983) 'Categorizing sounds and learning to read: a causal connection', *Nature*, 30: 419–21.

Bruce, T. (1997) *Early Childhood Education*, 2nd edn, London: Hodder & Stoughton.

Bruner, J.S. (1985) 'Vygotsky: "A historical and conceptual perspective" ', in J.V. Wertsch (ed.) *Culture, Communication and Cognition: Vygotskian Perspectives*, Cambridge: Cambridge University Press, pp. 21–34.

Carle, E. (1970) *The Very Hungry Caterpillar*, New York: Philomel Books.

Cooper, P.M. (2005) 'Literacy learning and pedagogical purpose', *Journal of Early Childhood Literacy*, 5(3): 229–51.

DCSF (2007) *Letters and Sounds: Principles and Practice of High Quality Phonics*, London: QCA.

DCSF (2008) *Every Child a Talker: Guidance for Early Language Lead Practitioners*, London: QCA.

DfEE (1999)

DfEE (2000) *Curriculum Guidance for the Foundation Stage*, London: QCA.

DfEE (2001) *The Revised Code of Practice for Pupils with Special Educational Needs*, London: QCA.

DfEE (2003) *Speaking, Listening Learning: Working with Children in Key Stages One and Two*, London: QCA.

Goswami, U. and Bryant, P. (1992) 'Rhyme, analogy and children's reading', in P.B. Gough, L.C. Ehri, and R. Treiman (eds) *Reading Acquisition*, Hillsdale, NJ: Lawrence Earlbaum Associates, Inc., pp. 49–64.

Gura, P. (ed.) (1992) *Exploring Learning: Young Children and Blockplay*. Froebel Blockplay Research, London: Sage.

Hendy, L. (1996) 'It is only a story, isn't it? Drama in the form of interactive story making in the early years classroom', in D. Whitebread (ed.) *Teaching and Learning in the Early Years*, London: Routledge.

Johnson, J. (2010) *Positive and Trusting Relationships with Children in Early Years Settings*, Exeter: Learning Matters.

Lave, J. (1991) 'Situated learning', in L. Resnick, J. Levine and S. Teasley (eds) *Perspectives on Socially Shared Cognition*, Washington, DC: American Psychological Association, pp. 63–82.

Lewin-Benham, A. (2008) *Powerful Children: Understanding How to Teach and Learn Using the Reggio Approach*, New York: Teachers College Press.

Maclean, M., Bryant, P. and Bradley, L. (1987) 'Rhymes, nursery rhymes and reading in early childhood', *Merrill Palmer Quarterly*, 33(3): 255–81.

Nutbrown, C. (1996) 'Wide eyes and open minds – observing, assessing and respecting children's early achievements', in C. Nutbrown (ed.) *Respectful Educators – Capable Learners. Children's Rights and Early Education*, London: Paul Chapman Publishing Ltd.

QCA (2000) 'A language in common: the assessment of English as an additional language', http://orderline.qcda.gov.uk/gempdf/1847210732.pdf.

Reddy, V. and Trevarthen, C. (2004) 'What we learn about babies from engaging with their emotions', *Zero to Three*, 24: 9–15.

Rinaldi, C. (2005) *In Dialogue with Reggio Emilia*, London: Routledge.

Siraj-Blatchford, I., Sylva, K., Muttock, S., Gilden, R. and Bell, D. (2002) *Researching Effective Pedagogy in the Early Years (REPEY)*, London: DfES.

Sutherland, P. (1992) *Cognitive Development Today: Piaget and his Critics*, London: Paul Chapman Publishing Ltd.

Sylva, K., *et al.* (2006) *The Effective Pre-School and Primary Education 3–11 [EPPE 3–11] Project*. The EPPE symposium at the The British Educational Research Association (BERA) Annual Conference. University of Warwick, England, 6–9 September 2006.

TTA (2001) 'School-based research consortium initiative, the evaluation, final report', http://eprints.soton.ac.uk/41341/.

Vygotsky, L. (1978) *Mind in Society: The Development of Higher Mental Processes*, Cambridge, MA: Harvard University Press.

Wells, G. (1986) *The Meaning Makers*, London: Hodder & Stoughton.

Wells, G. (2009) *The Meaning Makers: New Perspectives on Language and Education*, 2nd edn, Clevedon: Multilingual Matters.

4

Teachers and Children: A Classroom Community of Storytellers

Alastair K. Daniel

Once, when the world was still young . . .

One day, in a week of two Fridays . . .

Once, when weeks were as long as months, and years as short as days . . .

Once upon a time . . .

There are many ways to begin telling a traditional tale, but perhaps the most significant of them all is to close the story book. In this chapter we will explore speaking and listening in relation to storytelling, and in particular the role of the teacher as the principal storyteller in a classroom community of storytellers.

The publication of *Speaking, Listening, Learning: Working with Children in Key Stages 1 and 2* in (DfES 2003) highlighted the role of children's talk in the classroom and the need for teachers to take strategic interest in developing children's skills in speaking and listening, alongside those of reading and writing. Although at the time of writing we are uncertain about the future shape of the curriculum in England, this renewed awareness may yet be strengthened if teachers feel able to respond positively to the calls for developing the role of effective talk in children's learning which can be found in both the Rose Review (DCFS 2009) and the Cambridge Primary Review (Alexander *et al.* 2009). Few would deny that storytelling has an important role within speaking and listening and, in this context, professional storytellers may continue to enjoy demand for their services in school, but if storytelling is to achieve its potential, as both a model of talk and a means of engaging children with narrative, then it cannot be regarded simply as the preserve of the specialist teller of tales. Those who work in schools each day need to recognize that they are, themselves, storytellers, and that they have at their command a potent tool for classroom teaching.

Although, to date, specific references to story and storytelling in the primary curriculum have been concerned with the *child* as storyteller within literacy studies, the *teacher's role* as the principal storyteller in the classroom is essential. By experiencing imaginative storytelling that is embedded in pedagogic practice, children not only can be inspired to become creative and confident in their own tellings, but can also experience a sense of engagement that can do nothing but help their development as active and comprehending listeners – as well as enhance their understanding of curriculum content.

In this chapter, we are, therefore, concerned with developing the teacher's storytelling skills applied not only to the telling of tales, but across the curriculum. I will outline what I believe are six essential aspects to effective storytelling in the classroom, both in the specific telling of tales and in general teaching. These are:

1. The unmediated text – moving from reading to telling.

2. Narrative storytelling and narrative teaching.

3. The selection of suitable material.

4. The adaptation of the story.

5. The imaginative use of language – supported by expressive non-verbal communication.

6. The use of 'absence and completion' – engagement and story.

The unmediated text – moving from reading to telling?

Storytelling is a very different thing to story reading. While it may be excusable that in (what is arguably) a literate society stories are regarded as something to be read from a printed or written text, the reality is that we engage with the spoken narrative every day of our lives: listening to friends as they regale us with mishaps from their holidays, explaining the frustrations of the day to a partner, or watching the stand-up comedian who creates a whole act from a simple (and seemingly everyday) narrative idea. This is storytelling – even though we may not think of it as such – it is the telling of a tale that is immediate, expressive and unmediated by a written text. As such, it is a fundamental human activity.[1]

It would be foolish to deny the power of reading a book with a group of children but for many professionals the story book can, perhaps, provide a source of protection as much as a source of stories, the solid ground of the printed word preferred to the shifting sands of a memorized narrative. For all the benefits of reading to a class, however, there are some less positive aspects:

■   However creative you may be in your vocal production, and use of pace and rhythm, at the same time as you are mediating between the printed text and the listening children, the text mediates between them and your understanding of the narrative. The words that you use are not your own and, as such, represent neither your choice of language, nor natural speech patterns.

- The author of the printed text has aimed their work at a generalized readership of a particular age group (and perhaps social demographic) rather than your pupils specifically. Although words might be changed or the phrasing altered, the text leads both reader and hearer down a fixed path that allows little adaptation to a group of children.

- The book creates a physical barrier between you and your hearers; even rested across the knees, the paper and cardboard come between teacher and pupils.

- The pictures that form part of many books at this level represent the imaginative response of the illustrator to the narrative, which will not coincide with the imaginative response of the children. A picture in effect says: 'We are not talking of your imagined wolf, but the wolf in this picture.' While to put the book down and tell the story may seem a risky strategy (as there is no defined text), the story *told* has a flexibility and immediacy that set it apart from the read story.

- You can adapt language to the needs of the group and incorporate their responses into the narrative. In this way, the storytelling becomes a unique event for this group of children, at this specific time of telling and in this particular place.

- The absence of a physical object permits freedom of expression for the teller and removes a barrier between you and your hearers.

- It is frequently said 'the best pictures are on radio' and so, as a storyteller, you take your hearers on an imaginary journey that is individual to each one of them as they create characters, settings and encounters in their own heads.

- None of the above could possibly justify not reading to children, but it does suggest that the told story also has a place in the classroom.

Narrative storytelling and narrative teaching

One of the defining characteristics of storytelling is the weaving together of narrative ideas, and so the construction of coherent narrative is a necessary skill in order to give storytelling and teaching a clear comprehensive form.

I often commence lectures on storytelling with this example:

Answers to the question of how I solved the problem

$$\begin{array}{r} 14 \\ \times\, 3 \\ \hline 42 \\ \hline {\scriptstyle 1} \end{array}$$

either place me as the subject: 'You took the four and multiplied it by three . . .' or places one of the numbers as the subject: 'the three is multiplied by four . . .'. But whichever way, the description includes a character who acts or is acted upon: 'First, *you* took the three and multiplied it by four . . .' or 'First, *the three* is multiplied by four . . .'. These can be classified as:

- a quest (how to multiply two numbers);
- a change in circumstances (two separate numbers are resolved into one expression);
- a sense of time ('*First*, you took the four and multiplied it by three . . .');
- a sense of place ('You put the one *under* the line . . .').

The response is always in narrative terms. If something as abstract as describing the solution of a mathematical problem displays the same narrative features as a fairy tale, it is a simple step to seeing that as humans we make sense of the world through narrative, through story. This is hardly startling news and anyone interested in further reading should look at the work of Bruner (2002) and Haven (2007), among others.[2]

What is missing from this example are intentionality and affect. These human-izing elements can be introduced to narratives such as these by utilizing phrases such as 'I *want* to solve . . .', 'the one *wants* to go into the tens column, but it *finds a home* . . .'. Although this may appear to run counter to any distinctions that may need to be drawn between different kind of thought (in Bruner's (1986) terms, *paradigmatic* and *narrative*), I would suggest that narrative thought (the thinking of possibility, of 'what if . . .?') provides a context in which to explore the structures of paradigmatic thought (the thinking of pattern and verifiable truths).

As teachers, we enter the classroom already equipped as storytellers; the skills needed to transform the everyday storyteller into the teller of tales are neither mysterious nor arcane, but simply a heightened and deliberate variation of those deployed in the telling of stories in the staff room or pub. First among these skills, then, is the ability to identify and organize a clear narrative structure and to this end I use a simple rendering of the Actantial Analysis of the Lithuanian émigré semiotician A. J. Greimas.[3] At this point undergraduate students have been known to go slightly cross-eyed but, at its simplest, this analytical tool helps to make story-telling coherent and memorable. Sitting on the shoulders of Vladimir Propp (and his classification of Russian folktales), Greimas draws us to consider not individual characters, or character types (such as king, stepmother or child), but to the func-tions that the characters serve within the narrative.

Greimas identified six narrative functions:

1. *Subject* – the character around whom the narrative turns.

2. *Object* – that which the subject wants to achieve or acquire.

3. *Sender* – the person or force that moves the Subject to seek the Object.

4. *Receiver*[4] – the person that benefits from the Subject's successful quest for the Object.

5. *Helper* – the person or force that aids the Subject in their quest for the Object.

6. *Opponent* – the person or force that opposes the Subject's completion of their quest for the Object.

These form binary pairs:

Subject and Object
Sender and Receiver
Helper and Opponent

And are usually arranged as:

Sender → Object ← Receiver
↑
Helper → Subject ← Opponent

While a work of literature may generate a complex diagram, with more than one subject, a series of opponents and layers of objects, it is possible to reduce many folk tales (and other stories suitable for classroom use) to these simple binary pairs. Taking the example of *Little Red Riding Hood* (as told by the Brothers Grimm) (see Figure 4.1).

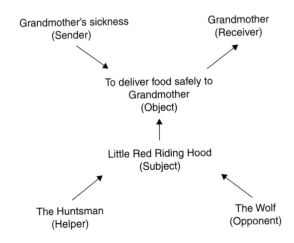

FIGURE 4.1 Little Red Riding Hood

If we accept that we understand ourselves and our world in narrative terms, and that simple narratives can be reduced to the functions of Subject, Object, Sender, Receiver, Helper and Opponent, then there is a clear implication for general teaching and specifically for creating narratives that assist children to become effective listeners and speakers. It suggests that in our own teaching we should be constructing narratives where these functions are clearly differentiated, and also assisting our students to do the same – and not just in specific times set aside for storytelling.

An application of this approach to storytelling can be illustrated by taking the example of the Norman Conquest. In order to understand the story we could consider the functions that operate in the historical narrative for the opposing leaders. Placing William as the Subject we can generate Figure 4.2, with Harold Godwinson (King Harold II) as the Subject, a contrasting schema would be generated.

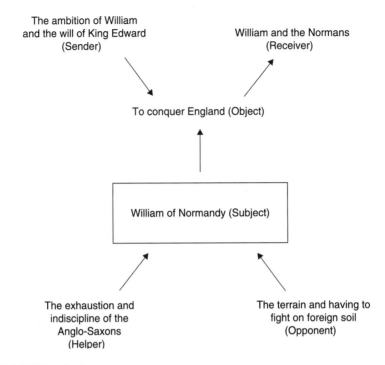

The ambition of William
and the will of King Edward
(Sender)

William and the Normans
(Receiver)

To conquer England (Object)

William of Normandy (Subject)

The exhaustion and
indiscipline of the
Anglo-Saxons
(Helper)

The terrain and having to
fight on foreign soil
(Opponent)

FIGURE 4.2 William the Conqueror

Naturally, neither schema provides a sufficient study of the Conquest. Not that children should be taught to make schematic diagrams of actantial function at Key Stage 2, but in trying to make sense of the story, this analysis helps us to identify the key elements that create a coherent narrative from the history. Take one of these elements away and the narrative is incomplete and fails to make sense. Hence by concentrating on narrative teaching, we are simply connecting with the way in which we naturally deal with information.

Returning to the teaching of multiplication, it is even possible to identify the six actantial functions of narrative in the solution to the algorithm (Figure 4.3). Without overt explanation, the children will understand that the teacher is the Sender who initiates the activity, but the Receiver is still to be identified. A simple introduction that explains that this revisit to multiplication is to remind everyone of the methodology before going on to more complex problems implies that the pupils are the Receivers of the benefit of the activity. Thus an actantial approach not only provides a useful model for unfolding memorable and comprehensible tales in dedicated times of storytelling, but also hones our communication skills in all areas of the curriculum.

One way of engaging pupils' storytelling skills with this approach to narrative is to use sets of story cards to help generate narratives. I use sets of cards which include archetypal characters (king, princess, child, etc.), places (castle, forest, desert, etc.), and situations (something lost, a curse, etc.) that groups or individuals can draw at

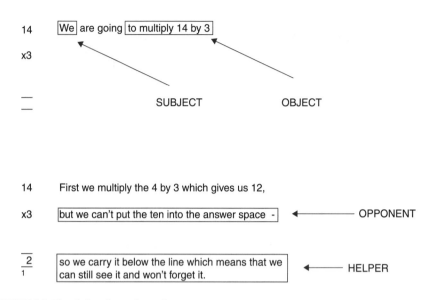

FIGURE 4.3 The six functions of narrative

random, and from which they then construct a simple narrative that can be told, acted out or represented in another way (commercial versions are available from educational suppliers and children's bookshops). A 'WHO' card, for example, can provide the main character (the Subject), another is drawn to give a character trying to stop that protagonist (the Opponent) and another to be the person who provides help (the Helper). The protagonist's objective (the Object) can be generated by a 'WHERE' card (setting providing a context for the story and its destination) or a 'WHAT' card (mirror, sword, magic lamp, etc.). The missing elements of the Sender and Receiver can be drawn out of the children's ideas, and identified as the motivational force behind the action. The randomness of such activities enables chance encounters with narrative that creates a sense of play. What is more, the creation of coherent narrative from apparently unrelated words or phrases engages children in imaginative activity that is open, co-creative and presents opportunities for meaningful dialogue.

Of course, storytelling is not synonymous with story-writing and a common teacher response to any exercise which develops narrative awareness is 'and now let's write a story'. Although committing a narrative to paper will be appropriate on many occasions in a child's education, the opportunity for children to engage in educationally contextualized oral retelling has potential for significant, and distinctive, learning. When children tell their own stories (to a partner or the whole class), they are engaged in meaningful and extended talk which develops a full range of oracy skills.

Narrative and memorization

With no written text to rely on, the teacher/storyteller relies on their abilities to memorize a story and the construction of a coherent narrative structure is key, not only to the children's comprehension, but also to the memorization process.

Various writers on the craft of storytelling have suggested methods for memorizing stories that have centred on creating a mental storyboard of images that can be linked together, drawing a 'spider diagram' showing the relationships between the major characters or writing a three-line précis of the tale. While I have often used simple storyboards/flow charts in order to remember strongly sequential narratives (such as creation myths), I have found that the actantial analysis outlined above as the most effective method of setting a story in my head in such a way that it has internal coherence when I tell it. Instead of trying to remember a list of events (which can become confused), with the schema, you simply have to remember the motivating and opposing forces that come to play on the protagonist as s/he pursues their quest. There are storytelling practitioners that advocate rote learning and, of course, the teacher should use whatever strategies enable them to be effective storytellers, but word-for-word learning kills the essential communal quality of the told tale. In a community of storytellers, language (verbal and non-verbal) is negotiated within the particular group, place and time; in the telling of a tale learned as a script, there is no flexibility. In addition, when the linguistic content is rigid, errors are easier to make and harder to recover from.

Above all, the busy teacher needs to find ways in which to memorize stories that suit their personality as well as the available time. Once the story is learned it becomes incorporated into the teller's personal repertoire and can be told and retold – remembering that the story should change with every telling. As the hearers change, so does the story.

Selecting suitable material

I would love to be able to say that I learned this or that story sitting at the feet of an old woman as she unfolded the traditions of her people to her gathered family, but sadly I am dependent on my collection of story books (picked up on travels, yes, but rarely found at the feet of the elderly). Of course stories can be, and are, drawn from all manner of sources and so in this section we will be looking at the way in which we, as busy professional people, can identify stories suitable for classroom use and to begin the process of adaptation.

Zipes (2004) writes:

The best storytellers are thieves and forgers. They steal their tales from everywhere – books, television, films, radio, the Internet, and even other living human beings . . . Storytellers appropriate their stolen goods, make them their property, and re-present them as if the goods were their own material, which, in many ways, they are because storytellers always forge the tales they steal anew.

I regularly use one tale that has stayed with me since childhood. *The Dog Gellert* was told to me as a small boy by my mother as I stood sobbing (always a sensitive child) next to the grave of the faithful hound slain in error by his master. The fact that I now know that both the tale and the grave are a romantic fiction has made no difference to the power of that narrative learned so many years ago and, whatever the origins of the tale, I tell it because of the emotional resonance it has for me as a childhood memory. This may seem a strange reason for choosing the story for classroom use, but it is vital that the teller has a real sympathy for the tales that s/he tells.

According to Grainger:

> The importance of finding short tales which have an instinctive and immediate appeal should not be underestimated . . . Finding tales that are waiting to be told, that the storyteller really wants to share, for whatever conscious or unconscious reason, remains important. The hunt is not a quick or easy one, but it is always worth the journey.

> (Grainger 1997: 147)

That phrase, *tales that are waiting to be told* is extremely felicitous and it certainly expresses my feeling when I come across a story that I would like to tell. For me, *The Dog Gellert* is a tale waiting to be told.

Between story collections in print and those available on the world-wide web, the teacher/storyteller faces an almost limitless supply of traditional and crafted tales from around the globe. With such a bewildering choice, it is prudent to apply some selection criteria that go beyond that initial moment of personal resonance. The final selection of a story needs to be appropriate to a specific group of children and meet their particular needs.

Selection criteria

A coherent narrative

The use of the Actantial Schema enables stories to be identified that are both suitable for classroom use and easy to learn. If the actants (Subject, Object, Sender, Receiver, Opponent and Helper) are not readily apparent on the first reading, the narrative will need additional work to ensure internal coherence. Storyboards/flow charts can help with sequencing.

Linguistic comprehensibility

The telling will need to be comprehensible to the children. This does not mean, however, that the language of the source text needs to be at the appropriate level – the language of delivery is dependent on you as storyteller rather than the original text.

Appropriate to the developmental level of the students

There is a huge a difference between the developmental levels of students between Foundation Years and Year 6. The story should be appropriate to the emotional and social development of the students.

Cultural relevance

It is essential to be aware of the culture within which you are working and its assumptions. For instance, in the Grimms' story of *The Fisherman and His Wife* the shrewish wife wishes in turn for a house, a castle and a palace. Realizing that she can't live in a palace as the wife of a fisherman, she wishes first to be the king, then emperor and then pope. In my own telling I have edited the papacy from the story on the grounds that few children outside the context of Roman Catholicism would understand the role of the pope, or why his status is elevated above that of king and emperor. If, however, the story was told during a class study of Henry VIII, the full version of the tale could enhance their understanding of the relationship between the Church and state in this period.

Story may be also be a means of valuing the various ethnic cultures present in the classroom setting and of building a bridge by which pupils can negotiate their way between the dominant and minority cultures:

> All cultures have their own histories, myths, legends and stories which are passed on through generations of children. These stories cross cultural boundaries; some are recognisably similar with subtle shades of difference, others will be particular within a specific cultural context. In either case the story itself becomes a powerful shared experience.
>
> (Wyse and Jones 2001: 255)

During a period of heightened tension between elements of the indigenous Flemish and minority Turkish communities in Belgium, I regularly told one of the Turkish Hodja folktales. The story is short, beautifully structured and amusing, enabling students from the majority culture to enjoy (and value) the playfulness of a tale from a culture to which some were antagonistic. At the end of these sessions Turkish students often spoke to me of their tradition and quizzed me of my knowledge of other Hodja stories.

Stories suitable for classroom use

A curriculum link

The story may be a means of supporting curriculum studies, or introducing themes. For instance, in science, a topic of the Solar System could be enhanced by a tale such as the Native American myth *How Grandmother Spider Stole the Sun* (Bruchac 1991). In this way, children explore the ways in which different peoples have tried to explain what they see in the night sky.

A socially constructive message

While this chapter does not have the scope in which to debate the rights and wrongs of story as a means of social manipulation within the education system, it has to be acknowledged that classroom storytelling exists within the organizational sphere of the school context. Just like any other activity in the classroom, story-telling cannot escape being a part of the structured environment of learning for the child, an environment which both reflects society and has the potential to effect change within society.

In addition to their role as a primary agent for constructing future society, every teacher faces social issues within the classroom itself, from bullying, to bereavement to the effects of family breakdown, among their students. Although we should beware of seeing storytelling as a panacea for the ills of society, the told tale can be a powerful tool in speaking for the marginalized and bolstering the cause of social justice within the school community.

Finding suitable stories

Faced with the array of possible sources for classroom storytelling, I would suggest the following process which reduces the amount of time that is wasted in the search for a suitable tale:

1. First make your choice of story collection. This choice may be based on a need to support the curriculum, to find material with a specific cultural relevance, or a tale with a socially constructive message. I tend to avoid most children's versions of story books; when I am looking for a 'tale that's waiting to be told', I am seeking something that expresses itself in language with which I am comfortable. When I retell the story to young people I tell my own version, and the language is then tailored to their needs. [Please note, however, I am not beyond cross-checking with children's versions to see how others have adapted tales.]

2. Scan the contents or the index and see if there is a title or reference that catches your attention.

3. Speed read the first and last paragraph (or two) of a few stories. This should enable you to identify the main protagonist and the theme.

4. Read through any story that seems to arrest your attention more than the others, but do not be afraid to reject them based on the suggested criteria and try the next story and so on.

Adapting the story

Once you have found a story that is *waiting to be told*, the next question is whether it has a Simple Coherent Narrative (or is adaptable to one); in other words, whether it is possible to easily identify the Subject, Object, Sender, Receiver, Helper and Opponent.

Once the structural elements have been identified, the tale needs adapting to the particular group to whom you are going to be telling. While linguistic comprehensibility will look after itself, the language content is something that will change with each telling of the story. Although you should avoid writing the story out word-for-word as you intend to tell it, you may wish to think about particular opportunities for the use of rhythm, rhyme, alliterative phrasing, onomatopoeia and imagery (and the original text may act as a source here).

As with all teaching materials, you will need to exercise professional judgement with regard to the appropriateness to the developmental level of the students of the tale. If the main theme of a story is the protagonist's Oedipal desires, then it is probably not going to be suitable for Key Stages 1 or 2 as it stands. However, you should not fear making adjustments to create a coherent narrative that is targeted at your particular group of children.

Although it may appropriate to use the Grimms' tale *Hans my Hedgehog* in full – including the hero washing his black skin until it is white in an exercise for undergraduates on the adaptation of traditional tales to classroom use, cultural relevance is extremely important and in the classroom there would need to be considerable editing to make the story useable.[5] Hence, as with *The Fisherman and His Wife*, if on a close reading a story has elements which are inaccessible, there is no problem with judicious cutting; the key point is that this is a personal telling of a traditional tale.

It is vital to realize that few children have had no exposure to traditional stories in some form and there will often be a very strong sense of ownership of a particular version. When I first started as a storyteller, I was often faced with children who would correct me ('No, that's wrong, the shoe was made of glass').[6] The storyteller, Sandra Pollerman, offered a solution during a seminar, suggesting that stories could end with the phrase: 'That was the story of _____, and that was how I told it' and I have used the formula since. This simple phrase allows one to claim ownership of the tale and justifies deviating from the commonly received form of a story (often, sadly, courtesy of the Disney Corporation). Bearing in mind the emphasis on a shared, communal, telling, I often modify the formula to: 'That was the story of _____, and that was how you and I told it.' The curriculum link can be established where it is desirable or necessary and a socially constructive message may be sought (avoiding any temptation to sermonize).

Related to the adaptation and editing of stories is the issue of *bowdlerization* or censorship.[7] The fear of violence and sexuality has led to what might be referred to as the Disneyfication, first, of European folk tradition and now that of other cultures.

Although some blame may be laid at the door of the 'Magic Kingdom', Disney has simply been the most successful of many forces promoting a romantic notion of childhood and society which, it can be argued, has little relevance to the world as children experience it – nor indeed to the world of traditional stories. We like to forget that Cinderella's ugly sisters had their eyes pecked out, that Snow White's step-mother danced to her death in red-hot shoes and that Manypelts was sought in marriage by her own father.

In his important work on the Freudian interpretation of fairy tales, *The Uses of Enchantment*, Bruno Bettelheim famously suggests that children have monsters, violence and desires deep inside their subconscious. The role of the folk-tale has been to give an imaginative language to that violence and to place the monsters and desires in a context that serves society's structures:

Adults often think that the cruel punishment of an evil person in fairy tales upsets and scares children unnecessarily. Quite the opposite is true: such retribution reassures the child that the punishment fits the crime. The child often feels unjustly treated by adults and the world in general, and it seems that nothing is done about it . . . the more severely those bad ones are dealt with, the more secure the child feels.

(Bettelheim 1991: 5)

In the traditional versions of Snow White and Cinderella, there is clear retribution for the wrongs done to the girls – retributive justice that will accord with the moral level of children at KS1 and 2. In the same way these stories reinforce social taboos in a symbolic form, taboos which it may be inappropriate to examine explicitly but work on a subconscious level (e.g. Manypelts and her father's incestuous intentions, Little Red Riding Hood climbing into bed with the older male Wolf).

It is possible that the lack of a truly enriched inner life may lead to frustration which can manifest itself as violence. We must, therefore, think hard before trimming the extremes from traditional tales to make them more acceptable or politically correct. From my own experience as a teacher of children with profound emotional and behavioural difficulties I would support the view that the child needs an imaginative capacity for violence in order to express their anger safely, but it must be made clear, however, that such an argument does not justify allowing the young access to violent films or images which do not provide an imaginative vocabulary or stimulate the imagination to creativity. Visual representations of violence force the child's imagination into a particular predetermined form which the shared story does not. However, sensitivity is still required if telling tales involving violence: too much descriptive detail and again you force the child into seeing mental images that may be inappropriate or frightening; too little, and the child fails to find a world where right is rewarded and evil pays the price of its crimes.[8]

The imaginative use of language – supported by expressive non-verbal communication

It has already been stated above that when searching for a story to tell, you should not be concerned about the language level of an original, source, text as the tale will be adapted to suit the children with whom you are working. However, the teacher should always be attuned to the creative use of language and there are often opportunities to play the 'thief and forger' adopting particular turns of phrase, or expressive language.

This flexibility to be creative in the retelling means children's linguistic understanding can be enhanced through storytelling. Freed from the printed text, the storytelling teacher can choose to emphasize adverbs or similes, to exemplify imagery, or to foreground other linguistic devices in the retelling. The strategic use of storytelling to support the teaching of systematic synthetic phonics formed the basis of a Leading Partners in Literacy project developed at Kingston University.[9] Having been placed in schools with a strong record in literacy teaching, students adapted short folk narratives to create stories which highlighted particular phonemes (a simple process when the key to the story is the underlying narrative structure, rather than words to be learned).[10] These story devices to target specific areas of language development were told, first, by the students and, then, by the children within discrete phonics sessions. In this way specific language knowledge was embedded within exchanges that were both meaningful and purposeful.

The issues around how children discern meaning in language is complex. While there is a very live debate over the rights and wrongs of children having access to books in which there are words that they are unable to decode using their phonological knowledge, the storyteller's quandary as to whether to use only the language with which children are familiar is not quite so contentious, but is related. Many years ago I heard an interview which, I believe, was with Neil Kinnock in which he talked about his teaching days, and the instruction he received to always throw the ball over the students' heads, never at their stomachs. In other words, the students have to reach up to grasp meaning, it does not always land in their laps. The narrative structure on which story is built acts as a linguistic scaffold – the imaginative context enables children to understand language at a more complex level than they could follow in a decontextualized setting.

Having said the above, modelling a developed vocabulary, a command of imagery and coherent construction will only work if they are supported by the non-verbal elements of communication. Hence, vocal tone, pace of delivery, gesture, physical tension and use of space all come into play. This is not to say that the teacher needs to ape a Shakespearian actor, but simply to ensure that all levels of their storytelling support the narrative, and do not conflict with the intended ideas, moods and structure of the story.

Absence and completion – engagement and story

The longer that I practise as a storyteller, the more convinced I become that the key to good storytelling – the key to good teaching – is the principle of *absence and completion*.

The word 'absence' can be used in many contexts, not all of them positive: absence of listeners, absence of attention, absence of understanding, absence of humour. When I speak of 'absence' I am specifically referring to moments where an element of the narrative is missing and has to be provided by the hearers. This absence is controlled by the storyteller and is intentional and contrived. Aimed at stimulating the imagination of the students, crafted moments of absence point that imagination along a particular path or paths without constricting it.

In this sense, absence may be manifest in a missing word or phrase that the students have to provide:

Storyteller: But Siput the snail kept on walking,
 he kept on walking,
 he kept on . . .
Students: . . . walking!

It may be in supplying information needed to complete the story:

Storyteller: The first animal to knock on the witch's door was the . . . the . . . You
know, I've forgotten; what animal do you think it was?

It could be visual absence where a person, place or object is 'seen' by the storyteller
in what is empty space, but an empty space that is filled by the imaginations of the
children.

Storyteller: [cupping hands and focusing eyes on the space between them] . . . and
the Lord God looked down at the body of the dead swallow and said to
the angels, 'You have chosen well . . .'

Or, the absence could be one of additional significance where an everyday object
gains a new meaning through the way it is used in the storytelling:

Storyteller: The fisherman rowed his little boat out into the blue sea [the storyteller
takes a long piece of blue cloth and creates ripples in it to signify water]

With moments of visual absence, the imagination is engaged in bridging the gap
between reality and the textual reference (between blue fabric and the sea). It also
anchors the whole group to a specific object or space creating a shared moment of
recognition and transformation.[11]

One of the main differences between the story that is read and the tale that is told
is the breadth of opportunities that the latter presents for creating moments of
absence, and through them engaging the hearers and making them active participa-
tions rather than passive hearers. While it might be only a slight exaggeration to
suggest that the presence of an audience would make little difference to many performance activities (whether storytelling, acting, dancing or singing), it is possible for
the storyteller's hearers to affect the telling of the tale without having to take an 'it's
behind you!' approach. I would echo the director Peter Brook who rejects the
activity of 'watching' a play because of its suggestion of passivity, preferring the
French word 'assistance' which has connotations of contribution to the event:

> In the French language amongst the different terms for those who watch, for
> public, for spectator, one word stands out, is different in quality from the rest.
> *Assistance* – I watch a play: *j'assiste à une pièce*. To assist – the word is simple: it is
> the key.
>
> (Brook 1968: 156)

By creating moments of absence and completion the storyteller assures the students
that their listening is valued and at the same time the children know that the story
cannot continue without them. This is a social event, and when the pupils are asked
to contribute to the story, and their assistance is incorporated into the narrative,
they see that what they bring to the story as integral to the telling and part of the
continuous whole.

Some final reflections

My formative experiences as a storyteller were from working with children with emotional and behavioural difficulties. Such students often experience problems with imaginative play and I found that closing the book and telling rather than reading a story had a dramatic effect on their ability to maintain attention and respond to the narrative – to the point that I was sometimes able to use storytelling techniques to calm distressed and hysterical pupils. At this point I need to counsel against using storytelling to practise quasi-psychological therapies. One of the features of contemporary storytelling is its association with various forms of spirituality and mysticism and there are those who wish to 'give prescriptions for self-healing through stories' (Mellon 1992).While such aims may be laudable, they presume a clinical expertise that few teachers possess and, what is more, distance storytelling from the prosaic day-to-day existence of classroom teaching. Even though storytelling in the classroom will neither mould the emotional nor cognitive development of children, it remains a powerful technique to be utilized as an element of a complete education.

To provide a meaningful experience of storytelling, whether teaching the physical properties of material science or telling the tale of Little Red Riding Hood, the same rules apply:

- A clear coherent narrative that is unmediated by a written text, that makes use of both imaginative language and well-crafted non-verbal communication.

- The use of material that is appropriate to the developmental level of the children and the cultural context in which they exist.

- The controlled and varied use of absence and completion that engages the children in the storytelling event.

Every time that I teach storytelling I find myself repeating the same mantra 'you are already a storyteller'; in the pub, round the dining table, in the staff room, we all tell stories to our families, friends and colleagues. The teacher who wishes to be an effective teller of tales in his/her class simply has to refine those storytelling skills they put to use every day.

Notes

1 Jerome Bruner (2002, 1986) and Kieran Egan (1989) have written extensively about the place of story in human interaction and learning.
2 Kendel Haven (2007) has examined much of the available research literature to construct what would appear to be an unassailable case for story being at the heart of human development, and from this position offers approaches to teaching that take full account of the narrative mind.
3 While Greimas's work does not often appear in primary education textbooks, along with Roland Barthes, he was one of the fathers of the Paris school of semiotics and pioneered narrative structuralism.
4 Greimas's narrative *receiver* is strictly the one who receives the contract to act in pursuit of the *object*. For our purposes, however, the notion of the *receiver* as the one in receipt of the benefit

of a successful achieved *object* is more useful – and indeed a widespread interpretation/simplification.

5 In fact, I do use an edited version of *Hans my Hedgehog* as it presents a male hero who is vulnerable and unwanted – a role often reserved for girls in popular story collections.

6 The article that enables Cinderella's transformation from put-upon servant to princess varies (along with her name) from culture to culture: the glass shoe in France becomes the fur shoe in Eastern Europe, and the golden shoe in China. In some traditions, the transformational object is a hat, and in others a ring; in Egypt, the girl's sandal is carried to Pharaoh by the gods.

7 Thomas Bowdler (1754–1825) published an expurgated edition of Shakespeare in which, among other 'improvements', King Lear is reunited with his daughter Cordelia, who go on to live happily at the end of the play.

8 The irony in British culture is a counter-movement that led to the removal of a story of theft, wife battery, child abuse and murder, from the public houses where it had previously been told and its assimilation into the culture of childhood. If you doubt that such a thing is possible, then I would suggest a stroll along the beach at Eastbourne (or any of a number of seaside towns) this summer, and take an informative break watching a Punch and Judy show.

9 The Leading Partners in Literacy projects were sponsored by the TDA (Training and Development Agency) between 2008 and 2011 to encourage collaboration between providers of Initial Teacher Education and schools with a proven record in teaching literacy.

10 As an example, I moulded language around the narrative frame provided by the traditional tale *The Old Woman and Her Pig*, and incorporated characters, actions and descriptions which emphasized the consonant digraphs and /sh/, /ch/ and /th/. This (and a couple of other tales) were produced by the university's media department and distributed on DVD, but earlier versions of two of the tales can be viewed at http://storytent.co.uk/video.html.

11 The use of absence and completion is a contrived and strategic extension of the play in which children engage naturally – as the cardboard box becomes the train through the child using their imagination to cross the gulf from reality to fantasy, imaginative bridges are built by the group to the world of story – bridges anchored to cues of absence provided by the storyteller.

Bibliography

Alexander, R.J. *et al.* (2009) *Children, their World, Their Education: Final Report and Recommendations of the Cambridge Primary Review*, Abingdon: Routledge.

Bettelheim, B. (1991) *The Uses of Enchantment*, London: Penguin Books.

Brook, P. (1968) *The Empty Space*, London: Penguin Books.

Bruchac, J. (1991) *Native American Stories*, Colorado: Fulcrum Publishing.

Bruner, J. (1986) *Actual Minds, Possible Worlds*, Cambridge, MA: Harvard University Press.

Bruner, J. (2002) *Making Stories, Law, Literature, Life*, Cambridge, MA: Harvard University Press.

DCFS (2009) *Independent Review of the Primary Curriculum* (the Rose Review). Available at: http://publications.education.gov.uk/eOrderingDownload/Primary_curriculum-report.pdf (accessed September 2010).

DfES (2003) *Speaking, Listening, Learning: Working with Children in Key Stages 1 and 2*, Nottingham: DfES.

Egan, K. (1989) *Teaching as Story Telling*, Chicago: University of Chicago Press.

Egan, K. (1992) *Imagination in Teaching and Learning*, London: Routledge.

Grainger, T. (1997) *Traditional Storytelling in the Primary Classroom*, Leamington Spa: Scholastic.

Greimas, A.J. and Cortes, J. (1982) *Semiotics and Language: An Analytical Dictionary*, trans. L. Crist *et al.*, Bloomington, IN: Indiana University Press.

Grugeon, E. and Gardner, P. (2000) *The Art of Storytelling for Teachers and Pupils*, London: David Fulton.

Haven, K. (2007) *Story Proof: The Science behind the Startling Power of Story*, Westport, CT: Libraries Unlimited.

Mellon, N. (1992) *The Art of Storytelling*, Shaftsbury: Element Books.

Rosen, B. (1988) *And None of It Was Nonsense: The Power of Storytelling in School*, London: Mary Glasgow Publications.

Toolan, M. (2001) *Narrative: A Critical Linguistic Introduction*, 2nd edn, London: Routledge.

Wyse, D. and Jones, R. (2001) *Teaching English, Language and Literacy*, London: RoutledgeFalmer.

Zipes, J. (1995) *Creative Storytelling*, London: Routledge.

Zipes, J. (2004) *Speaking Out: Storytelling and Creative Drama for Children*, London: Routledge.

Dynamic Talk: Speaking, Listening and Learning through Drama

Colleen Johnson

Sometimes when I'm in role I think, 'This is how I'll talk when I'm grown up.'
(Ella, age 9)

Introduction

Drama talk can be the most dynamic talk in the classroom. Through drama we can create a myriad of contexts in which children are able to experience diversity in spoken language. Such experiences can help develop skills in speaking and active listening, through paired, group and whole-class work, helping build children's confidence in their own oracy. The range is comprehensive and may encompass speaking *as* a character or planning *for* a scene, dialogue *in* performance or *responding to* performance, whole class discussions both *in* role and *out of* role. Such experiences, aided by effective teacher questioning, can stimulate children's critical reflection upon the ways in which talk enhances their learning. With its potential for affording sustained and purposeful talk, which is rich with possibilities for learning, drama is a must in the classroom.

Talk is at the forefront of recent primary initiatives,[1] and teachers are being urged to respond to the need to plan creatively and constructively for a range of activities which will foster the development of speaking and listening. In this chapter, it is argued that drama can stimulate the best in whole-class teaching through discursive and interactive talk, fostered and modelled by the teacher. Through drama, the teacher can create contexts for exploratory talk, developing hypothesis and opinion.[2] Good quality independent group work can be maintained when such talk continues while the children are working without teacher support. Further, drama offers the teacher excellent opportunities for the assessment of children's speaking and listening, using, for example, the planning and observation checklist suggested by Jones in Chapter 2.

During the first decade of this millennium, drama practitioners welcomed their subject's apparent return to the curriculum and its heightened status, with reference to fostering talk in the classroom. This is in evidence specifically in the speaking and listening group discussion and interaction and drama requirements of Speaking, Listening and Learning.[3] However, many teachers may well have had little or no experience of drama in their own professional training, largely focused on the core curriculum subjects, to the detriment of Foundation subjects and the arts in particular. It is understandable then that many are reluctant to attempt to teach a subject in which they may have had insufficient grounding. For the teacher with little or no experience of drama, therefore, what follows are tried and tested approaches for the non-specialist which can be incorporated within lessons such as literacy and personal, social, health and moral education (PSHME). All activities took place *in* the classroom. After all, in most schools, space is at a premium and access to larger areas such as the hall or the gym may be limited. In addition, such activities may easily stimulate further reading or written work. In this case it is useful for the children to be working in their own classrooms where relevant resources are at hand. The 'drama for talk' examples which follow reflect both Key Stages 1 and 2.

Anita's story

A Year 4 teacher incorporated drama in her teaching of speaking and listening, literacy and moral education. She devised a scheme of activities to help children explore issues surrounding bullying. She began by showing the children a letter purported to have been written from a 13-year-old girl to her mother, before leaving home. She read:

> Dear Mum,
>   It's happened again and today was worse than ever. Even my so-called friends are being horrible. I've had enough and I'm never going back to that school.
>   Don't worry about me. I'll be OK.
>   Love Anita.

Group discussion and interaction

The children were invited to suggest what might have happened to make Anita want to run away. Most were of the opinion that she must have been bullied and evidently over a period of time. There was speculation on the nature of the bullying which Anita had been experiencing. Various examples were offered including teasing, sending spiteful text messages, name calling and stealing her equipment. The children were asked to make notes on what was being discussed as these could be used later to help them in preparation for short improvised scenes.

Group improvisation

The teacher organised the children into groups of five. Each group was asked to create a short dramatic representation of one of the bullying incidents which Anita may have experienced. She stressed that it was not necessary for all in the group to take part in the improvisation itself but that all should be involved in the devising process. This allows for shy or reluctant children to contribute at a level at which they feel comfortable.

She added that some groups may decide to show a scene which might not necessarily include the incident as it happened but could, for example, show a prank being planned, a group of teachers confronting the bullies or a conversation between Anita and those not directly involved, after the event. This added a challenging dimension to the children's discussion and led them to think beyond action-based drama to that which might involve more reflective dialogue.

The teacher directed the children to think carefully about the effect which they would like their scene to have on the audience and how they might best achieve this. For example, how could they best convey the feelings of certain characters by facial expression or by physical proximity to one another in the scene? How might they achieve suspense within the scene or deepen empathy for a particular character? Again an added dimension was evident. Having to place themselves in the position of audience as well as directors and actors engaged the children in meta-cognitive process and enriched their exploratory talk.[4]

Each scene was watched in turn. The teacher encouraged the children to critically reflect upon the performances by asking them to say 'what worked well and why'. This helped the children to consider the ways in which those who had created the scene had used drama conventions such as mime, improvisation, characterisation and staging and to what effect. This reflective process fosters the growth of critical vocabulary for dramatic activity and enhances learning *in* drama.

In one scene 'Anita' had remained at a distance from the four playing her 'friends'. One child commented that this had made her 'really separate from everybody else. She is on her own'. This provoked responses from others in relation to feelings of isolation, which may be experienced by victims of bullying. In another scene, however, 'Anita' was in the middle of a tight group of 'peers' and their physical proximity heightened the claustrophobic atmosphere of the scene. A child commented, 'When they are that close, it is scary. No one else can hear what they are saying to you'. Others said, 'You can be on your own in a group when they are all against you' and 'They made it looked like Anita was trapped'.

Encouraging the children to comment constructively on performance, the teacher led discussion about the effects within the scenes and how they had been achieved. The participants were visibly gratified to hear, via the audience's feedback, how well they had succeeded. Critical appreciation and praise from peers can sometimes be more rewarding than that from teachers or other adults.

The teacher facilitated the children's learning *through* drama by asking them to make connections between what they had seen or discussed so far, and events in their own lives. In one scene, a parent had been seen talking with her friend about how her daughter's attitude to school seemed to have changed in recent days. When discussing this scene, one child said, 'It makes you realise that if you are not happy, it affects your Mum or your Dad'. And another added, 'Yes, you think you won't tell them if something's wrong but then they know something's wrong anyway and it makes it worse because they don't know what to do.' Several spoke about the sorts of bullying which they had experienced, or witnessed. The teacher encouraged them to consider examples from literature and television dramas. Here the teacher was capitalising on the children's engagement with the medium of television, which provoked animated conversation between children on a daily basis.

Written tasks followed which the children approached enthusiastically. They were required to chart the build-up of a scene in which they had taken part, or helped devise and to write character sketches, focusing on small details to evoke sympathy or dislike. Research shows drama enhances the quality of children's written work, stimulating their imagination and giving real purpose to the task in hand.[5]

Still image

The children were asked to return to their groups to make a 'still image' to represent their scene. This requires children to organise themselves into creating a three-dimensional image to represent a dramatic moment or a visual 'summing up' of a situation. This strategy serves a number of purposes:

- It helps create a visual *aide-mémoire*.
- It is less time-consuming to view a series of still images than improvised scenes.
- It involves highly focused discussion as children negotiate both meaning and conveyance of shared meaning to an audience.
- It requires less physical movement than a whole improvised scene in preparation and is therefore a useful strategy for the teacher anxious about possible rising noise levels.

The still images were presented in an agreed chronological order and the teacher exploited further opportunities for speaking and listening by introducing another strategy.

Thought tracking

Here those in the image are invited to contribute the immediate thoughts of the characters they are representing. The teacher said, 'At this moment I am thinking . . .' She moved around the image touching each character on the shoulder, inviting them to speak. One image showed a group of Anita's peers talking about having hidden her lunch box. Guided by the teacher, they spoke their thoughts in turn:

Brilliant – no way she will find it.

I'm glad it isn't me they are being mean to.

She'll be hungry.

Hope we don't get found out.

Another way of combining these strategies is to have those observing volunteer the thoughts of the characters in the image. This makes an already active learning situation even more interactive. To exploit literacy links, the children could be invited to invent captions to accompany the images, to write dialogue or create diary entries for characters.

Teacher and children in role

The teacher explained that she and the children would be acting together in their drama. She would be in role as the school's head teacher. Concerned about the negative publicity which Anita's disappearance had caused for the school, the head teacher had decided to call a meeting of student counsellors, teachers and parent governors to discuss ways forward. She organised the class into three groups: parents, teachers and student counsellors and the meeting began. In role, she said:

> Welcome everyone to this emergency meeting. I'm delighted to say that Anita has returned home safely but her mother is insistent that she will not be returning to our school. We must recognise that we have a bullying problem here and we urgently need to do something about it.
>
> You have been invited to attend because it is recognised that all of you have some expertise to offer in helping develop a policy on bullying. I suggest that we begin by dividing into our groups. Would each allocate a leader to head up the discussion and a scribe to make notes and to write up agreed key points, in order to feed back to us all when we reconvene?

She was using formal language to set the tone and to underline the seriousness of the endeavour. The status of the role of 'the head' helps the teacher feel in control of the class while working within the drama. Similar status roles in other dramas might include detective inspector, business manager or expedition leader.

The mantle of the expert

Here the children took on the role of 'experts' with knowledge and experience collectively greater than those of the teacher in role. When children adopt the mantle of the expert, the roles of teacher and pupil are temporarily reversed. The children are the 'ones in the know', who have the expertise to apply to the task in hand – in this case helping develop a working anti-bullying policy – while the teacher in a higher status role, nevertheless, is the 'one who needs to know' seeking their help and guidance.[6]

Children in role as experts rise to the challenge of using spoken language appropriate to a situation, which is uniquely afforded them through drama. They are *in* the role of another – usually an adult or older child – but it is still their own use of language demanded by that role which is being nurtured. In the continuing reflective discussion, the children demonstrated an appreciation for the ways in which drama had helped them engage in heightened language. It is important for the teacher to encourage reflection, out of role, on the levels of sophistication and quality of the language some children are able to demonstrate in role, especially as experts, and for the children to consider how they access such language, a metacognitive process fundamental to learning. As Ella (aged 9) said, 'Sometimes when I'm in role I think, "This is how I'll talk when I'm grown up." '

Back in the whole group, individuals fed back on behalf of their cohort. The 'student counsellors' made several suggestions, including the implementation of 'buddy systems' where younger and less confident children might be befriended by older students, who would 'look out' for them and offer support and guidance.

The 'teachers' suggested that more could be done in the classroom to raise awareness about the effects of bullying on victims. One 'teacher' said, 'We should have films about what happens when they run away from home'. Another said, 'Some children just think they are having a joke. They don't mean to really hurt'. Another added, 'I agree. Sometimes they think they are only teasing but they don't mean to be really nasty'.

The 'parents' offered their perspective, 'We want more meetings with the teachers because sometimes your children don't tell you anything about what's going on at school'. And 'If we don't sort it out, people won't send their children to this school'.

This was serious, purposeful talk. Ground rules for dialogue were observed, children responded appropriately to the contributions of others in the light of alternative viewpoints and spoken argument was clearly presented. Opinions were qualified and agreements were reached. The activity demonstrated the quality of learning achievable through exploratory talk facilitated by, in this case, the strategies of teacher in role and mantle of the expert.

Out of role, the children were encouraged to reflect upon the range of talk in which they had been engaged and to consider how their own use of language appropriate to the role had given the drama credibility. Discussion showed raised awareness of the effects of bullying upon the immediate victim, families and the community. The children, through their roles, had been able to identify proactive strategies for creating a school ethos which would make bullying less likely to thrive. The role of the 'innocent bystander' was explored and the ways in which the children become part of the problem if they do not go to the aid of the victim or, more realistically, to get help from someone else, usually an adult. The activity demonstrates how powerful a tool drama can be in facilitating personal, social and moral development.

The Gruffalo's Child

A Year 1/2 (vertically grouped) class had been reading the *The Gruffalo's Child* by Julie Donaldson and Axel Scheffler (2004). This is the story of a bored young creature, the Gruffalo's child, whose curiosity gets the better of her. Despite warnings from her father, the Gruffalo, she heads off into the deep dark wood in search of the Big Bad Mouse, where she experiences the fright of her life.

The teacher used a number of drama strategies in order to develop the children's ability to listen with concentration, to use talk in order to plan effectively, to work collaboratively and to act out well-known stories. She began by recapping on the first part of the story when the Gruffalo was warning his daughter to stay away from the wood and showing the illustration of that moment. She asked the children to listen carefully of the description of the Big Bad Mouse because they would all be playing the part soon. She read:

> The Gruffalo said that no gruffalo should
> Ever set foot in the deep dark wood.
> 'Why not? Why not?' *'Because if you do*
> *The Big Bad Mouse will be after you.*
> *I met him once,'* said the Gruffalo.
> *'I met him a long time ago.'*
> 'What does he look like? Tell us, Dad.
> Is he terribly big and terribly bad?'
> *'I can't quite remember,'* the Gruffalo said.
> *'The Big Bad Mouse is terribly strong*
> *And his scaly tail is terribly long.*
> *His eyes are like pools of terrible fire*
> *And his terrible whiskers are tougher than wire.'*

She asked the children to find a space in order to pretend that they were each the Big Bad Mouse. She said, 'On the first signal [the shaking of a tambourine] you can move around – and remember, the Big Bad Mouse moves quietly through the woods – but on the second signal you must freeze.' The children spent some time moving around and getting into character. The description of the Big Bad Mouse makes him 'larger than life' and is therefore ideal for such an activity with Key Stage 1 children who enjoy creating exaggerated movements in order to represent giants and monsters.

She said, 'If the Big Bad Mouse could speak, what would he say?' As she moved between the children, she invited some of them in turn to speak:

I'll eat you up!

Keep away from my woods!

I like to scare gruffalos!

Grrrowl!

Then she made an opportunity for the children to see each other's work so far. She asked those in one half of the room to 'freeze' so that those in the other half could look at the various Big Bad Mice. She asked them to comment on what they were seeing with, 'What words come into your head when you look at the Big Bad Mouse?' and, 'How would you describe the look on this Mouse's face?' There were several comments:

I like Nerssi's because how he stares make his eyes pools of fire.

Anna's making her hands like claws – her fingers are jagged.

That one [pointing to a Mouse crouching behind a table] is very frightening because he is ready to pounce.

The children were learning to comment critically on performance and those 'freezing' in character were learning about how what they were doing was impacting upon their audience.

Teacher and children in role

The teacher explained that she would now be playing the part of the Gruffalo and that they would be the Gruffalo's children. They were to try to persuade her to let them go into the wood. She suggested that they turn to each other to discuss possible persuasive arguments. After a few minutes, the whole-class improvisation began.

> Please, Dad, can I go to the wood?
> *It's too dark in there.*
> Can I go with a torch?
> *Absolutely not.*
> Can I go with my friend?
> *No, no.*
> I will take some cheese for the mouse.
> *No. He will still be after you.*

It was evident that permission would not be granted so, out of role, the teacher suggested that, just as in the book, they consider going without their Dad's permission. She introduced the next strategy.

Conscience alley

This strategy allows children to explore the moral dilemma within a story or a situation and to articulate and explore conflicting viewpoints. In this case, they were to consider the reasons both for and against setting off into the woods.

The teacher organised the children into two lines facing each other. She said, 'You are all Gruffalo children. Those of you in this line [pointing to the one the left] are going to give reasons *for* going into the deep dark wood and those of you in this line [the one on the right] are going to give reasons for *not* going'. She gave them some time to think and then she moved down the line inviting each child to speak, one at a time, first from the left line, second from the right, and so on. Their responses began as follows:

I want to meet the Big Bad Mouse.

Dad says don't go.

We can go together.

Then I'll be in trouble.

We can go at night when he's asleep.

I'm scared.

We can take a torch.

Then the Big Bad Mouse will see us.

This process helps generate new thinking and a range of views but for the less confident child who is challenged by having to think on the spot in this way, s/he can simply repeat a statement already made, therefore requiring concentrated listening.

At the end of the conscience alley exercise, the teacher gave the children opportunities to discuss some of the reasons offered both for and against the journey and asked if the activity had made them think of anything in their own lives, or in books and on television. One child talked about the film of J.K. Rowling's first Harry Potter Book, *Harry Potter and the Philosopher's Stone* (Rowling 2004). He said, 'Harry went back to find Hermione but everybody had to leave the school, but he did it'. Several children had seen the film and were keen to discuss that incident. The teacher asked them what they thought about Harry's decision to disobey on that occasion. There was animated discussion and several points of view were given:

Well, he shouldn't have done it because it was dangerous.

She was his friend, so that's fair.

He does magic, so he is OK.

He did it for the right reasons.

But what if he'd been killed?

Then there wouldn't be any more Harry Potter books!

This last comment provoked gasps of horror, as well as laughter!

These young children were engaging in debate on moral issues. The teacher ended the activity by saying that it was clear that there was determination from several Gruffalo children to go on the adventure so, in their next drama, they would all be playing those who had decided to go.

Whole-class improvisation

The teacher gathered the children on the carpet and explained that in their drama she would now be acting alongside them as a Gruffalo child. She reminded them that as their Gruffalo Dad wouldn't allow them into the wood, they would have to go without him finding out. She asked, 'How should we do this?' and the children offered suggestions about creeping quietly out of the house so as not to disturb the Gruffalo. Stories in which people are required to move quietly with stealth are useful in the Key Stage 1 classroom both for helping the teacher feel 'in control' and keeping the noise level down so as not to disturb other classes. This is where a classroom full of furniture becomes a valuable resource for the story: it serves both as an interior of a house through which the children must move quietly as well the dark wood with bushes and trees to provide hiding places and cover.

The teacher began by reading from the story:

> One snowy night when the Gruffalo snored
> The Gruffalo's Child was feeling bored.
> The Gruffalo's Child was feeling brave
> So she tiptoed out of the gruffalo cave.
> The snow fell fast and the wind blew wild.
> Into the wood went the Gruffalo's Child.

As the children moved through the 'wood', she asked them to 'freeze'. She introduced the thought tracking strategy, saying, 'As I entered the deep dark wood, I thought to myself . . .' She invited each child to speak the character's thoughts aloud as she moved among them. They responded:

I feel shaky.

I don't want to see a ghost.

What will happen to me?

I hope I meet the Mouse!

My dad will be very angry.

Upon their safe return from the encounter with the 'Big Bad Mouse', the teacher invited the children to go beyond the usual end of the story. One of Schleffer's illustrations shows how the little mouse had been able to dupe the Gruffalo's child into thinking he really was a Big Bad Mouse. He had climbed a tree and positioned himself so that the light from the moon fell upon him and cast a long shadow on the ground, making him appear enormous.

Paired work

The teacher organised the children into pairs: one child was to play the Gruffalo Dad and the other, the Gruffalo's child. She set the scene: 'The Gruffalo Dad has woken to find his child missing. He is worried and cross, hoping and waiting for her return.' Her instructions to the Gruffalo's children were:

If you find your Dad awake, although he will be angry, at least you can explain to him how the little mouse had tricked him to thinking he was a Big Bad Mouse, then perhaps he will no longer be afraid to go into the deep dark wood.

This activity demanded sophisticated use of subject-specific language and could be used to help the teacher assess levels of understanding in relation to how shadows are created and vary in size.[7] This is an example of how drama can inform assessment in other curriculum areas, such as science. By going on an imaginative journey beyond the traditional end of the story, the children were able to enlighten the Gruffalo with their expert knowledge and understanding.

Each of the drama activities explored in the two examples above can be delivered within a lesson, and need not necessarily occur on the same day. In fact, giving time for children to think back on what they have done in their previous drama can lead to further reflective talk, and allows for what Fisher (2004) calls 'soft thinking' – that which takes place over days rather than hours. The strategies can be applied to the exploration of other themes and texts and throughout the primary school. The processes of drama are largely transferable between different ages and key stages. The levels of sophistication of the language used will be dictated by the maturity of the group and by the teacher's skill in guiding and challenging the children's thinking.[8]

With imagination and willingness to take the occasional risk, the primary teacher will benefit enormously from adding drama to her teaching repertoire. If teachers are to create 'sparks that make learning vivid' (DfES 2003) in the classroom, then drama is the box of matches.

The best bit of drama was I talked like the Gruffalo and it was weird and wonderful.

(Thomas, age 6)

Notes

1 See The Rose Report (2006) and Every Child a Talker (2008).
2 See Johnson (2006).
3 See nationalstrategies.standards.dcsf.gov.uk/node/88194.
4 See, for more discussion, Johnson (2004).
5 For more discussion, see Johnson (2002).
6 Johnson (2006) explores Dorothy Heathcote's 'mantle of the expert' approach in the classroom.
7 See National Curriculum for units 1D: Light and Dark to 3F (Parsons 2003).
8 See, for more details, Johnson (2004).

Bibliography

Clipson-Boyles, S. (1998) *Drama in Primary English Teaching*, London: David Fulton Publishers.
DfES (1999) *Opportunities for Drama in the Framework of Objectives*, London: HMSO.
DfES (2003) *Excellence and Enjoyment: A Strategy for Primary Schools*, London: HMSO.
Donaldson, J. and Scheffler, A. (2004) *The Gruffalo's Child*, London: Macmillan.

Every Child a Talker (2008) Available at: http://www.nationalstrategies.standards.dcsf.gov.uk/node/277287.

Fisher, R. (2004) 'What is creativity?' in R. Fisher and M. Williams (eds) *Unlocking Creativity*, London: David Fulton.

Fleming, M. (1994) *Starting Drama Teaching*, London: David Fulton Publishers.

Heathcote, D. and Bolton, G. (1995) *Drama for Learning: An Account of Dorothy Heathcote's 'Mantle of the Expert' Approach to Education*, Portsmouth, NH: Heinemann.

Hendy, L. and Toon, L. (2001) *Supporting Drama and Imaginative Play in the Early Years*, Buckingham: Open University Press.

Johnson, C. (2002) 'Writing aloud: drama and writing', in M. Williams (ed.) *Unlocking Writing: A Guide for Teachers*, London: David Fulton.

Johnson, C. (2004) 'Creative drama: thinking from within', in R. Fisher and M. Williams (eds) *Unlocking Creativity: Teaching Across the Curriculum*, London: David Fulton.

Johnson, C. (2006) 'What did I say?: speaking, listening and drama', in R. Fisher and M. Williams (eds) *Unlocking Literacy*, London: David Fulton.

Parson, R. (2003) *KS2 Science: Light and Shadows*, London: CGP.

Rowling, J.K. (2004) *Harry Potter and the Philosopher's Stone*, London: Bloomsbury.

Rose Report (2006) Available at: http://www.literacytrust.org.uk/assets/0000/1175/Rose_Review.pdf.

Winston, J. (2000) *Drama, Literacy and Moral Education 5–11*, London: David Fulton.

Winston, J. et al. (2001) *Beginning Drama 4–11*, London: David Fulton.

Woolland, B. (2003) *The Teaching of Drama in the Primary School*. Harlow: Longman.

CHAPTER

6

Letting Talents Shine: Developing Oracy with Gifted and Talented Children

Mary Williams

Introduction

In this chapter the role of speaking and listening, as it relates to gifted and talented children – across the Foundation Stage and Key Stages 1 and 2 – will be explored drawing on findings from a DfES Key Stage 1 Gifted and Talented project – 'Nurturing Young Talent' (NYT) now published (Koshy *et al.* 2006).[1] Oracy is at the heart of learning and occurs in most subjects of the curriculum in some form or another, although it develops initially as young children learn through play. Therefore, consideration will be given to the teacher's role in supporting the speaking and listening of gifted and talented pupils in literacy and across the curriculum.

All children – especially higher ability pupils – need to be motivated through challenging activities that involve them in deep levels of thinking and discussion with others during whole-class or group activities across the primary school curriculum and in Early Years settings (DCSF 2008). On an individual level, they need to be aware that they use 'inner speech' as the medium in which to think. As part of reflection on learning, opportunities for pupils to gain metacognitive awareness need to be given, as this offers yet another important dimension to thinking, i.e. by getting them to think about *how* they have learned something, as well as to share *what* they have discovered in the course of any investigation.

In terms of literacy, oracy underpins learning to read and write. Therefore, the interrelationship of speaking and listening to reading and writing will be examined to show how the precocious oral abilities that many gifted and talented children possess can be utilised to the full. The need for some of these pupils to be given a listening agenda will also be explored. Practical ways to challenge higher ability pupils will be suggested, in particular through the use of 'dialogue and questioning', 'discussion', 'presentation' and 'drama' across the Programmes of Study of the English Curriculum – speaking and listening, writing and reading. The premise that creative, problem-solving tasks are vital if gifted and talented children are to remain focused and to learn effectively will provide the backdrop to the debate.

The rights of gifted and talented pupils

To put the discussion into perspective, the rights of gifted and talented children need some consideration first. Until the setting up of the Gifted and Talented unit at the DfES in 1999, the educational needs of higher ability pupils had not been a high priority in the UK, Ofsted suggesting that the needs of the more able were not adequately addressed (Ofsted 2001, 2003). In addition, the needs of younger gifted and talented children have quite often been neglected (Koshy and Robinson 2006).

Gifts and talents, whatever they may be, need nurturing, as they are unlikely to develop on their own. All children should be given a curriculum that provides them with the 'optimal match' (CTY 1994) with their learning potential and nowhere is this more important than for gifted and talented pupils. This match will be achieved when an appropriately challenging curriculum is adjusted to match the child's pace and level of learning. Higher ability children have the right to a stimulating, challenging and creative education: something that is of vital importance if early potential is to flourish (DfES 2007).

Consequently, gifted and talented children require a differentiated curriculum that will meet their needs along with those of the rest of the ability spectrum in the class. This is not always easy to achieve, particularly in classrooms where there is a wide range of ability. To leave higher ability pupils to take care of themselves is risky because, as most teachers would agree, idle, unchallenged minds will soon find alternative, and sometimes inappropriate, ways of keeping amused. Reassuringly, however, gifted and talented do not require a curriculum that is radically different from other pupils in the class but one in which the pace is faster and the level of instruction deeper and where the accent is on them reflecting about what they are doing. According to the QCA (2001), there are five crucial dimensions to the work they should be given:

- breadth;
- depth;
- acceleration;
- independence;
- time for reflection.

Teachers can set all the children in a class the same task but with different, more challenging outcomes being required from higher ability pupils. Activities should be planned so that they become progressively more difficult as pupils work through them, based on the assumption that the more able will reach these quicker. Sometimes higher ability pupils can be set different tasks from the rest of the class, specifically geared to their own interests to provide them with essential motivation for learning, such as when they are supported in finding out more about a personal interest.

Therefore, to make the most of their education, gifted and talented pupils should be given tasks that demand high levels of commitment from them through an enriched curriculum (Renzulli 1994) that captures their imaginations and nurtures their potential. This will be achieved via creative, problem-solving tasks that sometimes involve collaboration with peers (good for their sociability) that often require an oral outcome. Ways of developing such a curriculum for gifted and talented pupils will now be looked at in more depth.

Thinking across the curriculum

All children need to be given time to think and to express their ideas across a range of curriculum subjects. They need to know how to discuss ways to solve problems in creative and systematic ways. They need to be able to outline their findings so that they are accessible to other children in the class, as well as to pupils of similar ability to themselves. This is unlikely to be achieved without direct input or modelling by teachers about how best to undertake these activities. One of the problems with oracy teaching – or the lack of it – in the past has been that it was assumed that as talking comes naturally to most people, it could be left to its own devices. Equally, although often they are orally adept, gifted and talented pupils may need help to become active and sympathetic listeners. This is essential if they are to become socially confident, as well as intellectually able. In order to be successful across subjects of the primary curriculum, children need to be encouraged to think about what they are learning and how they are learning it. This will best be achieved while carrying out stimulating, creative tasks.

Encouraging gifted and talented children to think

The important relationship between 'speaking and listening' and thinking has been acknowledged for a long time.[2] Gifted and talented pupils, in particular, need the match and pace of the curriculum to be accelerated and deepened (as above). This can be gained through challenging them to higher levels of thinking through motivating them to solve interesting and relevant problems. To achieve this, teachers need to ask questions that require reflective and elaborated responses and demand higher order thinking (Bloom 1956; Fisher 2001). This should involve analysis synthesis and evaluation (Koshy and Casey 1997; Koshy et al. 2006).

High levels of thinking like this occur when children generate outcomes that show imagination and originality and are capable of being thoughtfully evaluated. Essential to this is a questioning classroom, where teachers and pupils ask unusual and challenging questions; where new connections are made; where ideas are represented in different ways – visually, physically and verbally – and where innovative approaches to finding solutions are encouraged. Through such lessons children develop new thinking as they generate and extend ideas in collaboration with each other and their teachers. To assess whether a particular lesson has stimulated the children to think creatively, look for evidence of pupils doing the following:

- applying their imagination;
- generating their own questions, hypotheses, ideas and outcomes;
- developing skills or techniques through creative activity;
- using judgement to assess their own or others' creative work.

(Fisher and Williams 2004)

Encouraging gifted and talented children to be creative

There are several keys to unlocking creativity.[3] Most of these are speech dependent: be it through actual discussion with others or via 'inner speech' as pupils reflect upon what they are doing. These keys include:

- motivation;
- inspiration;
- gestation;
- collaboration.

(ibid.)

Creativity is a critical element in fostering ability. It takes children beyond the here-and-now into realms of thinking that involve using the imagination to solve problems that transcend curriculum subjects. Being creative depends on the use of multiple intelligences (Gardner 1993), with one of these being 'linguistic'; therefore, children need stimulating problem-solving tasks to encourage them to think creatively.

With young children, this can often be achieved through play. In the Early Years Foundation Stage (DCSF 2007), play is seen as both a context for children's learning as well as a means of keeping motivation alive. Indeed, the value and importance of play as integral to children's learning and development cannot be underestimated (Moyles 2010). In the UK, the Foundation Stage (for children between the ages of 3–5 years) and Key Stage 1 (from 5–7 years) is where the potential of play as a means of learning about the world and each other can be maximised. It is counterproductive to start formal learning too soon because children learn best in ways that are holistic and context-specific. Learning through play is beneficial because, at the time, the play activity is the child's world with a reality of its own, but to have purpose, it needs to be carefully planned. Here is an example of an activity devised for Key Stage 1 gifted and talented children.

In this example from the NYT project (Koshy et al. 2006), children from a school in the London Borough of Hounslow were asked to solve the following problem – how can you transfer water from one water tray to another using a variety of pipes and containers? (The trays were too far apart for water to be tipped straight from one to the other.) The children selected for this activity had already shown an ability to be experimental and to take risks in a previous water-based activity. A large percentage of children in this school were using English as an additional language (EAL) so it was decided to set up the task using a mixture of gesture and simple verbal interaction. Throughout the task the children found ways of communicating with one another, providing a useful platform on which social interaction and oral confidence could grow. Above all, they revealed spatial and interpersonal intelligence in interpreting the task as well as emergent scientific concepts about water.

Once completed, the activity was reviewed by the staff involved and the following conclusions were reached. Tasks for higher ability EAL learners need to be:

- culturally accessible to all;
- related to previous experience;
- child-centred;
- not too language dependent;
- large-scale and motivating to appeal to all genders;
- open-ended – lasting for more than one session with children being given as much time as they need to complete them;
- resourced easily with overnight storage being considered from the outset.

To make sure that play is purposeful, as in the example above, it must be challenging, so that all children, but particularly those who are gifted and talented, are encouraged to think deeply and learn to persevere while engaging in imaginative and interesting activities. They can be encouraged to explore new objects or ideas if asked to think about them in terms of:

- Does it (object, artefact or photograph) remind you of anything?
- Have you done anything like this yourself before?
- What does it smell (taste, feel, look or sound) like?

Their imaginations need to be fostered as they are asked probing questions with language being used increasingly to mediate understanding, for example, when adults respond to what children are doing and/or saying by asking these sorts of questions:

- 'Do you mean that . . .?',
- 'I think I understand what you are saying. You think that . . .?'
- 'What would happen if . . .?'
- 'What else do you need to think about?'
- 'Is there another way of doing that?'
- 'How does that help?'

(Williams, in Fisher and Williams 2004)

Adults have sometime been reluctant to intervene in children's play because they are afraid that they will disrupt the imaginative flow, but high levels of interaction involving questioning, the recall and reformulation of ideas by the child, will deepen its quality. Therefore, through high levels of questioning, gifted and talented children can be encouraged to think deeply by being asked to evaluate what did or did not work.

The role of the teacher

The role of the teacher will be critical in developing children's 'gifts and talents'. It will involve them in planning an appropriately differentiated curriculum and in asking searching questions (as above). In particular, they will need to be aware of the important role that speaking and listening play in education, for example, in doing the following:

- identifying gifts and talents;
- teaching gifted and talented pupils a variety of learning techniques;
- knowing how to give gifted and talented pupils metacognitive awareness.

Identifying gifts and talents

Problems about how to identify gifted and talented pupils still remain. Characteristics established from research undertaken in Kent suggest that oral ability has a large part to play in this, as can be seen in many of the attributes listed below:

- is continuously demanding
- is very curious
- possesses a vivid imagination
- learns more quickly than other children
- has a good memory
- has great physical energy
- can concentrate for long periods if interested
- begins to speak and read earlier than chronological peers
- has a wide vocabulary
- pays great attention to detail
- has a well-developed sense regarding social matters, e.g. leadership, taking turns, self-awareness, nuances in interaction, 'tunes in' to what is going on
- frequently asks questions, sometimes speculative or philosophical in nature
- shows a sense of humour that may be unusual or odd
- challenges by asking 'why'.

(Baczala 2003)[4]

Teaching gifted and talented pupils a variety of learning techniques

There are various ways that gifted and talented children can be challenged through speaking and listening learning techniques. These include:

- challenging dialogues and probing questioning;
- presenting;
- drama;
- providing a listening agenda;
- working in a group.

Challenging dialogues and probing questioning

Learning occurs most successfully when gifted and talented children engage in challenging dialogues with adults (and each other) as part of solving problems or investigating new objects or ideas (Vygotsky 1978). As a means of getting pupils of higher ability to be creative in their thinking, they need to be provided with cognitive challenges that often involve them in working with each other towards specific, motivating goals as in the water play challenge above. Tasks that offer this should include information processing and questioning as part of challenging dialogues between children and their teachers.

The adult's role in such dialogues is to ask probing questions that:

- make challenging cognitive demands of the child;
- manage the response – by providing models of how to synthesise disparate items of learning;
- help the child to see a task/problem through sequentially;
- help the child to select appropriate materials to solve the problem set;
- check that the child's response is appropriate;
- keep the child *actively* involved;
- pace questions asked, so that the number of probing questions asked keeps up the momentum;
- give shape to a session – by drawing the threads of learning and understanding together in a plenary and inviting children to do this for themselves.
  (adapted from Meadows and Cashdan 1988 and Fisher and Williams 2004)

In this activity from an 'Upside Down Day' project undertaken as part of the NYT venture in Dorset in (Koshy *et al.* 2006), the whole class (5- and 6-year-olds) were introduced at first to the idea through a drama activity that centred on them waking up to find that everything was upside down to what it normally was. The discussion that this engendered was highly dependent on a challenging dialogue between pupils and teacher. Also, as this activity was to be shared among four schools, ideas for it were set out clearly in the accompanying documentation, including suggestions for a series of probing questions that included the following:

- What made you think about . . .?
- How do you . . .?
- What were you thinking when . . .?

- How would your life be different?
- Think of something that would be a problem.
- How would you solve it?

The children were asked to record their thoughts in speech or thought bubbles that were entered on 'mind maps' relating to the central themes that had emerged in the initial dialogue, e.g. it is dark not light, people are walking in the sky, you have lunch before breakfast, etc. Gifted and talented children were identified by the 'special' insight they showed, for example, one child wrote about it snowing in summer, a mouse chasing a cat and the sea being yellow and the sand blue, while another attempted to write words backwards.

Presenting

Sometimes higher ability pupils can be asked to present findings from work across the curriculum, either individually, in pairs or as a group. Preparation for presentations will be needed so that pupils are analytical and systematic in their thinking, as they decide what to include, what to leave out and the order in which various points should be introduced. A proforma could be prepared like the one below to assist this process.

Box 6.1 Preparing a presentation

Ask yourself these questions and note down the answers so that they can be shared with others:

- What do I already know about the subject?
- Why am I interested in it?
- What else do I want to know?
- How and where will I find this out?
- What questions are still unanswered or have arisen during my investigation?
- Does anyone in the audience know the answers to any of these?
- Does anyone want to ask any questions?

Using artefacts or pictures to make the presentation more interesting should be considered. PowerPoints and the interactive whiteboard can also be used to facilitate the use of source material from the internet, and so on.

Drama

Another way of getting higher ability pupils to share their knowledge is through the use of the drama technique of 'hot-seating'. (This was used in 'The Upside Down Day' project (above) so that children could share their ideas before attempting to write them down and during which they were challenged to justify their opinions by their teacher and other children.) Gifted and talented children can also take on 'the mantle of the expert' for a particular subject or focus and can be questioned about what they know about it by other children in the class (Johnson, in Fisher and Williams 2006). They are the ones in the know and the challenge is for them to share what they have found out with others in an interesting and accessible way. In Chapter 5, Johnson provides further ideas and contexts in which to develop and extend children's talk in a creative context.

Providing a listening agenda

Gifted and talented children may need to be given a specific focus during some direct teaching inputs or discussions as they can be impatient and disruptive when not allowed to speak or answer first. A way to do this is to set them a 'listening' agenda and this also ensures that they do not hog the limelight all the time, as this can be very demotivating for other pupils in the class. It involves giving them something specific to listen for or a challenge that asks them to 'analyse, synthesis and evaluate' the contribution of others. To improve their powers of analysis, this can take the form of summing up the evidence offered in a debate, or at the end of a discussion relating to an investigative piece of work, e.g. in science or history.

A listening agenda could include:

- Listening to a poem and being asked to discuss it on several levels – literal, figurative, emotional, inferential and deductive.
- Assessing the motivation of a particular character from a story or poem that has been read out loud to the class.
- Taking a passive role in a group as scribe or balancer (see below), including assessing whether the mode of address adopted by the speaker was appropriate to the task in hand.
- Listening out for particular information in a presentation or during direct input on a subject by the teacher.
- Listening to information given by another (or others), making notes about it and writing it up in the form of a newspaper article.
- Listening to a persuasive speech or reading in order to comment on the features that made it effective or not.
- Summing up on a particular theme/lesson as a result of findings offered by several children to assess whether a consensus has been reached or whether there is disparity between sources.[5]

Working in a group

By implication, much of the work suggested above will require gifted and talented children to collaborate with one another. This, in itself can be quite a challenge for them, as they can be highly individualistic and easily irritated if others do not keep up with their pace of learning. Such work will only be effective if pupils know how to operate successfully in a group.

In addition to the subject-based, problem-solving nature of any task pupils, need to understand how to work in a group (Williams 2006). Therefore, during any reporting back session, children need to evaluate the effectiveness of the discussion itself. To facilitate this, they can be given roles within the group such as chair, scribe or *balancer*. This last role can be usefully given to higher ability children, as they have to listen very carefully to each contributor in order report back whether certain individuals dominated the discussion in order to determine who took the lead, so increasing their understanding of group dynamics. This may have a salutary effect on them by making them aware of how it can feel to others when someone always hogs the limelight. The role of *scribe* could also be given to gifted and talented children who tend to take the automatic lead during discussions. This gives others a chance to speak and might make the scribe more sensitive to the needs of others in the class: all part of the process of socialisation. In these more passive roles, they could be asked to decide whether those who speak the most actually make the greatest contribution to the discussion and should give evidence-based reasons for any conclusions they reach. In a more active way they could be in the *chair* as this would involve them in analysing and evaluating the contribution of others as they sum up what has been learned.

Finally, to ensure that gifted and talented are sensitive towards others when engaging in dialogues with them or when taking on the role of an expert, they should be encouraged to use a 'praise sandwich' so that others in the class feel that their contributions have been valued, i.e. offer something positive on the top and bottom, with an area for growth or contention in the middle.

Knowing how to give gifted and talented pupils metacognitive awareness

Gifted and talented children should be given challenges that involve them in higher levels of thinking such as analysis, synthesis and evaluation (as above). This brings together thinking, questioning and dialogue skills as shown in Table 6.1.

TABLE 6.1 Thinking, questioning and dialogue skills

THINKING SKILLS (NC)	CHARACTERISTIC QUESTIONS	FEATURES OF DIALOGUE
Information-processing	What is it about?	Relevant information is shared
Reasoning	What does it mean?	Reasons are expected
Enquiry	What do we need to know?	Questions are asked
Creative thinking	Can we add to it?	Ideas are developed
Evaluation	What do we think about it?	Judgements are made

Source: (Fisher and Williams 2002).

Through such high levels of thinking, gifted and talented children will be challenged to achieve at levels commensurate with their learning potential. Levels of thinking will be deepened even further if attention is paid to metacognition.

The term 'metacognition' refers to an individual's own awareness and consideration of his or her cognitive processes and strategies (Flavell 1979). It relates to the human capacity to be self-reflective, not just to think and know, but to think about how you think and know. Vygotsky (1962) argued that when the process of learning is brought to a conscious level, children become aware of their own thought processes and this helps them to gain control over the way they learn. It is not just about the integration of information with existing knowledge, but involves directing the learner's attention to what has been assimilated and understood, and the relationship of this, to the processes of learning itself.

Metacognition includes knowledge of self, as a thinker and learner, in relation to a task and in relation to a particular context. It develops the thinking ability of the learner as the levels of thinking become gradually deeper as implicit understanding becomes explicit. This works in the following way.

Box 6.2 Levels of awareness

1. *Tacit use*: Children make decisions without really thinking about them.
2. *Aware use*: Children become consciously aware of a strategy or decision-making process.
3. *Strategic use*: Children are able to select the best strategies for solving a problem.
4. *Reflective use*: Children can reflect on their thinking, before, during and after the process and evaluate progress and set targets for improvement.

(Williams and Fisher 2002)

However, getting children to think about thinking is not easy, it is a complex teaching skill that depends on three key factors, i.e.

- the task must be worthy of serious thought;
- the thinking and reasoning of pupils must be valued;
- time must be given for thinking about their thinking.

It can be made more accessible through 'modelling'. Teachers can help children to think metacognitively by modelling their own thinking processes as they engage in a range of tasks. After this, some higher ability pupils may be capable of 'modelling' themselves. This gives them an oral challenge, as they need to reveal their thinking processes to other children. If pupils are to be involved in this, they will need to rehearse what they are going to say either with their teacher, or with each other if they are working in a group or as a pair. Asking oneself metacognitive questions will be useful in this respect (or these questions can be asked by the teacher). Metacognitive questions might include:

- How did you start to solve the problem?
- Did you go up any blind alleys?
- What was particularly useful in working it out?
- Did you consider any alternative ideas?
- Why did you reject these?

- How did you figure it out?
- Would you go about a similar task in the same way?

Significantly, metacognitive awareness gained in this way can help children to make conscious decisions about how to tackle similar learning tasks in the future (Williams 2006).

Speaking and listening and literacy

Oral ability underpins learning to read and to write, so it is a vital component of literacy learning. Little direct guidance was given on how to teach higher ability children in the National Literacy Strategy (DfEE 1998) although some attempt to identify what gifted and talented pupils are able to do was offered later on:

- They are able to orchestrate the various reading cues at an early age.
- They are *active readers* who can generalize from their reading experience.

And in writing, they are able to do the following:

- latch on quickly to the conventions of different types of writing;
- *think in original ways and experiment with new styles;*
- manipulate language, sentence structure and punctuation;
- *use apt terminology and varied vocabulary.*

(DfEE 2000a)

Implicit in this are several references to 'speaking and listening' and thinking skills (in italics above) but it was not until the English National Curriculum (1999) set out teaching objectives for 'speaking and 'listening' separately (although the two are closely related), as well as for group discussion and interaction and discussion that this was given true weight.[6]

It is important to make use of the 'precocious oral ability' that many higher ability children possess to help them become fully involved in the Literacy Hour. They need to be asked to justify the language choices, or the conclusions they have reached as part of shared, guided or independent work. They can share what they have earned in a particular lesson, or from an investigation, during the plenary session where they can be encouraged to 'think aloud' (see above) by telling others what they were thinking about as they went about a task. This gives less able pupils metacognitive understanding while providing a challenge for the more able as they have to put themselves across in a way that is accessible to others.

Speaking and listening and reading

Through problem-solving activities, gifted and talented children can be challenged to demonstrate what they have understood from reading a range of texts in a variety of ways. They can be required to offer opinions about the personality and motivation of particular characters in novels. Giving children access to an idea by discussing how they think they would experience it, if it happened to them, can be stimulated by reading them carefully chosen extracts from stories and poems as part of text-level work. Higher ability children need to be set challenges that captivate them on an emotional, as well as intellectual, level. They can respond to themes in stories by offering evidence-based reasons for their thoughts about the issues raised. This will take them deeper inside the author's thinking and help them when they start to write on similar themes for themselves. Discussion with a response partner will help to increase understanding as long as preparatory work on how to go about this is undertaken (see questions below).

Similarly, children can be asked to justify conclusions reached as a result of researching into a particular problem. This may take the form of an individual enquiry but may involve pupils in high levels of discussion with similar ability children, either in their own class during group work or perhaps by making links over the internet with higher ability children from other schools. Findings can be shared with other pupils, possibly in a higher class or with others in their own (see Box 6.1 on how to prepare for a presentation). To provide appropriate depth and challenge through reading, more complex texts should be made available to gifted and talented children, who should be asked searching questions about them, for example:

- How do you know that?
- How did you learn that?
- What evidence do you have for that?
- Are there words in story that led you to think that?
- Can you think of another word that means the same as?
- What do you think s/he meant by the words . . .?

Searching for information via the internet can provide another reading challenge. Whatever the source, children need to be taught to discriminate between sources and to be aware of the possibility of bias.

Speaking and listening and writing

There are several ways this might occur including through:

- oral composition;
- writing conferences;
- being a response partner.

Oral composition

To encourage higher ability pupils to develop their writing teachers should help them to understand the processes involved (Hodson and Jones 2001). Oral composition is a crucial part of the writing process and has been highlighted as an important factor in giving young children the confidence to write. It helps to avoid the blank page syndrome that puts so many off. One device to avoid this was used by a NYT project school in the London Borough of Richmond, based on an idea from 'The Shape Game' by Anthony Browne. The teacher drew a number of non-representational shapes on a piece of paper and the gifted and talented children in the group were asked to say what they reminded them of. After much discussion a consensus was reached and the teacher made additions to the drawings to make them represent the objects concerned. After this the children were asked to tell a story that included as many of the objects as possible and initially, they worked on this together; as they were doing this, many indulged in spontaneous dramatic improvisations in order to make the point. In the pieces of writing they went on to produce individually it was evident to the teacher that their use of descriptive language devices had significantly improved.

Writing conferences

Once writing is underway, writing conferences can be used to challenge higher ability pupils. During these they can be asked to justify the language choices they have made, or to offer critiques of other children's writing (see 'response partners' below) such as in guided writing in the Literacy Hour. Sometimes these conferences will be with the teacher or a small group of other children but, on occasions, they can take place during the plenary session of a Literacy Hour.[7]

Being a response partner

Gifted and talented children can work as response partners for the writing of children of similar or lower ability while they work in pairs, although care needs to be taken to ensure that they are not always in a lead position as this could have a negative affect on interpersonal relationships within a class. Some planning needs to go into this.

Box 6.3 How to be a good 'response partner'

---

1. Listen carefully to your partner read his/her work.
2. Tell your partner what you liked about the writing.
3. Think how it might be improved:

   a. Will the audience understand it?
   b. Will they find it interesting?
   c. Is there anything missing?
   d. Can you suggest any words or changes?
   e. Is it the right length?

4. Suggest how the writing might be improved.

(Fisher and Williams 2006)

Collaborating with less able children can be quite a challenge for gifted and talented children as they are often highly individualistic and can become irritated if others do not keep up with their speed of thought. They need to be aware that it is important to show sensitivity towards others. This is made easier if they have been taught how roles operate within a group (see 'working in a group' above).

Some final reflections

Speaking and listening are both vital ingredients of effective learning. They underpin learning across the curriculum. Gifted and talented children often possess sophisticated oral ability but are not always so good at listening to the views of others. If they are not challenged appropriately – either in terms of speaking or listening – they easily become disillusioned and demotivated, so it is vital that teachers respond to their needs appropriately to ensure that they remain interested in learning and fulfil their potential. Ways of achieving this have been suggested in this chapter that are not too difficult to implement in classrooms where the demands on busy teachers, who have to cater for pupils across the ability spectrum, are heavy. All children, but particularly those who are gifted and talented, need to be encouraged to think deeply about how, as well as what, they are learning as part of creative, problem-solving tasks. Specific techniques to help them achieve this have been discussed with this in mind as, without nurturing the gifts and talents of all children, society will be impoverished. In the past, many geniuses came to the surface *despite* their education. Many more are likely to shine if appropriate attention is given to them when lessons are planned, to ensure that the talents they have are not hidden from view. Competence and confidence in speaking and listening are the keys to unlocking this.

Notes

1 The NYT project for pupils in Key Stage 1 was funded by the Gifted and Talented unit at the DfES with research support being offered by Brunel University's BACE centre. Some 14 local authorities took part and the final report was published in 2006.
2 See Williams (2000), for more about this.
3 See Fisher and Williams (2004), for more details.
4 This source is not actually from the Key Stage 1 NYT research project although the Medway division of Kent Local Authority is involved.
5 See DfES (2003), for suggestions for more listening activities.
6 In the early stages of the National Curriculum, 'speaking and listening' fought hard to be recognised as being of equal importance to reading and writing (see Cox 1995). It was not until 2001 that it was properly acknowledged.
7 See Williams (2002), for more about teaching in the Literacy Hour.

Bibliography

Baczala, K. (2003) *Guidance on Gifted and Talented Children in the Foundation Stage*, Kent: Medway Council.

Bloom, B.S. (1956) *Taxonomy of Educational Objectives*, Vol. 1, London: Longman.

Center for Talented Youth (CTY) (1994) *Philosophy and Program Policy*, Baltimore, MD: Johns Hopkins University.

Cox, B. (1995) *Cox on the Battle for the English Curriculum*, London: Hodder and Stoughton.

DCSF (2007) *Early Years Foundation Stage*, London: DCSF.

DCSF (2008) *Every Child a Talker: Guidance for Early Language Lead Practitioners*. London: DCSF.

DfEE (1998) *The National Literacy Strategy*, London: HMSO.

DfEE (1999) *The National Curriculum for England: English*, London, HMSO.

DfEE (2000a) *National Literacy and Numeracy Strategies: Guidance on Teaching Able Children*, London: QCA.

DfEE (2000b) *Curriculum Guidance for the Foundation Stage*, London: QCA.

DfES (1999) *Excellence in Cities*, London: DfES Publications.

DfES (2003) *Speaking, Listening, Learning with Children in Key Stages 1 and 2*, London: QCA.

DfES (2007) *National Literacy and Numeracy Strategies: Gifted and Talented Education*, London: QCA.

Fisher, R. (1999) *First Stories for Thinking*, Oxford: Nash Pollock

Fisher, R. (2001) 'Philosophy in primary schools', *Reading*, 35(2): 67–73.

Fisher, R. and Williams, M. (eds) (2004) *Unlocking Creativity*, London: David Fulton.

Fisher, R. and Williams, M. (eds) (2006) *Unlocking Literacy*, London: David Fulton.

Flavell, J. (1979) 'Metacognition and cognitive monitoring: a new era of cognitive developmental enquiry', *American Psychologist*, 34: 906–11.

Gardner, H. (1993) *Multiple Intelligences*, New York: Basic Books.

Hodson, P. and Jones, D. (2001) *Teaching Children to Write: A Process Approach to Writing for Literacy*, London: David Fulton.

Johnson, C. (2000) ' "What did I say?": Speaking, listening and drama', in R. Fisher and M. Williams (eds) *Unlocking Literacy*, London: David Fulton.

Koshy, V. (2001) *Teaching Gifted Children 4–7*, London: David Fulton.

Koshy, V. and Casey, R. (1997) *Effective Provision for Able and Exceptionally Able Children*, London: Hodder and Stoughton.

Koshy, V., Mitchell, C. and Williams, M. (2006) *Nurturing Gifted and Talented Children at Key Stage 1: A Report of Action Research Projects*, (Research Report 741), London: DfES.

Koshy, V. and Robinson, N. (2006) 'Too long neglected: gifted young children', *European Early Childhood Education Research Journal*, 14(2): 113–26.

Meadows, S. and Cashdan, A. (1988) *Helping Children Learn*, London: David Fulton.

Moyles, J. (2002) 'Foreword', in A. Craft (ed.) *Creativity and Early Years Education*, London: Continuum.

Moyles, J. (2010) *The Excellence of Play*, Maidenhead: Open University Press.

Ofsted (2001) *Providing for Gifted and Talented Pupils: An Evaluation of Excellence in Cities and Other Grant-Funded Programmes*, London: Ofsted.

Ofsted (2002) *National Literacy Strategy: The First Four Years 1998–2002*, London: Ofsted.

Ofsted (2003) *Excellence in Cities and Education Action Zones*, London: Ofsted.

QCA (2001) *Working with Gifted and Talented Children*, London: QCA.

Renzulli, J. (1994) *Schools for Talent Development*, Connecticut: Creative Learning Press.

Vygotsky, L. (1962) *Thought and Language*, Cambridge, MA: MIT Press.

Vygotsky, L. (1978) *Mind in Society*, Cambridge, MA: Harvard University Press.

Wallace, B. (2002) *Teaching Thinking Skills across the Early Years*, London: David Fulton.

Williams, M. (2000) 'The part which metacognition can play in raising standards in English at Key Stage 2', *Reading*, 34(1): 3–8.

Williams, M. (ed.) (2002) *Unlocking Writing*, London, David Fulton.

Talking to Think:
Why Children Need
Philosophical Discussion

Robert Fisher

Thinking has to be learned in the way dancing has to be learned.

(Nietzsche 1888)

Philosophy is good because it gets you to use parts of the brain you don't use in other lessons.

(Karl, aged 10)

'Why is speaking and listening important?' I asked a group of 9-year-olds. 'It helps to think,' said Andrea. 'It helps to build your brain,' said Dan. 'You learn more,' said Pat. They were surely right. Human intelligence is primarily developed through speaking and listening. The quality of our lives depends on the quality of our thinking and on our ability to communicate and discuss what we think with others. Talk is intrinsic to literacy and to our ability to form relationships with others. It is the foundation of both IQ (verbal intelligence) and EQ (emotional intelligence). Every lesson therefore should include some time for 'talking to think'.

This chapter is about a special form of 'talking to think' based on an approach called 'Philosophy for Children' (P4C).[1] It is a form of dialogic teaching that emphasises the development of critical and creative thinking through questioning and dialogue between children and teachers and between children and children. Researchers have reported striking cognitive gains through this approach in the classroom.[2] Philosophy for Children can help enhance communicative skills as well as develop habits of intelligent behaviour. These habits of intelligent behaviour include being:

- *Curious* – through asking deep and interesting questions.
- *Collaborative* – through engaging in thoughtful discussion.
- *Critical* – through giving reasons and evidence.

- *Creative* – through generating and building on ideas.
- *Caring* – through developing awareness of self and care of others.

Philosophical discussion develops the kinds of thinking, as Karl says, that children may not use in other lessons, including *philosophical intelligence* – the capacity to ask and seek answers to existential questions (Fisher 2008b). Second, philosophical enquiry provides a means for children to develop *discussion skills* – the capacity to engage in thoughtful conversations with others. Third, philosophical discussion of complex objects of intellectual enquiry such as stories enhances *critical thinking* and verbal reasoning – the capacity to draw inferences and deductions from all kinds of texts. Fourth, philosophical enquiry helps develop *creative thinking* – the capacity to generate hypotheses and build on the ideas of others. Fifth, doing philosophy with children helps develop *emotional intelligence* – the capacity to be self-aware and caring towards others, providing essential practice in *active citizenship* and participative democracy. The chapter concludes with a warning about the challenges that can arise from engaging in talk for thinking.

Being curious: asking open questions

Studies of interaction in the classroom over the past 50 years have consistently shown that it is teacher-talk that dominates the classroom and that in much of this talk there is a lack of open questioning.[3] Such studies show that often in teacher-led discussions that closed questions predominate, children only make brief responses, teacher-talk rarely challenges children's thinking and that pupil–pupil discussion (rather than gossip) was rare.

An open question is one that allows for a range of possible answers. A closed question allows for only a true or false answer. One of the problems that results from teachers using too many closed questions is that it leads over the years to a decline in curiosity of children. The need to test and 'cover' the curriculum leads to students asking fewer questions the older they get.[4]

Open questions, like those used by Socrates in ancient Greece, have many potential benefits. Like closed questions they can offer cognitive challenge, but they also do the following:

- encourage more flexible thinking;
- allow depth of discussion;
- test the limits of knowledge rather than one item of knowledge;
- encourage better assessment of children's beliefs;
- offer the possibility to clear up misunderstandings;
- result in unanticipated and unexpected answers, new hypotheses and connections to previous knowledge.

A 10-year-old child, when asked in a P4C session, 'Is there a difference between knowing something and believing something?' replied, 'Yes, there is, because, for example, I believe in Father Christmas, but I know he doesn't exist!'

Teaching for thinking requires a community approach to enquiry in the classroom, not one or two voices creating single viewpoints, but many voices creating multiple viewpoints. The community of enquiry is sustained by the use of complex open-ended questions and elaborate explanatory responses – by teachers as well as children. For example, a teacher using a story that includes the theme of truth (such as Aesop's fable 'Mercury and the Axe') might prepare a number of open-ended prompt questions to encourage children to discuss the nature of truth. Box 7.1 presents a list of such questions that have been used in many primary classes:[5]

Box 7.1 Thinking about telling the truth

Key question: What is truth?

1. Do you think this is a true story? Why?
2. What do we mean when we say something is true?
3. What do we call something that is not true? What does 'false' mean?
4. What is a lie?
5. What do we call a story which is not true? What is fiction/a fable/a fairy tale?
6. Which character in the story was honest? What does 'honest' mean?
7. Which character in the story was a liar? What does 'liar' mean?
8. Is it better to tell the truth or lies? Why?
9. Have you ever told a lie? Can you say when or why?
10. Is it ever right to tell a lie? Is it ever wrong to tell the truth?

Here is an excerpt from one such classroom discussion, prompted by the teacher using questions like those above:

Child 1: Sometimes you say something you think is true. It's not a lie if you think it is true.

Child 2: I disagree with that because you could think something was true and say it was true when it was not true.

Teacher: Can you give an example?

Child 2: Well, if you could say it is raining because you thought it was raining and it was only birds on the roof. You can say something you think is true although in fact it is not true.

Child 3: You can only tell if something is true if you or somebody sees it with their own eyes and ears. That is why there are many people who think things are true, like ghosts or witches, that sort of thing. But you might be wrong so you have to check it first before you say it's true.

Child 4: It's not true because you say it is, but it might be.

If Howard Gardner (1999) is right that the human mind contains many forms of intelligence, then philosophical intelligence (what he calls 'existential intelligence') may be one of these. All humans have the capacity to ask and respond to existential questioning about ideas and conceptual problems – *Why? How do you know? What do you mean by . . .?* These questions lie at the heart of talking for thinking. Such talk involves processing information at the literal level and trying to find deeper meaning at a conceptual level, for example by asking questions such as *What is love?, What is truth?, What is beauty?* But can children engage in this kind of questioning?

What research into P4C has shown is that even young children have the capacity to engage in philosophic questioning, like Tom, aged 5, who asked: 'Where does time go when it stops?' Tom may not of course fully understand his question, but he is full of curiosity and wonder. This capacity to question lies at the heart of intelligent behaviour. But as he gets older it is likely that Tom will ask fewer questions in school. However, the practice of P4C would help to sustain and develop his ability to question and interrogate the world. It has a well-researched pedagogy called 'community of enquiry' and teaching programmes through which the habits of intelligent behaviour can be developed. These habits will help them face the conceptual problems and conflicts that face them in an uncertain world. An 8-year-old expressed the problem we all face: 'The trouble is people are telling you different things, and sometimes your mind tells you to do different things too!'

Gardner (1999) argues that 'Students should probe with sufficient depth a manageable set of examples so that they come to see how one thinks and acts in the manner of a scientist, a geometer, an artist, an historian'. In terms of philosophical intelligence, this means showing students what it is like to think and act as a critical speaker, listener and thinker. Michael Ross is a teacher who has used P4C with his primary school classes for many years. He does this, he says:

> for the simple reason that philosophy in itself is one of the basic activities of human beings – the questions about life – Why are we here? What is it all about? What ought I to do? etc. may be ignored due to the pressures of everyday life but they are all ultimately addressed by everyone at various periods throughout their lives.

The following are some of the questions raised by a group of Year 3 and 4 children (7–9-year-olds) who had asked if they could discuss God at their next philosophy session in the community of enquiry.[6] The questions reflect the breadth of their vision and imagination:

- Who made God?
- Who is God?
- How was God made?
- How old is God?
- How did God make the world?
- Why was God made?
- Is God real?
- How did He make us?

- What does Heaven look like?
- Why is God so special?
- Why does God make thunder?
- Why did God make us?
- Why did God make the devil?
- Why does God kill us?
- Why did God make swear words?

The unique value of P4C is that it is the only well-researched thinking approach that focuses specifically on developing questioning, and in particular the kinds of questioning that enable children to think and act with philosophical intelligence.

Collaborating in thoughtful discussion

A community of enquiry seeks to create the optimal conditions for group discussion. One of the prime benefits of this is that it helps children to internalise the ground rules for intelligent discussion. Recent research shows how important this process is in children's thinking. One study by Wegerif describes how teaching the ground rules for effective discussion helped groups to solve non-verbal reasoning test problems. These same children then did statistically better than matching control classes at individual non-verbal reasoning tests.[7] Simply learning how to discuss in reasonable and reflective ways seems to help improve children's reasoning and problem solving skills.

What is important is to establish the ground rules for such discussion. One teacher did this by listing and discussing with the children all the 'talking' words they could think of, such as 'argument', 'discussion' and 'reason'. The children in groups then discussed and agreed the meaning of each word (with the help of dictionaries and thesauruses). Then they discussed in groups 'the most important rules that people talking in groups should follow' and were asked to come up with no more than six of these. They then discussed as a class the different sets of rules and agreed a final list to display in the classroom as shown in Box 7.2:

Box 7.2 Our rules for talking and listening

- We only talk one at a time.
- We all listen to the speaker.
- We respect what people say – no 'put downs'.
- We try to give reasons for what we say.
- We say what we mean.
- We can disagree and say 'Why?'

The aims of P4C focus not only on questioning, but on developing discussion and thinking skills. The discussion skills that underlie any learning conversation include: information-processing, enquiry, reasoning, creative thinking and evaluation.

P4C helps develop:

- *Information-processing skills*: through seeking the meaning of concepts and ideas and using precise language to express what we think. 'Philosophy is good,' as Paul, aged 10, said, 'because it helps you understand what you mean.' Information is sought during discussion by use of questions such as: *What do we know from this?, What do we not know?, What do we need to know?*

- *Enquiry skills*: through asking relevant questions, posing problems, and engaging in a process of serious and sustained investigation. Enquiry is facilitated during philosophical enquiry by questions such as: *What do we want to find out?, What question(s) do we want to ask?, What are the problems?*

- *Reasoning skills*: through reading, discussion and writing to draw inferences and make deductions, give reasons for opinions. As Carl, aged 11, said: 'Philosophy helps me to give reasons and explain what I mean.' Reasoning is encouraged by questions such as: *What can we infer?, Are there good reasons for believing it?, Can we explain what it means?*

- *Creative thinking skills*: through being playful with ideas, suggesting possible hypotheses, apply imagination to their thinking, and to look for alternative explanations and ideas. As Ravi, age 10, says: 'It can be fun playing with ideas, like thinking impossible things and wondering if they are impossible.' Creativity is encouraged by questions such as: *Can we build on that idea?, Is there another possible viewpoint?, How could it be different?*

- *Evaluation skills*: through applying their own judgement to contestable issues, develop criteria for judging the value of ideas, evaluate the ideas and contributions of others, and practise being self-critical and self-correcting. As Paula, aged 13, said: 'Philosophy gives you the confidence to speak and think for yourself.' Evaluation can be guided by questions such as: *What have we learned from this enquiry?, How has our thinking changed?, What do we still need to think about?*

P4C integrates all these aspects of thinking into one process. Nothing achieves these ends more effectively than open-ended group discussions of ideas and questions in which young people are interested, assisted by a philosophically aware teacher.

Being critical and creative

What philosophical enquiry offers is a tried and tested strategy for helping children apply critical and creative reasoning to stories and other texts. The teaching strategy, which is based on whole-class discussion, is called the 'community of enquiry'. It is not a new strategy, but one that is gaining popularity, because it works in making children more reflective and critical readers. Teachers in more than 30 countries world-wide find that philosophy is adding value to the primary curriculum by providing a 'Fourth R' – Reasoning, to the basic curriculum. In Brazil alone, more than 30,000 children are involved in a P4C programmes that are helping to raise standards of literacy.

How does it work in the classroom? Ideally the group sits in a circle or horse-shoe, the aim being that everyone can see everyone else. The following are typical stages in a lesson:

Box 7.3 A P4C talking to think lesson format[8]

- *Focusing exercise* – sharing the learning objectives, remembering the agreed rules, and using a relaxation exercise or thinking game to ensure alert yet relaxed attention.
- *Sharing a stimulus* – presenting a story, poem, picture or other stimulus for thinking.
- *Thinking time* – children think of what is strange, interesting or unusual about the stimulus and share their thoughts with a partner.
- *Questioning* – children ask their own (or partner's) questions which are written on a board, these are discussed and one is chosen to start the enquiry.
- *Discussion* – children are asked to respond, building on each other's ideas, with the teacher probing for reasons, examples and alternative viewpoints.
- *Review* – review the discussion (e.g. using a graphic map), invite last words from children to reflect on the discussion, making links to real situations and possible 'homework'.

Children tend to expect to have their questions unequivocally answered by grown-ups, not discussed by other children. They are often not used to having their attention focused on a particular issue for a length of time, to discuss questions in a systematic and sustained way or to consider things from a variety of viewpoints. But if they have a stimulus (for example, a story), then even young children can respond to questions in ways that can be called philosophical. This may mean helping them to move from the concrete and literal aspects of the story to the conceptual and the abstract, moving the discussion from *what* happened in the story and *why* to thinking about *what it means*.

Discussion can be moved to philosophical levels through use of Socratic questions (Fisher 2008a). Socratic questioning means using a series of questions to progressively engage higher levels of thinking – including literal, analytical and conceptual levels of thinking. The following are examples of questions that engage these three levels of thinking:

- Literal (or factual) questions ask for information
  - What is this about?
  - Can you remember what happened?
  - What do you have to do?
- Analytic questions call for critical and creative thinking
  - What question(s) do you have?
  - What reasons can you give?
  - What are the problems/possible solutions here?
- Conceptual questions call for abstract thinking
  - What is the key concept (strategy or rule) here and what does it mean?
  - What criteria are we using to judge this (or test if it is true)?
  - How might we further investigate this concept (strategy or hypothesis)?

This excerpt of discussion of the story *The Monkey and her Baby* (Fisher 1999) with 6–7-year-olds shows the teacher trying to move the children's thinking on through a Socratic questioning:

Teacher: Why did the mother think that her baby was best?
Child 1: Because it was beautiful. She thought it was beautiful.
Child 2: She thought it was beautiful because she was the mother.
Teacher: What does it mean to be beautiful?
Child 1: It means someone thinks you are lovely.
Child 2: You are perfect . . .
Child 3: Good to look at.
Teacher: Can you be beautiful even if no-one thinks you are lovely?
Child 1: No. You can't be beautiful if no-one thinks you are beautiful.
Child 2: You can be beautiful inside, you can *feel* beautiful.

Paul, a reluctant reader, aged 8, suddenly sees the point of it all during a philosophical discussion of a story: 'Oh, I get it. We're not supposed to just read the story. We're supposed to think about it.' For him, it is a revelation. Although still struggling with the mechanics of reading, he finds he is able to make a personal response, to question, to discuss inferences and meanings using challenging texts during the shared reading session. For John, aged 10, philosophy not only gives him time to think in a serious, structured and sustained way, but also: 'It helps you ask questions. It shows you there can be many answers to one question [and] it makes you think that everything must have a reason.' For Michelle, aged 10, the community of enquiry gives you a chance to self-correct your thinking. She says: 'In philosophy lessons you can say what you really think and sometimes you change your mind.'

It is not only children who find 'the philosophy effect' stimulating and challenging. An increasing number of teachers build regular philosophy sessions into their literacy work, and report encouraging results. The national organisation for the use philosophy with children (SAPERE) report evidence from Ofsted inspections which have praised the role of philosophical discussion in raising standards of literacy in infant and junior classes (www.sapere.org.uk).[9]

One teacher reports that philosophical discussion has added 'another dimension' to her teaching, one that will provide 'added value' to her Literacy Hour. 'The results for me were truly inspirational,' says Morag Macinnes, 'and show that the approach is suitable for all children . . . and shows also that stories and collaborative discussion develop thinking skills.' So which skills are being developed?

The National Literacy Strategy (1998) described shared reading as the class reading together, 'discussing ideas and textual features, engaging in a high level of interaction'. There is no higher level of interaction with children than a philosophical discussion in a community of enquiry. The skills identified in the Literacy Strategy are those routinely developed in a philosophy for children session, including:

- linking the story to personal experience;
- interrogating and evaluating the story;
- identifying themes and ideas;
- distinguishing between opinion and evidence in the text;
- identifying implicit meanings;
- developing a critical reading stance.

Philosophy for children fulfils the criteria for high level discussion of texts, but it offers more. It is about training children not only to answer but also to ask questions, to interrogate texts, so that they not only learn how to be active, critical readers, but how to be critical and reasonable thinkers as well. Research shows that the practice of P4C enables children to obtain higher achievement scores in tests of verbal reasoning. But skills alone are not enough, what must be added to these to make them effective is the awareness of when and how we may use these skills to make a difference. Being reasonable means being more than rational. To be reasonable, we need to be mindful of self and others.

Caring – being mindful of self and others

P4C does not overlook the emotional aspects of living and learning together. The community of enquiry creates the conditions that foster emotional engagement and self-expression. It creates conditions that engender awareness of and new feelings towards others. The child will better understand, refine and control his/her feelings if he/she can reason, explain and discuss in an optimal way. Discussion in a community of enquiry requires the group to develop trust and the ability to co-operate, and to respect the views of others. They develop insight into the problematical nature of knowledge, and the need to subject what they read, see and hear to critical enquiry. Through this process they develop self-esteem as thinkers and learners.

The two sets of dispositions or attitudes which philosophy for children aims to foster are being mindful of oneself and of others. Both derive from the dialogical nature of the process, developing individual skills through co-operative activity. P4C pioneer Matthew Lipman calls these aspects 'caring' thinking (Lipman 2003). Caring thinking involves learning to collaborate with others in a community of enquiry, developing empathy and respect for others. It means being guided by questions such as:

- What do others think?
- Can I understand what they think?
- Can I learn from what they think?

By taking part in a community of enquiry children develop personal qualities such as the need to listen to and respect others, and the self-confidence to speak their mind, challenge others and change their views.

P4C develops and strengthens what Goleman calls 'emotional intelligence'. Studies that show that a youngster's life chances are at least as much affected by emotional intelligence as they are by other aspects of intelligence (Goleman 1997). Emotional intelligence includes:

- *Self-awareness* – knowing how/what you are feeling and how it impinges on your work, having a realistic awareness of one's abilities.
- *Self-regulation* – handling emotions so they facilitate the task in hand, being conscientious.
- *Resilience* – sustaining motivation, persevering in the face of setbacks, striving to improve.
- *Empathy* – sensing what other people are feeling, and using that information in our dealings with them, being able to have a rapport with a wide range of people.
- *Social skills* – reading social situations, using skills to persuade, lead and negotiate.

Philosophical discussion can develop all these personal qualities. It does so by making thinking relevant to children's personal needs and quest for answers. It is less a curriculum and more a way of life. It has more to do with what the Greeks called *phronesis* (practical wisdom) than it has to do with *tekne* (skills), more to do with the intellectual behaviour than competence. It is to do with the dispositions to behave intelligently when confronted with problems, uncertainties and puzzling questions. It is about persisting on a task, sustaining the enquiry, pursuing the question. It is about encouraging mindfulness and resisting impulsivity, thinking before acting, allowing others their say. It is about listening with understanding and empathy, devoting mental energy to attending to what others say, perceiving other points of view and sensing their emotions. It is about the metacognitive capacity to know oneself, to be aware of one's own thoughts and feelings and their effects on others.

John Stuart Mill argued we do not learn to read and write, to ride or swim merely by being told how to do it, we learn by doing it – similarly, only by involving children in democratic processes of discussion and decision-making will they ever learn how to practise it (Fisher 2008b). In a democratic society, beliefs must be self-accepted rather than uncritically imbibed, freely chosen rather than externally imposed. The nurturing of the 'reasonable person' lies at the heart of education in citizenship.

The exercise of philosophical enquiry, like any educative practice, is most effective when it is participatory, proactive, communal, collaborative and given over to constructing meanings rather than receiving them. P4C, with its emphasis on inclusive, democratic practice provides a powerful means for children to share experience and explore meaning. They can learn to express their views with confidence, to raise doubts and questions, and to challenge the thinking of others. Through engaging in a community of enquiry, children learn how to do the following:

- ask their own questions and raise issues for discussion;
- explore and develop their own ideas, views and theories;
- give reasons for what they think and believe;
- explain and argue their point of view with others ;
- listen to and consider the views and ideas of others;
- change their ideas in the light of good reasons and evidence.

The oral nature of P4C is crucial to its radical democratic role. Children are soaked with written and visual information. They need to be given a voice, a voice to question, to challenge, to construct and deconstruct the meanings around them. As Jason, aged 10, says, 'Everyone is telling you things and not getting you to think things through'. P4C is a way to engage critically with their given world, and to find a space to think things through. Like other groups in society, such as women, ethnic minorities and the poor, children's views have been marginalised and their claims to knowledge and to reason have been devalued. P4C opens up a space for thinking, for sharing beliefs and for creating knowledge, as in the following excerpt from a discussion by a group of 9-year-olds on whether it is right for parents to smack their children.

Child: I think Sophie's was a good idea why smacking children is wrong.
Teacher: What was the idea?
Child: Well, she said it was wrong because smacking you doesn't tell you why it was wrong, it just tells you that if you do it you will get smacked. That means you'll do it again, if you can get away with it and not be smacked. But if you are told why it is wrong . . . whatever it is . . . then you are less likely to do it again. Because you know why it is wrong. If you understand the reason . . .

P4C has been shown to be effective in teaching democratic community values. It gives children a voice and a vote in deciding the focus and the course of the enquiry. P4C offers an arena for the free flow of their views, a space for creativity and dialogue.

Some final reflections

P4C does not just provide a 'talking shop', or an exercise in free-flowing discussion. Research suggests that programmes that promote thinking skills have positive effects on academic achievement.[10] The research evidence from a wide range of small-scale studies across the world indicates that the philosophy for children programmes can make a difference to various aspects of a child's academic performance. Findings from my Philosophy in Primary Schools research project echo worldwide research into P4C programmes, show positive effects on:

- pupils' achievements in academic tests;
- children's self-esteem and self-concept as thinkers and learners;
- the fluency and quality of children's questioning;
- the quality of their creative thinking and verbal reasoning;
- their ability to listen to others and engage effectively in class discussion.

Research shows the positive effects of philosophical discussion extend across the curriculum.[11] As Jemma, aged 10, said: 'Philosophy can help in all your lessons, no matter what you're learning.'

Teachers generally feel that philosophical discussion adds a new dimension to their teaching and the way their pupils think. Children become more ready to ask questions, to challenge each other and to explain what they mean. As Kim, aged 9, put it; 'The important thing is not to agree or disagree but to say why.' Children too value what P4C has to offer, not only as a stimulus to learning in the classroom but as a life skill. As Camilla, aged 10, put it: 'Philosophy helps you make the most of your mind.'

A warning

It can be challenging when children are encouraged to think for themselves. Uncomfortable consequences can arise from developing philosophical habits in children. This was illustrated for me at the end of a community of enquiry with Year 2 children (6-year-olds). We had been discussing their chosen question after a Story for Thinking lesson when the discussion dried up. I then posed the class a question that I hoped might further stimulate their philosophical thinking. 'How do you know I am Mr. Fisher?' I asked. There was silence. This is good, I thought, for they are really thinking this through. The silence dragged on and I began to wonder whether any of the class would respond. Suddenly a child's hand went up. 'How do you know *you're* Mr. Fisher?' he asked.

When children develop the habits of intelligent behaviour, the results can be unpredictable. When they learn how to interrogate ideas within texts and in the world they will also learn to interrogate you and what you say. Talking for thinking with children is an intellectual adventure that may be full of unexpected challenges.

Notes

1 Philosophy for Children is a programme for teaching thinking developed by Matthew Lipman (Lipman 1981). It has since been adapted and developed for use in many countries (Fisher 1998). See the Institute for the Advancement of Philosophy for Children research on Philosophy for Children at http://cehs.montclair.edu/academic/iapc/research.shtml.
2 See Trickey and Topping (2004) and summaries of research at: www.sapere.org.uk.
3 For a useful summary of classroom research on dialogue, see Alexander (2004). For further activities to stimulate dialogue in the classroom, see Fisher (2009).
4 A trend noted in Dillon (1988).
5 For the story 'Mercury and the Axe', and further questions and suggestions on ways of using the story to create a community of enquiry, see Fisher (1999: 45) and other books in the *Stories for Thinking* series.
6 I am indebted to Julie Winyard for this example. See also Winyard (2005), which has further examples of P4C dialogue with her class of Year 3 and 4 pupils.
7 See Wegerif (2002). For more on his 'Thinking Together' approach, see www.thinkingtogether. org.uk.
8 For other descriptions of the stages of a P4C lesson, see Haynes (2008) and Robert Fisher's 'Stories for Thinking' series.
9 See Trickey (2010), available at: www.sapere.org.uk.
10 For reviews of research into teaching thinking, see McGuiness (1999), and Fisher (2005a, 2005b).
11 For example a three-year thinking programme, including a P4C, resulted in a school getting its best ever English test results (Fisher 2003). In Clackmannanshire, researchers reported:

- Pupils gained on average 6 points on measures of cognitive abilities after 16 months of weekly enquiry.
- Pupils and teachers perceived significant gains in communication, confidence, concentration, participation and social behaviour after 6 months of enquiry.
- Pupils doubled their occurrence of supporting their views with reasons over a 6-month period.
- Teachers doubled their use of open-ended questions over a 6-month period.
- Pupils increased their level of participation in classroom discussion by half as much again following 6 months of weekly enquiry.
- Pupils' improved cognitive abilities were sustained two years into secondary school.

Bibliography

Alexander, R. (2004) *Towards Dialogic Teaching*, Cambridge: Dialogos.
DfEE (2000) *The National Curriculum: Handbook for Primary Teachers in England*, London: DfEE.
Dillon, J.T. (1988) *Questioning and Teaching*, London: Routledge.
Fisher, R. (1996) *Stories for Thinking*, Oxford: Nash Pollock.
Fisher, R. (1997a) *Games for Thinking*, Oxford: Nash Pollock.
Fisher, R. (1997b) *Poems for Thinking*, Oxford: Nash Pollock.
Fisher, R. (1999) *First Stories for Thinking*, Oxford: Nash Pollock.
Fisher, R. (2000) *First Poems for Thinking*, Oxford: Nash Pollock.
Fisher, R. (2001) *Values for Thinking*, Oxford: Nash Pollock.
Fisher, R. (2005a) *Teaching Children to Think*, 2nd edn, Cheltenham: Nelson Thornes.
Fisher, R. (2005b) *Teaching Children to Learn*, 2nd edn, Cheltenham: Nelson Thornes.
Fisher, R. (2008a) *Teaching Thinking: Philosophical Enquiry in the Classroom*, 3rd edn, London: Continuum.

Fisher, R. (2008b) 'Philosophical Intelligence: why philosophical discussion is important in educating the mind', in G. Hand and C. Winstanley (eds) *Philosophy in Schools*, London: Continuum.

Fisher, R. (2009) *Creative Dialogue: Talk for Thinking in the Classroom*, London: Routledge.

Fisher, R. and Williams, M. (eds) (2004) *Unlocking Creativity*, London: David Fulton.

Fisher, R. and Williams, M. (eds) (2005) *Unlocking Literacy*, 2nd edn, London: David Fulton.

Gardner, H. (1999) *Intelligence Reframed*, New York: Basic Books.

Goleman, D. (1997) *Emotional Intelligence: Why It Can Matter More than IQ*, New York: Bantam Books.

Haynes, J. (2008) *Children as Philosophers*, London: Routledge.

Lipman, M. (1981) 'Philosophy for children', in A.L. Costa (ed.) *Developing Minds: Programs for Teaching Thinking*, Alexandria, VA: Association for Supervision and Curriculum Development.

Lipman, M. (2003) *Thinking in Education*, Cambridge: Cambridge University Press.

McGuiness, C. (1999) 'From Thinking Skills to Thinking Classrooms: a review and evaluation of approaches for developing pupils' thinking', Research Report No. 115, London: Department for Education and Skills.

Nietszche, F. (1888) *The Will to Power*, New York: Vintage.

Trickey, S. (2010) *Promoting Thinking for Learning Through Collaborative Enquiry: An Evaluation of 'Thinking Through Philosophy'*. Available at: www.sapere.org.uk.

Trickey, S. and Topping, K.J. (2004) 'Philosophy for children: a systematic review', *Research Papers in Education*, 19(3): 365–80.

Wegerif, R. (2002) 'The importance of intelligent conversations', *Teaching Thinking*, 9: 46–9.

Winyard, J. (2005) 'Cunning little vixens', *Teaching Thinking and Creativity*, Spring: 30–6.

Conveying the 'Right' Kind of Message: Facilitating the Voices of Bilingual Learners

Geeta Ludhra and Ruth Lewis

Introduction

For teachers and Newly Qualified Teachers (NQTs),[1] who have never taught pupils with English as an Additional Language (EAL), it can seem both daunting and challenging. In the UK, the 2007 Standards for Initial Teacher Training (ITT) require an understanding and practical engagement with pupils from diverse backgrounds, yet many teachers (and trainees) may lack confidence in this area. Through experience, professional training, and pedagogic knowledge, cultural and linguistic diversity will be seen as an asset, enriching and broadening the language curriculum. Teachers have a professional duty and responsibility to develop their own understanding and knowledge of bilingual pupils' needs in line with the QTS Standards, the statutory inclusion principles outlined in the National Curriculum,[2] the Race Relations (Amendment) Act and the five aims of the Every Child Matters Agenda. These should be integral features of their teaching and learning approaches with all pupils.

In today's classrooms, teachers are faced with increasingly challenging pressures to assess, test and measure academic achievements, yet bilingualism may not feature highly as one of those achievements. As Wrigley (2000) points out, 'the ability to understand, communicate and think in two or more languages is in itself a great achievement'. Many bilingual learners achieve well academically although it is recognised that particular groups still underperform. Garcia's[3] more global, pluralistic and twenty-first-century perspective of bilingualism posits 'that bilingual education is *the only way* to educate children in the twenty-first century'.

Clearly, the role (and ethos) of the teacher (within the broader school culture) are central as they convey powerful discourses about the value of additional languages and cultures through their daily practices, conversations with pupils, staff, parents/carers, and through the classroom environments they create for pupils. Within increasingly multicultural and multilingual school contexts, most teachers will find themselves working with bilingual pupils at some stage in their careers and therefore pedagogic and theoretical knowledge during training is vital. Statistics indicate that between 10–13.5 per cent of pupils in UK maintained schools are learning English as a second, third, or indeed fourth, language and over 300 languages are spoken by pupils in UK schools. In some inner London schools, this figure can be over 90 per cent where bilingual pupils form the majority of the school population. The challenge for teachers then is to determine what a child who ostensibly 'doesn't speak a word of English' can actually understand. Although some children may appear to speak little or no English, assessments, collaborative discussions and systematic observations may reveal a multitude of linguistic competencies 'under the surface' of the initial silence or assumed 'confusion'. A teacher's holistic judgements of the child's language repertoire and abilities will involve working in partnership with language specialists (bilingual teaching assistants if available) and family/carers as the primary educators.

Bilingual learners (or pupils with EAL) do not form a homogeneous group; differences in language bring with them alternative sets of beliefs, value systems, customs, ways of living, and so forth. Bilingual learners will vary not only in their levels of spoken English, but come from a range of linguistic, socio-economic, historical and cultural positionings. It is therefore important that teachers do not make naïve assumptions but view 'differences' as new ways of thinking, opening doors to more three-dimensional and global perspectives for learning in the primary classroom.

The aim of this chapter then is to locate the teaching of bilingual children within an historical context and essentially, to provide teachers (and those beginning their training) with pedagogic principles, signposting to theoretical readings and suggested strategies. In considering the latter, 'strategies' need to be considered with caution: 'one size does not fit all' and teachers must use them as a starting point, adapting and modifying suggestions based on their professional judgements and the needs of each unique child. Strategies will become more meaningful once some guiding principles and theories are understood. Finally, it is recommended that in reading this chapter, language (talk) is viewed within the broader context, by considering how it informs complex notions of power,[4] culture and identity in society.

Historical context and background to EAL teaching

Towards the end of the 1960s, the UK government became aware that there were an increasing number of pupils arriving in schools speaking little or no English. In an effort to provide support for these children, specialist training courses for teachers were set up in large urban areas such as Leeds, Liverpool and London. The funding, from the Home Office, was referred to as Section 11. The term used to classify these children was 'immigrants' and the specialist teaching as English as a Second Language (ESL or E2L). As a result, ESL/E2L pupils were often taught in separate classrooms from their peers and in some cases attended specialist full-time units until they were considered able enough to cope in the mainstream context. Often there was no attempt to link pupils' learning of English to the mainstream curriculum. This would have been very difficult, as the groups of ESL pupils were often from different age groups and there was, at this time, no National Curriculum to guide teachers. Many of the strategies and materials were based on teaching English as a Foreign Language or resources developed for pupils with learning difficulties.

During the 1970s and 1980s, concerns grew among educators, parents and some politicians that the pupils of ethnic minority families were in many cases receiving a second-rate education and that that the withdrawal of pupils from the classroom was not actually providing the benefit originally intended. Parents complained that teachers ignored their children's home culture and language, making pupils feel inferior to their peers.[5] It was also discovered that in some Local Education Authorities (LEAs), Section 11 funding was being misused. Furthermore, withdrawing pupils from the classroom on the basis of what could appear to be skin colour rather than language needs was seen as a form of racism.

Consequently, policies and practice began to change. Specialist English language teachers developed partnership teaching strategies with class teachers. In the best examples of practice, two teachers working together would provide good role models for the pupils and develop interactive communication strategies across all areas of the curriculum. In this way, bilingual learners could be supported 'in' the mainstream classroom alongside their peer group and access the National Curriculum in a more inclusive approach. In some LEAs, community language staff were employed to help with translation and interpreting for pupils new to school or recent arrivals who arrived as midterm admissions. Specialist staff were also able to support schools to communicate effectively with parents/carers who had limited levels of English.

During the 1990s, the descriptive term 'English as an Additional Language' (EAL) was introduced into the government literature. It is used for pupils who are learning English 'in addition' to their first language on entry to school. Some bilingual pupils, may speak, read and write in more than two languages at home, making the description 'English as a second language' (ESL or E2L) a narrow depiction of their language skills. The term EAL is intended to recognise that in learning English as the prime language of instruction, pupils are 'adding' to their existing language repertoire and not 'subtracting' from it.

In 1999, the funding of EAL teaching was transferred from the Home Office to the Department for Education and Skills (DfES), and distributed to LEAs via the Standards Fund (known as the Ethnic Minorities Achievement Grant (EMAG)). There have been numerous government initiatives that have affected the ways in which education for EAL pupils is delivered in the classroom. The more inclusive model of guidance for EAL pupils in the Primary National Strategy (PNS) has meant that the emphasis has changed dramatically. EAL pupils are expected to achieve national targets alongside their peers. The emphasis is on whole-class teaching with appropriately differentiated tasks for individuals or groups. There are extra teaching assistants in the classroom (depending on funding) and various accelerated learning programmes for those pupils who have not met expected literacy targets.

In 2003, the DfES announced the first national strategy to tackle underachievement among minority ethnic pupils. The *Aiming High* (DfES 2003a) strategy included targeted activities on narrowing achievement gaps and provided valuable funding for Primary National Strategy (PNS) EAL programmes in 21 LEAs. LEA consultants worked with schools between 2004 and 2006 to support mainstream staff meet the needs of bilingual pupils (including advanced bilingual learners who had developed high levels of language competency).[6] The training drew on the principles of key theorists in the field of EAL pedagogy – Cummins (2000), Gibbons (2009), Baker (2007) – and emphasised the role of the first language in developing additional languages, where bilingualism was seen as an asset. The framework places importance on the need to transfer language skills from L1 to additional languages so that cognitive challenge and engagement remain high. The 2006 EAL professional development materials further emphasised the central role of talk in relation to language development for bilingual pupils. This was a move away from the strong emphasis on reading and writing skills advocated in the National Literacy Strategy at that time.

Multilingual approaches in the classroom

Bilingual (or multilingual) learners are those children who have access to more than one language at home or at school. It does not necessarily imply that they have full fluency in both or all languages. Baker (2007) highlights useful definitions in considering the overlapping dimensions of bilingualism and multilingualism. Offering bilingual children the opportunity to continue to use their first language alongside English will support their overall academic achievement and provide them with the opportunity to engage in cognitively demanding tasks. Monolingual teachers often ask how they can provide this support, particularly if they do not share the same first language. The Multilingual Resources for Children Project has produced a useful book on the subject *Building Bridges: Multilingual Resources for Children* (see Baker 2007). This includes a section on creating the right ethos and resources for speaking and listening.

Creating the 'right' conditions for 'dynamic' bilingual talk

The role of talk for bilingual pupils (and all learners) cannot be over-emphasised. It is through talk that bilingual pupils will learn to articulate and explore ideas, make connections across languages (through 'code-switching' at times) and learn new concepts. As highlighted throughout this book, facilitating talk in the class-room requires time, patience and, most importantly, strategic planning for language skills and curriculum content (the 2006 PNS for EAL learners emphasised the centrality of high quality planning). This section draws on two analogies from key writers in the field – Baker's (2006) 'language gardener' example and Garcia's (2010) analogy of the 'banyan tree'. Baker (2006) positions the teacher (or parent/carer) in the role of the 'language gardener'. They carefully nurture the young seeds (the minds of the pupils) with the necessary conditions for healthy growth (fertile soil, water, sunlight). In this way, multilingual approaches for language development can be better understood. They are more likely to be successful where the 'right' kind of conditions are created and nurtured within the classroom, whole school and wider community. Garcia (2010) draws on the image of the complex web of branches on the 'banyan tree' when discussing notions of 'dynamic bilingualism'.[7] The banyan tree takes many years to grow in this 'dynamic' fashion (mirroring the complex and interconnected language practices and challenges facing bilingual learners).

The 'double curriculum'

Bilingual pupils therefore are faced with complex challenges: those of learning the grammatical structures and functions of a new language alongside curriculum content and skills. Leung (Leung and Creese 2010) refers to this as the 'double curriculum' and Gibbons (2009) uses the phrase: 'Learning to learn in a new language' where often quite abstract and complex demands are placed on early stage EAL learners. Unrealistic, or unchallenging, tasks (such as copying or colouring in exercises) are often the result of poor background knowledge or weak pedagogic knowledge. Alongside the language learning processes of this 'double curriculum', some bilingual pupils will encounter more social and emotional difficulties, experienced as part of settling into a new country, culture and way of living and learning. These difficulties will be heightened if the school marginalises and devalues their first language and culture. Negative messages can be conveyed in implicit ways, yet pupils are often able to 'tune in' to them and sense what is expected or valued very early on.

Suggested strategies

The message to teachers is to show pupils that their languages and cultures are valued and that they are capable individuals who can 'enjoy and achieve' within a 'safe' and supportive environment. Teachers need to take some time to develop an understanding of the underlying pedagogies which underpin the following strategies:

- Explicit (and meaningful) celebration of linguistic diversity through multilingual displays (including 'working wall' displays),[8] appreciating and listening to music from different countries (in assemblies), storytelling and rhyme singing in other languages. It is important that schools do not pay 'lip service' to the above and attempts to be more inclusive do not convey 'tokenistic' or 'one-off' gestures.
- Explicit recognition and use of other languages within the class and school community to show how the first language is 'genuinely' valued and celebrated as an achievement (some schools offer language classes so the building links between teachers are essential). This 'bridges' the gap between home and school language experiences and as Ludhra's EAL project research (Ludhra and Jones 2008) revealed, there was a heightened recognition within the wider school community.[9]
- Pre-teaching of new concepts and technical terminology in the child's first language in order to provide greater confidence and familiarity. By being

'future-orientated', teachers can plan for oral language rehearsal opportunities prior to whole-class encounters in forthcoming lessons. This will enable them to make more confident responses to questions and discussions, rather than sitting there quietly.

■ Creating a language register for the class (and whole school community) in a prominent space within the school so that pupils (and families/visitors) can view the languages (and cultures) of staff and their peers. This provides a useful network of support for setting up bilingual language buddies.

The above highlight just a few general strategies and clearly their success is dependent on the ethos and philosophical values of senior management and staff in the whole school community.

Supporting new arrivals and meeting their diverse needs

Welcoming newly arrived pupils and providing effective induction programmes has become a standard feature of many city and isolated schools. Although 'new arrivals' carry varying definitions in documentation, in the context of the 'PNS New Arrivals Excellence Guidance Programme', they are defined as those pupils who have arrived as a result of international migration. The 'New Arrivals Programme' outlines underlying principles, exemplar induction frameworks and useful resources to support their arrival and integration to the school. All schools will have different induction approaches, depending on their views of integration and resources available.

Statham (2008) raises important dilemmas in relation to integration and learning of English, taking us back to the approaches of the 1960s where the belief was that English should be taught in grammatically progressive stages (even if decontextualised and abstract). However, as teachers are well aware, these stages do not necessarily equate with the curriculum language of the classroom and therefore pupils could feel even more isolated. Withdrawal approaches for induction are contrary to the beliefs of current government thinking.[10] As Statham (2008), Datta (2001) and Gibbons (2002)[11] all raise, real meaning making and collaborative language experiences take place in the classroom. In line with socio-cultural processes and Vygotskian (1978) theory, these participatory environments allow new arrivals to listen and engage in dialogues with more experienced peers and adults, allowing them to learn in the 'Zone of Proximal Development' (ZPD).

The dilemma then, as raised by Leung (Leung and Creese 2010) is how bilingual learners are expected to learn English alongside academic curriculum language (the 'double curriculum'). Leung (ibid.) challenges aspects of classroom integration approaches as being naïve and 'conceptually ill equipped' for additional language teaching and learning. His concerns focus on unrealistic expectations for instant results and progress in English and a lack of specialist staff.[12]

Clearly frameworks provided in government guidance which advocate that the majority of EAL teaching should take place in the mainstream will need to be adapted (and questioned at times) in how realistic they are in meeting individualised needs and addressing language development. The New Arrivals Excellence

Programme poses an interesting question in relation to the inclusion of 'pupil voice' (increasingly part of the government's agenda) in whole-school issues. The following provides an example of how the teacher drew on the whole-class community to support a new arrival.

> Ludhra asked her Year 4 class to write an induction programme (including useful 'survival' language, visuals and maps) for a new pupil. In cases, advanced bilingual pupils or bilingual staff provided translations. Pupils worked in pairs to discuss and write suggested induction frameworks from the pupil perspective. This activity engaged the whole-class community.

So, providing for new arrivals starts at the planning stage before they cross the school threshold is vital. Where teaching staff, pupils, parents and carers work in partnership, their induction is likely to be more effective, resulting in them feeling 'safe' and confident. Once the new arrival enters the school, it is important for relevant staff to gain as much prior knowledge as possible by posing the 'right kind of questions'. Hall (2001: 17) reinforces this: '[T]he answer to concerns about a child's lack of learning progress will only be as good as the questions asked.' The child should not be overwhelmed with assessments and instructions too early on as the primary aim should be to make them feel comfortable within the school environment. When assessments are conducted, they should reflect the complexity of bilingualism and consider carefully the benefit and purpose of the test or assessment. Gravelle (2000) poses three pertinent questions for consideration at the planning stage:

a. What do learners bring to the task?

b. What does the task demand of them?

c. What support needs to be planned?

By engaging with these questions at the planning stages, teachers are more likely to provide an inclusive curriculum drawing on previous observations, records from discussions and first language assessments. Sometimes, the fact that EAL learners (or new arrivals) 'speak no English' overshadows the knowledge and skills they have gained from their first language or from previous educational contexts. Building on Gravelle's (ibid.) questions, we outline a more detailed and modified question framework.

1. What do I already know about this pupil's language competencies, schooling experiences and social experiences?

    a. What did their previous schooling look like?

    b. Have they experienced formal education as such?

    c. What do they like and dislike?

    d. What do assessments in language one reveal about their spoken language proficiency (the ability to use complex language structures and vocabulary)?

e. How can I build on existing language competencies (with the support of a specialist maybe) to ensure high levels of cognitive and academic challenge within my lessons?

f. How can I provide a meaningful and relevant context for talk that draws on familiar experiences? Is there ICT or multimedia software to support language development?

g. Are there opportunities for collaborative first language work with first language buddies?

2. What language demands will the lesson objectives place on the bilingual pupil?

a. For example, will the lesson objectives require them to explain, describe, evaluate, explain, predict and so forth?

b. How will language (particularly technical terminology) be modelled and 'scaffolded' within or before the lesson?

3. What support needs to be planned?

a. What visual, audio and practical resources are available to support the bilingual pupil and meet the objectives of the lesson?

b. How can the adult (or more knowledgeable peer/advanced bilingual learner possibly) 'scaffold' the talk of the learner across languages?

In all of the above, assessment for learning (AfL), plays an integral role in tracking the pupils' progress and setting challenging, yet realistic targets. The QCA report (2000) *A Language in Common* provides valuable guidance on assessing EAL pupils' stages of language development through extended scales in National Curriculum levels. In April 2005, the Department for Education and Skills issued guidance on the assessment of pupils learning English as an additional language where they advised schools to use the QCA fluency scales for summative assessment. However, as highlighted by Garcia (2010), stages need to seen with caution. Although they provide a useful starting point, it is vital to remember that even advanced bilingual learners will need support, so they should not be forgotten about but seen as being on a language continuum.

Creating a welcoming environment

It is important at an early stage to welcome a new arrival (and their parents/carers) in a friendly and encouraging manner. If there is a pupil in the class who speaks the same language, it can certainly encourage the recent arrival to communicate and set them at ease with some common understanding. In any case, it is important to ensure that some members of the class are willing to be 'buddies' and introduce the new arrival to the routines of the classroom and school. It is helpful to remind the class to speak in a normal tone of voice and avoid baby talk or excessively loud talk that can appear patronising or make the child stand out as being 'different'. Learning how to pronounce and spell the new pupil's name correctly and teaching it to the class, will help the new child feel included and important (avoid anglicised or shortened versions as an easy way out unless the child prefers this). Names are important and form part of the child's identity. It is also useful if a few words or phrases, such as greetings from the new pupil's home language are taught to the class and dispersed within the curriculum at appropriate slots.

The classroom should reflect a variety of other cultures, in terms of pictures, posters, books, resources and artefacts. Contextually relevant materials will encourage talk about them as pupils will be more enthusiastic. The most important thing about helping children to acquire a new language for learning is to provide them with a secure and welcoming environment where they will develop the confidence to 'take risks' with talk as a natural part of learning across the curriculum. When 'taking risks' and experimenting with new language, it is important that teachers (and language buddies) model the 'correct' language structures with care and discretion. It is also important to recognise different accents and dialects as acceptable but standard English versions are to be highlighted alongside these. Constant correcting will only serve to diffuse their confidence and enthusiasm, resulting in possible silence.

The importance of gathering background information

Gathering background information on any new arrival enables the teacher to take into account the whole child: their particular social, cultural, religious (and medical) needs. This may prove particularly useful for children from refugee or asylum seeker families which require a sensitive treatment and understanding of the past. If the parents and child speak limited English, then an interpreter (and bilingual buddy) can help to build a relationship between home and school. In this way, school expectations, rules and timetables can be explained. The information gathered will prove invaluable in terms of making effective provision, planning for teaching and learning and building on prior experiences (in line with Gravelle's earlier questions). A useful checklist might include some of the following and this draws on the pro-forma illustrated in Hall.[13]

- Full name
- Date of birth and age
- Correct pronunciation of name/preferred name to be used at school
- Literacy skills in additional languages
- Out-of-school language classes (if attended)
- Competency in English
- Prior experiences of formal learning
- Prior life experiences that may impact learning (this might include life in a refugee camp, loss of a close relative, living in a war-torn country or other traumatic experiences)
- Parental attitudes, expectations and language proficiency in English
- Information about siblings, relatives and friends living locally
- Religion observance (festivals, prayers)

- Dietary needs
- Housing arrangements
- Medical history.

It is important not to make assumptions about a new pupil and either underestimate their capabilities or overestimate their understanding. Children may initially need a little time to settle into their new surroundings before they begin to speak in English. Clearly they will develop a sense of the atmosphere of the school, staff and pupils before experimenting with language. They may have been to an English-medium school in Asia or Africa and experience difficulty in 'tuning in' to different pronunciations. They may also have difficulty in making their spoken English understood which could be distressing for them. Contrary to views portrayed in some of the literature, not all bilingual pupils (or new arrivals) will suffer from notions of 'culture shock' or 'culture crises' (the school clearly plays a key role in this). Some pupils find it relatively easy to move between two (or more languages) and negotiate their importance and use in different contexts. Many bilingual pupils come from very supportive families who have high aspirations for them to achieve.

Of great importance is that bilingual pupils (and new arrivals) are not wrongly identified as having Special Educational Needs (SEN). As Hall (2004) points out, different types of targeted provision will need to be offered and a lack of English proficiency does not equate to SEN or learning difficulties. In some cases, however, some bilingual children may experience learning difficulties and careful assessments would need to be made before placing them on the special needs register. Some refugee/asylum seeker children may not have experienced any formal schooling so will require support to include aspects such as handwriting skills, oral skills, classroom, playground and assembly behaviour. In cases, teachers may need to be sensitive of particularly traumatic events that may need a lot of emotional support and understanding.[14] As one parent of a newly arrived pupil commented to his child's teacher 'Never mind his SAT's results. I long for the day when my son will learn to smile again'. So for most parents, their child's well-being and happiness will be of primary importance and this is in line with the outcomes of the Every Child Matters Agenda (particularly to 'enjoy and achieve').

Sometimes teachers may forget that their new arrival already speaks at least one other language. It is therefore incorrect to say 'She doesn't speak a word!' It is through the skilful approaches of the teacher that the child will be able to transfer their existing language experiences to the new language of learning. Cognitive theories of language transfer in bilingual learners are usefully outlined and illustrated by Baker (2007) and draw on the prominent work of Cummins (1996) and different historical shifts in bilingualism.[15]

Silent time

It is easy to forget that it is mentally exhausting learning a new language and pupils may feel very tired (as well as excited) during their first few weeks of induction. Some may prefer to remain silent for weeks (or even months) before they speak or contribute in class. It is important that they are given the chance (and time) to assimilate what they are hearing. This may feel very frustrating for the teacher especially when it can be seen that the child can understand you and perhaps talks to friends in the playground more readily. The pupil's attitude will depend partly on their personality. An extrovert child will often be desperate to communicate and young children, in particular, may talk to you in their home language in an effort to make themselves understood. Whilst it is important to encourage pupils to speak whenever there is an opportunity, it is usually counterproductive to try and force them or put them under unnecessary pressure. Having said the above and in acknowledging the 'silent period', teachers should also question their own teaching approaches where pupils have not contributed for some time (the 'silent period' should not be used as an excuse for prolonged silence). So, how could they as teachers enable the child to progressively make small contributions within lessons to build their confidence and status within the class? The teaching assistant could conduct speaking and listening observations to inform this process. Part of their speaking and listening targets could relate to making small oral contributions. It is important to recognise that some children are perfectionists and will not speak until they feel confident enough to talk in whole phrases or sentences. Children need to feel as if they can 'take risks' with language and explore language structures without being made to feel 'stupid' or inadequate. The example below illustrates a successful scenario.

Box 8.1 A successful scenario

A Chinese girl who had been in school in England for two years and could follow complex instructions easily was refusing to speak to her teacher. She would mouth the words in her reading book but it was impossible to hear whether her intonation or pronunciation was correct. Her classmates all said, 'She doesn't speak, Miss.' Her parents, who spoke English well, were very concerned about her. A mother tongue assessment in Cantonese showed that she was performing at a very high academic level for her age. After working in a small group context, drawing on role play and choral work to support the understanding of stories, she suddenly began to speak aloud when given the role of a cat. This play was then performed in front of the whole class and when she made her contribution, her classmates were astounded and clapped and said, 'She can speak!' She received much praise from the teacher and from then on voiced regular contributions to classroom discussions.

Each child will need a different approach to 'break' the possible 'silence' and teachers need to find what appeals or interests them. Some pupils who have come from a particular education system may have been taught that it is very rude to look the teacher directly in the face and will look away or hang their heads when spoken too. This can be taken for rudeness and children may mistakenly be punished for this. Some children may see it as rude to raise questions and therefore passively continue in silence without understanding the meaning of the work. In the UK, critical questioning, thinking and debate are in line with current initiatives. This may not relate, however, to the experiences of all pupils.

The teacher's role

Organising the classroom

In any primary classroom there are certain key principles which will help to support EAL pupils in their language development. It is important that all pupils and adults working in your classroom respect purposeful talk as a learning and thinking tool. It is worth spending some time setting criteria with the class to identify what the qualities of being a good listener and speaker are.[16] If all the pupils in your class are using speaking and listening rules, then it is much easier for EAL pupils to become active listeners and speakers themselves. With the heightened status of talk within classrooms, speaking and listening rules should be displayed alongside the general rules of behaviour (often called the 'golden rules'). These could be translated and include visual prompts (or even photographs) to enhance easy understanding.

By drawing on rules for high quality talk and dialogue, and praising pupils when they address them, high standards are set. In schools where there is a whole-school policy on speaking and listening, you may find that teachers using badges, stickers and certificates to encourage 'good listening'. For bilingual pupils, valuing and praising their contributions will raise their self-esteem and provide encouragement for making more contributions.

Teacher talk

The teacher plays a vital role both in modelling language for the EAL child and in speaking in a way which is accessible. The following suggestions may be shared with teaching assistants, parent volunteers, students or any other classroom helpers.

- Be consistent in classroom routines and language. For example, ringing a bell, clapping your hands and holding up your hand as a signal for silence will create confusion. It is best to use one agreed signal that the children are used to. If making changes, ensure that they are discussed beforehand.

- Give instructions that are direct and unambiguous, e.g. 'Come and sit on the carpet.' followed by 'Can I see everyone sitting on the mat, please' could potentially confuse EAL pupils, particularly those at the early stages of learning English.

- Avoid giving too many instructions at once. An EAL pupil may find it difficult to retain a lot of information at once and may therefore appear not to be listening. Often they will respond either to the first or last thing that the teacher said. Some teachers find 'prompt boards' with visual messages/reminders useful. This way if they forget, they can refer to them.

- Paraphrase and recycle messages in different ways so that learners have different opportunities to access understanding. Gibbons in her 2009 keynote address at the NALDIC conference, referred to this concept as 'message abundancy'. This process allows pupils to 'get more than one bite of the apple'.

- Allow EAL pupils more thinking time. When posing direct questions, use talk partners to help pupils rehearse their answers before answering in front of the whole class.

- In questioning, use clarification checks. For example 'Can you tell me two things that I have just said?' and 'Check first with your partner,' rather than, 'Do you understand me?'

- Tell pupils in advance that you will be asking them questions. This again gives them thinking time to rehearse ideas. If the pupil lacks confidence, the response could be fed back to the teaching assistant rather than in front of a whole class.

- Differentiate your questioning and plan for suitable questions. As stated earlier, good questions need to be planned out before the lesson. Bloom's taxonomy model provides a useful hierarchy of question stems.

- Model and scaffold procedures and texts in preparation for activities and writing tasks. Ensure that pupils know how to do a task as well as what to do. In cases, this may require some pre-teaching or familiarity exercises to acquaint them with some of the more academic language demands. As Gibbons (2009) stresses, scaffolding approaches should result in 'high challenge/high support' contexts.

- Use 'hands-on' practical activities to support the use of new language. For example, cookery, science and craft activities work well when organised into groups and will provide effective 'high quality' dialogue opportunities. Where possible, set up first language buddies for first language dialogue if pupils feel comfortable to converse.

- Encourage active oral participation. Elicit (and expect) lengthier responses to questions as they grow in proficiency and confidence, providing relevant prompts where necessary. Allow for pupil initiation of questions and praise pupils for good examples of questioning (these may be displayed on a class question board).

Opportunities to practise and rehearse new language

Accessing language across the curriculum

It is worth remembering that every lesson is a language lesson and is full of opportunities for language to be taught (and rehearsed) across the curriculum. Every subject area has specific characteristics. For example, PE provides opportunities for pupils to follow and give instructions as well as higher order language skills:

Throw the ball to your partner.
Curl up, tuck your heads in and do a forward roll.

Evaluate the effectiveness of their sequence:

What worked well and why?
How could that roll be improved?

Science involves the language of instructions, describing a process and reporting back.

1 Put some cold water in the bowl.	First we put cold water in the bowl.
2 Add one teaspoon of salt.	Then we added one teaspoon of salt.

History creates opportunities for thinking chronologically, and asking questions and retelling past events.

Question: When was Mary Seacole born?
Answer: She was born in Jamaica in 1805.

Gibbons (1991) warns against 'restricting children to using set phrases and predetermined language within a particular learning activity'. She advises that 'An important concept in language acquisition is the notion of the learner needing to hear models of language which are *comprehensible* but also *beyond what the learners are able to produce themselves*'. In order to plan effective speaking and listening activities across all areas of the curriculum, it is advisable to become aware of the range of language functions that are typically used in the primary classroom over the course of a typical week.[17] Gibbons (ibid.) provides a useful list of the more common functions of language (e.g., planning, predicting, explaining, hypothesising, comparing, describing, and so on). All of these language functions can be embedded in the National Curriculum.

Strategies and resources

The following strategies and resources have proved useful in developing communication skills in the classroom for all pupils, but particularly EAL learners. They can be appropriately adapted for all primary age groups. While emphasising the importance of speaking and listening, the strategies are part of an integrated approach to developing all four literacy skills.

Home-made books

These are easy and inexpensive to make. They could be text-free, offer limited text or include the pupil's own language (alongside English possibly). They provide supportive language or visual structures, stimulate speech and offer restricted vocabulary (word banks) which are helpful for children at the earlier stages of the bilingual continuum. In addition, by incorporating the language of making books, the physical process also becomes a language learning experience:

- instructions such as cut, stick, copy and draw;
- prepositional words such as top, bottom, centre of, cover, back page;
- book words such as front, back, cover, pages, contents, index.

Children can 'read' these books to a variety of audiences and use them for reading practice with family or peers. They can also become part of the class library along with audio versions of the story.

Storytelling with puppets and story sack materials

These can prove beneficial for bilingual learners as they provide a practical context for language learning and opportunities for exploratory talk. The kinds of stories that best meet the needs of EAL beginners are:

- Those with repetitive, predictable storylines (e.g. *The Little Red Hen*).
- Those with natural language structures and vocabulary.
- Those clearly supported by good quality illustrations.
- Those that span cultural and age boundaries, e.g. traditional tales.
- Activities that will support pupils' access to the story and encourage them to name the characters, complete the dialogue and begin to retell the story could include: Story props, e.g. puppets or magnet board figures to rehearse and familiarise the language and structure of the story.
- 'Picture Book Maker' software allows children to create their very own animal picture book (with optional text) using an interactive website.[18] 'Clicker 5' is another useful multimedia story-making tool with picture grids and audio facilities.
- Story maps/story mountains/story finger puppets (a series of pictures or finger puppets used to help pupils retell events and describe characters). Pie Corbett's work promotes the use of these (see his 'Story Maker's Chest' with a range of visual and practical resources to help children generate ideas).
- The use of comic strips would be a modification but would require more a complex range of reading skills.
- Bilingual story books with the accompanying recordable 'TalkingPEN'. This allows pupils not only to hear the story in different languages but also record their own retellings of the story, making it more personal (see Mantra Lingua bilingual books).
- Story grids for picture sequencing accompanied with matching sentences (children could use a washing line with pegs to explore different variations of the story).
- Songs and rhymes that will reinforce the language of the chosen story.
- Role play (including hot seating) – acting out the story with short scripted parts of a repetitive dialogue. By using repetitive actions, the story is more likely to be committed to memory.
- 'Small People' and/or 'Shoebox Theatres' to act out the scenes from a story (Key Stage 2 pupils may find this a helpful strategy when asked to create stories with alternative endings).
- 'Talk Box': Screen off an area of the classroom or build a large, decorated box with a tape recorder inside where individual pupils can be encouraged to record

stories, poems, songs or messages in English or other languages for their teacher or friends to listen to at a later date. The privacy and regular use of this system encourage reserved pupils to take risks and learn to correct their speech for themselves. Teachers will also have evidence of progression if the audio tapes are dated, saved and analysed.

Songs, rhymes and poetry

Songs, rhymes and poetry for young learners of English should be a natural part of everyday life in the classroom. Many young bilingual learners will mouth the words of songs and rhymes and join in the actions long before they will sing them aloud. Being part of a group who will carry on singing even if they forget the words will give them the confidence to develop a repertoire of songs and rhymes often before they can speak in full sentences. Obviously choosing songs which have a repetitive refrain or chorus is always helpful.

Making props to match the rhymes adds a three-dimensional aspect which aids understanding for children who are not sure what five currant buns look or taste like, for example. Bilingual parents can also be encouraged to teach songs from their own cultural background in some early year settings, they are encouraged to take part when dropping off or collecting their children.

When selecting poems, it is important to use those from a range of cultural backgrounds as well as with different features. Such poetry can be of great benefit to bilingual learners. It can give opportunities to read and repeat the same piece of text and in addition the rhythm and rhyme 'warm up' a familiarity with the language. Pupils can also benefit from sharing poems through performance and the videoing of these can be used as examples for them to self-assess. A class can be divided into groups to work on either the same piece of text or different poems depending on the experience of the pupils. It is important that the groups contain at least one experienced reader and the bilingual learners who are at the earlier stages of learning English are carefully grouped with more able peers. By choosing appropriate poems that can offer repetitive refrains or simple structures, all the children can participate and bilingual learners will be provided with scaffolds by these approaches.

Using key visuals

For many years, specialist EAL staff have been using a variety of grids and charts to scaffold pupils' thinking and ability to express their thoughts verbally across all areas of the curriculum. Key visuals (Figure 8.1) provide visual and diagrammatic means of representing information which is 'less dense' (and daunting) than pages of text. They may take the form of food chains, Venn diagrams, timelines, branching diagrams or flowcharts.[19]

Children's language can be supported further by providing them with sentence support structures. These are structures which will enable them to express their thoughts and ideas using language and sentence constructions which are not part of their normal everyday speech.[20]

Learning prompts help EAL pupils to articulate their ideas and provide a 'frame' for a particular form of language structure. They may include highlighted key vocabulary diagrams and/or other scaffolds to learning in the form of key visuals. They help the pupils to organise their thinking around the focused activity and facilitate the recall of key words and phrases rather than large chunks of text.

- T CHARTS

Hot	Cold

These are useful for teaching concept language, e.g. big/small, hot/cold, like/don't like. Pictures can be discussed and sorted into appropriate categories, labelled and then used as a basis for writing repeating sentences.

These charts can be further divided to include more categories.

Paper	Glass	Tin	Cardboard
News			

- STRUCTURED SEQUENCE CHARTS

These are useful for follow-up to practical activities and storytelling, e.g. cooking, science.

1	First we boiled the water.
2	Next we put the noodles in the saucepan.
3	Then we cooked the noodles for 8 minutes.
4	Lastly we put soy sauce on and ate them.

FIGURE 8.1 Learning prompts – key visuals

Choose a feature from the text

There was good example of ....
in the ....text when the writer said
....

Find the thesis of the text

In the ....text, it was clear that the writer
believed ....

Find the arguments of the text

In the ....text, the writer wants the reader to ....
....

Looking for patterns

The writer did not use ....in the
....text because ....
....

FIGURE 8.2 Sentence supports

Children learning EAL will usually acquire basic conversational English relatively quickly (according to Cummins (2000), this is acquired within two years). However, the acquisition of academic English required to access the curriculum takes much longer. Cummins (ibid.) argues it can take between 5–7 years to acquire academic language proficiency (up to 10 years in cases), depending on the school environment.

Some final reflections

Within the space of this chapter only the cornerstones of principles and strategies to support bilingual learners have been touched upon. Journals showcase valuable case studies and academic research in the field at both a national and international level will prove useful for academic writing in this area.[21] As raised in the Introduction, spoken language cannot be seen in isolation to notions of power, culture and identity and pupils will easily 'pick up' messages about their 'acceptable' use. Government policy, educational initiatives, senior management in schools and governing bodies play a vital role in conveying particular messages and discourses. Schools need to engage in critical dialogues about the kind of messages they want to convey and how they actually align to their language policies, culture and ethos. Alexander (2000) refers to the school as an institutional setting (a micro-culture), that can convey, filter and selectively modify messages coming from the top. In this way, schools (and teachers within classrooms) act like 'cultural channels' or 'cultural interfaces'. By conveying the 'right kind of messages' and building relationships with bilingual learners (their families and communities), teachers will facilitate the articulation of bilingual 'voices' in their classrooms so that are heard and not 'silenced'. As Cummins (1996: 244) helpfully summarizes:

> Educators concerned with preparing students for life in the 21st century must educate them for global citizenship. The potential to achieve this goal is obviously greater in a classroom context where cultural diversity is seen as a resource rather than in one where it is either suppressed or ignored.

Therein lies the challenge for teachers working within a linguistically and culturally diverse society.

Notes

1 Newly qualified teachers' perceptions of their training to prepare them for meeting the needs of bilingual learners are repeatedly rated poorly in relation to other training Standards. The NQT Survey results reveal marginal increases in scores. Access the Newly Qualified Teacher Survey: Five Year Analysis, available at: http://dataprovision.tda.gov.uk/.

2 See the National Curriculum inclusion overview. This statement can be accessed as a pdf on: http://www.ttrb.ac.uk/attachments/caf8c5cc-c904-4e8a-9825-1d5814e102ee.pdf.

3 Ofelia Garcia's (2009) book provides a more advanced, yet global overview of bilingual education in the twenty-first century. Her keynote address at the 17th annual NALDIC conference provides an imaginative reconceptualisation of bilingualism, which moves beyond seeing it as two monolingual codes. This speech can be accessed on YouTube in parts.

4 See Cummins (2000). This book (particularly the introductory chapters) provides valuable insights into the links between notions of language and power.

5 The Bullock Report (DES 1975) stated that the home and school cultures and languages should not be seen as separate.

6 See Ludhra and Jones (2008). This paper reflects on the EAL pilot study (2004–06) for advanced bilingual learners.

7 See Garcia (2010). 'Dynamic bilingualism' views language practices as more complex than just two separate languages. Language is seen as a lifelong development of skills on a 'bilingual continuum' that never ends (in contrast to language categories for children).

8 'Working wall' displays were an integral feature of the 2004–06 EAL PNS pilot study. Many schools use them today as they display 'work- in-progress' and key vocabulary that is currently part of classroom teaching and learning. For EAL learners, it is useful if key visuals or graphic organisers are used in these displays so that information is easily accessible. Where appropriate, translations would also be useful.

9 Ludhra and Jones (2008). See examples of vignettes within the paper, particularly the school newspaper club.

10 The Swann Report (1985) 'Education for All' recommended that pupils learning EAL should be taught alongside their peers in the mainstream classroom to ensure full access to the curriculum and avoid stigmatisation.

11 See Gibbons (2002). Chapter 2 provides a useful overview.

12 Ludhra, as part of her work in the EAL National Pilot Project (2004–06), found that this was also the case in the school in which she worked. It was only after the consultants had worked

with staff to 'uplevel' their expertise and pedagogic knowledge of language acquisition theories that they understood some of the principles behind EAL development and drew on first language approaches in the classroom.

13 See Hall (2001). Chapter 4 provides a useful overview on the importance of gathering background (see proforma on pp. 76–7).

14 Books like *The Colour of Home* by Mary Hoffman (about a new boy called Hassan who arrives from Somalia) usefully address such issues and provide valuable starting points for the exploration of emotions related to new arrivals. Exploring their experiences through talk in subjects like PSHE or drama could prove valuable.

15 See Baker (2006). Chapter 8 provides an excellent overview of the balance theory, iceberg analogy, and thresholds theory, drawing on Professor Jim Cummins' BICS (basic interpersonal communication skills) and CALP (cognitive academic language proficiency) framework for language development.

16 The Primary National Strategy (DfES 2006): Excellence and Enjoyment Professional Development Materials, includes a useful video clip of a Year 2, Term 1 class engaged in instructional talk in the context of cooking. The video clip illustrates how the teacher has modelled features of what makes a good listener, speaker and observer. Teachers' TV also features some useful video clips to support talk for bilingual learners and good practice in schools.

17 Ludhra, as part of the EAL Pilot Project, worked with EAL consultants and staff to evaluate the range of language functions planned over a typical week. Year group teams engaged in language-specific planning dialogues at weekly meetings and discussed the cognitive demands of different language functions in relation to pupils' language abilities. Such dialogues promoted high levels of challenge while considering suitable scaffolding.

18 Picture Book Maker can be accessed via the London Grid for Learning (LGfL) KS1 English website on: http://portal2.lgfl.org.uk/learningresources/curriculum/english/ks1/Pages/EnglishKS1.asp.

19 There is a website that provides templates for key visuals as word documents. For free access, see: http://www.milton-keynes.gov.uk/emass/DisplayArticle.asp?ID=27465.

20 The Sue Palmer big books provide a range of key visuals, graphic organisers and sentence structures in line with the genres to be studied as part of the primary framework for literacy.

21 Useful journals to support your wider reading include: *International Journal of Bilingual Education and Bilingualism* and *Bilingual Research Journal*. The NALDIC website and *NALDIC Quarterly* journal produce useful case studies and research findings.

Bibliography

Alexander, R. (2000) *Culture and Pedagogy: International Comparisons in Primary Education.* Oxford: Blackwell.

Baker, C. (2006) *Foundations of Bilingual Education and Bilingualism*, 4th edn, Clevedon: Multilingual Matters.

Baker, C. (2007) *A Parents' and Teachers' Guide to Bilingualism*, 3rd edn, Clevedon: Multilingual Matters.

Conteh, J. (ed.) (2006) *Promoting Learning for Bilingual Pupils 3–11: Opening Doors to Success*, London: Paul Chapman.

Cortazzi, C. and Jin, L (2002) 'Seven keys: developing writing for EAL pupils', in M. Williams (ed.) *Unlocking Writing*, London: David Fulton Publishers, pp. 116–30.

Cummins, J. (1996) *Negotiating Identities: Education for Empowerment in a Diverse Society*, Ontario: California Association for Bilingual Education.

Cummins, J. (2000) *Language, Power and Pedagogy: Bilingual Children in the Crossfire*, Clevedon: Multilingual Matters.

Datta, M. (ed.) (2001) *Bilinguality and Literacy: Principles and Practice,* London: Continuum.

DES (1975) *A Language for Life: The Bullock Report*, London: HMSO.

DfEE (1999) *The National Curriculum*, London: HMSO.

DfES (2003a) *Aiming High: Guidance on the Assessment of Pupils Learning English as an Additional Language.* Nottingham: DfES Publications.

DfES (2003b) *Speaking, Listening, Learning: Working with Children in Key Stages 1 and 2,* Nottingham: DfES Publications.

DfES (2004) *Every Child Matters: Change for Children,* London: HMSO.

DfES (2006) *Primary National Strategy: Excellence and Enjoyment. Learning and Teaching for Bilingual Children in the Primary Years (Professional Development Materials),* London: HMSO.

Garcia, O. (2009) *Bilingual Education in the 21st Century: A Global Perspective,* Oxford: Wiley-Blackwell.

Garcia, O. (2010) 'Reimagining bilingualism in education for the 21st century (Keynote presentation). *NALDIC Quarterly,* 7(2): 4–11.

Gibbons, P. (1991) *Learning to Learn in a Second Language,* Newtown, Australia: Heinemann.

Gibbons, P. (2002) *Scaffolding Language, Scaffolding Learning: Teaching Second Language Learners in the Mainstream Classroom,* Oxford: Heinemann.

Gibbons, P. (2009) 'Challenging pedagogies: more than just good practice', *NALDIC Quarterly,* 6(2): 4–14.

Gravelle, M. (2000) *Planning for Bilingual Learning: An Inclusive Curriculum,* Stoke-on-Trent: Trentham Books.

Gregory, E. (1996) *Making Sense of a New World,* London: Paul Chapman Publishing.

Gregory, E. (2008) *Learning to Read in a New Language,* London: Sage.

Hall, C. *et al.* (2004) *EAL at Key Stage 1: Framework for Early Stages,* London: Hounslow Language Service.

Hall, D. (2001) *Assessing the Needs of Bilingual Pupils: Living in Two Languages,* 2nd edn, London: David Fulton.

Leung, C. and Cable, C. (eds) (1997) *English as an Additional Language: Changing Perspectives,* Watford: NALDIC.

Leung, C. and Creese A. (eds) (2010) *English as an Additional Language: Approaches to Teaching Linguistically Minority Students,* London: Sage Publications.

Lewis, R. *et al.* (2005) *Access and Inclusion: Beginners in English in Primary Schools,* London: Hounslow Language Service.

Ludhra, G. and Jones, D. (2008) 'Giving the "right" kind of message: planning for the first language and culture within the primary classroom', *English Teaching: Practice and Critique,* 7(2): 56–70.

Parker-Jenkins, M., Hewitt, D., Brownhill, S. and Sanders, T. (2007) *Raising Attainment of Pupils from Culturally Diverse Backgrounds,* London: Paul Chapman.

QCA (2000) *A Language in Common,* London: QCA Publications.

Statham, L. (2008) *Counting Them In: Isolated Bilingual Learners in Schools,* Stoke on Trent: Trentham Books.

Vygotsky, L. (1978) *Mind in Society: The Development of Higher Psychological Processes.* Cambridge, MA: Harvard University Press.

Wrigley, T. (2000) *The Power to Learn: Stories of Success in the Education of Asian and Other Bilingual Pupils.* Stoke on Trent: Trentham Books.

Useful resources and websites

Department for Education (DfE). Look under EAL publications: http://www.education.gov.uk/.

Hounslow Language Service: http://www.hvec.org.uk/HvecMain/index.asp.

Mantra Lingua: www.mantralingua.com.

Multiverse Website: www.multiverse.ac.uk.

NALDIC (National Association for Language Development in the Curriculum): www.naldic.org.uk.

National Literacy Trust: http://www.literacytrust.org.uk/.

Story sack resources: http://www.storysack.com/.

Inclusive Approaches to Communication with Children who Have Special Educational Needs and/or Disabilities

Nicola Grove

The focus of this chapter is the use of strategies to promote effective communication for children who have special educational needs and/or disabilities (SEND) and are being taught in mainstream classrooms. The perspective adopted here integrates medical and social models in an interactionist approach, considering three principal dimensions of inclusion: what the child brings, the skills and attitudes of those who interact with the child and the context within which the child functions (Lewis and Norwich 2005; Lindsay *et al.* 2008). Children with special educational needs have always been educated in mainstream classrooms, whether or not they were labelled as such, and teachers since the dawn of time have differentiated their approaches to suit children with different aptitudes, interests and needs. So teaching for inclusion is nothing new – it has always been there. However, it is true to say that in the twenty-first century our understanding of differing needs is structured in a way that makes particular demands on teaching staff, and there are specific challenges and possibilities inherent in the current system for children who learn and interact with others in unorthodox ways. We know that school staff are positive and committed to the principle of inclusion, but that many feel that they lack a basic understanding of language and communication, and the specialist knowledge needed to make inclusion work (Mackenzie 2009; Sadler 2005; Sheehy *et al.* 2009).

Who are children with special educational needs?

Current estimates (DCFS 2009) suggest that overall, just over 20 per cent of the pupil population are likely to have SEND, although less than 3 per cent will have statements. This means that in an average class of 30 children, we might expect there to be around six with special needs (Lamb Inquiry 2009). Of course, not all of these needs are necessarily long-term. The needs are defined as those which affect a child's ability to learn and function well in the school community: cognitive and learning needs; language and communication needs; social emotional needs; sensory needs and physical needs. For children below the age of 7, the most common type of need was speech, language and communication difficulties, 42 per cent of all pupils at School Action Plus.[1] The underlying causes of persistent SENDs may include such examples as an extreme emotional response to a life event, or a physical condition resulting from a temporary but debilitating illness as well as permanent conditions such as deafness, autistic spectrum disorder or Down syndrome. These categories are identified through the annual schools' census of pupil levels, and are the officially recognized descriptors of conditions.

The needs of some children will be relatively clear-cut, but many children may have more than one underlying impairment or disability, or may have several educational needs arising from the primary condition. These will have complex effects on learning. For example, children with Down's syndrome and learning difficulties are almost certain to have some degree of hearing impairment; children with cerebral palsy (a physical condition) are likely to have visual problems which will affect their ability to handle visual tasks, say, in mathematics and geography (Stiers *et al.* 2002).

Beyond these categories, there is a strong link between identified special educational needs and social disadvantage: some 40 per cent of children eligible for free school meals, and around one-third of children from underperforming ethnic groups have identifiable SENDs. Children who are the youngest in the year are one and a half times more likely to be identified as having SEND than those who are the eldest in the year. Lamb (2009) points out that these data suggest that the problems are related to the social environment rather than intrinsic to children; the solutions therefore lie with the modification of the learning context. To break the existing link between low attainment and special needs, confidence, expectations, enabling environments and the skills and commitment of staff are what count, regardless of the impairments of the children. More than a decade of research and practice demonstrates that teachers and classroom staff should not feel overwhelmed by the diversity and complexity of conditions that affect children in their care, because there are many strategies that seem to work well for all pupils, whether or not they have SENDs.

Speech, language and communication needs (SLCN)

SLCNs can be caused by a range of factors, which interact in complex ways. The following is a summary of the causes of SLCN taken from a review by Lindsay and colleagues (2008), which contributed to the Bercow Report (2008).

Causes of SLCNs

- Primary: conditions affecting the speech and language system.
- Secondary to other problems, such as hearing impairment or learning disabilities.

- Reduced developmental opportunities due to social disadvantage. Approximately 50 per cent of children from most socially disadvantaged communities have delayed speech and language skills.

- Associated with English as an additional language, being relatively disadvantaged when there is a mismatch between the languages of home and school.

Although the prevalence of this category seems to decline after the age of 7, this does not mean that communication difficulties (in the broadest sense) disappear from the SEND population at this point. But as children grow older, other problems are seen as more important and are classified as the primary difficulties. There is a strong association between SLCNs, and subsequent learning, behavioural and emotional difficulties (Bercow 2008). A firm foundation in communication is needed for children to achieve their potential in both social and academic aspects of their education. Children with an inadequate grasp of vocabulary will be hampered as they face increasingly complex and abstract concepts in different subjects (Cummins 1984), and children with poor language skills will find it difficult to master literacy (Nation and Snowling 2004; Rose 2009). Most importantly, without effective communication, it is difficult to make friends, collaborate and learn from others, or to gain a sense of oneself as a valued member of a social group. Children who cannot understand what is going on, or cannot express themselves may present as disobedient or aggressive, when in fact the problem lies with communication.

By the time they enter school, it has been predicted that around 7 per cent of children will have significant problems with speech and language that will need to be addressed specifically, with around 1 per cent having severe difficulties that will need specialist provision (Lindsay *et al.* 2008). This leaves over 90 per cent whose difficulties must be addressed through strategic, inclusive approaches to teaching and learning. In this context, it is essential to provide an enabling environment, within which staff are confident and informed enough about good practice in communication to adapt learning tasks and teaching strategies to suit the needs of individuals and the whole class.

Communication problems

Communication and language themselves involve many different processes – there is a lot that can go wrong. Any act of communication involves every aspect of ourselves: hearing, seeing, feeling, moving, thinking, remembering, predicting, inferring, imagining, empathizing, decision-making, articulating. We use our faces, eyes, hands, bodies as well as our speech organs to express ourselves, and even small anomalies in any one of these behaviours can have quite profound effects. If you look someone too long in the eye, or don't look at them at all; if you stand too close or too far away; if you speak too slowly or too fast; if you persistently misread emotional signals – you are likely to disrupt an exchange just as much as if you fail to hear what is said, or cannot find the right words to express yourself. Both speaking and listening are processes that are highly vulnerable to disruption – because auditory signals are fast, transitory and decay quickly (therefore are hard to remember and store, even if you have very good hearing) – and production of intelligible speech requires very fine co-ordination of breath, lips, tongue and palate.

The upside is that if there are many ways in which you can compensate for a difficulty in one particular area, provided that the people you interact with are sensitive and responsive and the environment in which you are communicating is facilitative. This has clear implications for the teacher's role.

The process of communication

It is useful to consider what actually goes on when people communicate with each other, in order to understand where things can go awry for a child with special needs, and how to help them compensate for their difficulties. A distinction is usually made between two levels of processing information: the first level involving input and output: the senses (hearing, vision, touch, smell, taste) and the motor system (organs of articulation, hands, facial expressions and eye movements, body movements, and the second involving so-called central processes where the brain decodes and encodes meaning, retrieving information from memory and storing new information.

Input processes: perceiving and attending

We first have to actually notice that something is being communicated. This means that the signal has got to be sufficiently prominent, which is arguably the responsibility of the sender rather than the receiver of the message. It may seem obvious, but recent developments in the design of classrooms have emphasized how poor the acoustics and other features of school buildings are for teaching and learning (Shield and Dockrell 2004). Many teachers, too, can be helped by learning basic techniques of voice projection and management, since even mild voice problems seem to affect children's ability to process information (Rogerson and Dodd 2005).

Understanding requires us to pay attention to what is being communicated. Attention involves focusing, sustaining concentration, executing an action, and shifting between different tasks (Kelly 2000). This usually involves listening – but for a deaf child it would require watching and for a blind and deaf child, attending to a tactile signal. The point about attention is that it involves very active selection of a stimulus. We now know that the brain has an incredible capacity to screen out information that is irrelevant or uninteresting, so that even in noisy surroundings we can hear the words 'I love you' or 'Would you like another drink?' Selective attention is something that develops with age, and which may have to be specifically taught to children with SEND – it does not come automatically (Johnson and Gallow 2007). Of course, lack of attention may be the result of boredom, or insubordination, or laziness. But it is just as likely to result from a primary difficulty in screening out distractions or in understanding what is being said, or perhaps from hunger, tiredness or emotional or physical discomfort. It is important to note that children who look away from you while you speak to them may not be either insubordinate or bored, but trying to process what you are saying to them which is actually easier if you are not looking someone directly in the eye (Doherty-Sneddon

2004). It is also important to check that a persistently inattentive child does not have an undiagnosed problem (see Box 9.1).

Box 9.1 Think again about inattention

Jamie, aged 9, was always the first to put his hand up, talked loudly over other children and could rarely remember what had been said to him. Through discussion with his class teacher, Jamie identified that one of the main difficulties he had in class was with listening. She went through possible causes with him, and Jamie indicated that the problem was not boredom or lack of wanting to listen, but that he often could not hear what was said. A hearing test was arranged and Jamie was found to have an undiagnosed loss which meant he could not hear speech at a conversational level if there was ambient noise.

Even if a child is attending fully, he or she may have difficulties in understanding you because of problems with their receptive language system, or comprehension. This brings us to consideration of central processes.

Central processes: the language system

Generally, we make a distinction between language and communication, with communication being the broader process whereby people exchange both verbal and non-verbal messages, whereas language denotes the aspects of that message which are formally codified in a symbolic system. A distinction is also made between language and speech – with speech being only one of the ways in which language is realized. We now know, for example, that sign languages – which do not involve the vocal channel – share all the characteristics of spoken language systems: namely a grammar, a vocabulary and socially codified rules for their expression, or pragmatics. These aspects of the language system are sometimes referred to as Form, Content and Use:

- *Form*: languages are made up of patterns of elements – sounds in speech – which come together to make words and sentences and paragraphs. So the formal aspect of language covers both the structure of sounds (*phonology*), words (their *morphology*), and sentences (*syntax*). A child who has difficulties with the formal aspects of language may have difficulty perceiving certain sounds, may leave out word endings, or simplify long words, or find it hard to understand and/or produce complex sentences.

- *Content*: the term used to denote vocabulary and meanings, the semantics of the language. This covers the kind of words that we use – whether abstract (*glory, failure*) or concrete (*chair, cat*); the classes of words we use (nouns, adjectives, adverbs, verbs, etc.) and the way that words and meanings relate to each other (*king, prince, kingdom, govern, ruler; pen, pencil, rubber, draw, ruler*). Children who have difficulties with these aspects of language may find it difficult to learn new words, and have limited vocabularies; may not be able to recall the right word quickly and use lots of 'filler' words such as um, er, or hesitations or long-winded non-specific 'circumlocutions'; may overuse general terms such as 'that', 'thing', 'got', 'do' and may find it hard to acquire abstract language.

■ *Use or pragmatics*: this refers to the social use of both the content and the form of language. It covers the ways in which communication functions to perform certain social acts (such as *promising, insulting, begging, arguing, loving, narrating*) and the cultural conventions which dictate which forms and which meanings will be used in a particular social context – for example, the difference between greeting a close teenage friend and a Member of Parliament. Use of language also involves non-verbal aspects, such as intonation and prosody; and the way we use 'body language' – eye contact, gesture and social distance.

Pragmatics is critically important in understanding, as it affects the way we use our knowledge of the context and our previous experiences to make inferences about what people say and do. A lot of what is said is potentially ambiguous, so that we not only have to retrieve literal meanings, we also have to work out what is the most likely interpretation in a given situation. Inference is actively involved in the process of comprehension – we make assumptions based on attitude and prior experience about what someone is likely to say, do, mean, and while they are talking we are mentally completing their sentences for them – often to be surprised at what they actually say. We also use inference to work out how explicit we have to be in talking and what we think the other person knows.

Children may have difficulty with the social aspects of language because of their lack of experience of certain conventions and contexts, or because of emotional issues, or because they cannot hear or see properly, or because they find it hard to work out what other people are feeling and thinking. They may appear rude or shy or passive; may give you too much or too little information; may fail to understand use of non-literal meanings and seem very pedantic in their choice of words. Non-verbal aspects are affected, so that their speech sounds wooden or mechanical; they may stand too close or too far away when they talk to you.

Form, content and use are all involved in both comprehension (receptive language) and expression (expressive language). The relationship between comprehension and expression varies in children with SEND. In normal development, comprehension is in advance of expression, so that we generally assume that children can understand more than they say. In some children they will be about equal, and in others, comprehension may actually be lower than you would think from the way they talk. An illustration of this is provided in Box 9.2.

Central processes: memory

Both short-term (working) memory and long-term (storage) memory are involved in processing language. Working memory has been defined as the mental

Box 9.2 Comprehension and expression in a child with SEND

Marek is 7 years old and has hydrocephalus and spina bifida. He talks all the time, using full sentences. People therefore think that he understands complex sentences. However, if you listen carefully to Marek talking, he is using a lot of 'learned phrases' – like 'I was only thinking the other day', 'the point is . . . we had a great time, didn't we?' In fact, his understanding of language is at about the average of a 4½-year-old child. In conversation or instruction he needs short sentences, and a lot of time to process information. However, in drama and in literature, he will enjoy listening to and using rich language with lots of rhythm and intonation.

workplace in which information can be temporarily stored and manipulated during complex everyday activities (Gathercole and Pickering 2001; van Daal *et al.* 2008). The system involves an executive element which retrieves items from long-term memory and manages the task of sorting all the information which is arriving simultaneously; a system which holds in place the incoming sounds of speech so that they can be processed; and an element that does the same for visuo-spatial information. Long-term memory stores meanings and the way these are represented (whether in words, gestures or facial movements) and this system interacts with and is updated through working memory. There is considerable evidence that working memory and difficulties with auditory processing of information underlie many of the language difficulties in vocabulary and grammar that children demonstrate in the classroom (Leonard 1998).

Output processes

Once we have understood an incoming message, we may (or may not) construct a reply. In order to do this, a meaning and intention are generated centrally, and the appropriate words and sentence forms are assigned. We then have to actually articulate the message – through speech, gestures, face and body. In asking a question, for example, we not only formulate the sentence, we have to use a particular intonation, we lean forward and raise eyebrows, directing our gaze at the respondent. Some children with special needs may have primary difficulties at the level of motor output which means that their speech is unclear. Many children take some time to develop the complex sound systems of the language (typically, the earliest sounds to be produced are ones like m, b, w, l, whereas sounds which require more complex co-ordination come later: th, r, s). Some children with underlying physical co-ordination problems may continue to have difficulties producing sounds, or single words and short phrases may be clear but sentences are not. Other children may also show problems in producing clear hand gestures or the use of facial muscles – typically children with some form of cerebral palsy or severe dyspraxia (sometimes called developmental motor difficulties).

Difficulties and skills in communication for children with SENDs

Although there is no one-to-one correspondence between an identified condition or disability and single communication problems, there are nevertheless some communication difficulties that are consistently associated with some conditions. It is critical to remember that we are talking about predictions, not certainties and that that children have an extraordinary capacity to surprise. This is demonstrated in Box 9.3.

Box 9.3 Watch your preconceptions! The case of Johnny

I met Johnny (not his real name) at a storytelling festival where I was on the bookstall. Aged about 9 or 10, he had Down's syndrome and was there with his mum and brother. He was looking intently through the books and tapes. I asked him if he was enjoying the festival and he said yes he was. I asked which stories he had enjoyed most, but he misunderstood and thought I was asking about his usual favourites. Children with Down's syndrome have auditory processing difficulties and comprehension problems so you might expect him to like picture stories suitable for younger children. His best stories though were the *Iliad* and the *Odyssey* as told for adults by Hugh Lupton, a well-known oral storyteller. He listened to the tapes over and over again and could recite them by heart.

Children with autistic spectrum disorders

Autistic spectrum disorders tend to be associated with fundamental difficulties in communication, in understanding other people's emotions, and social conventions. Their thinking tends to lack flexibility and 'central coherence' – that is the ability to see things as a whole and to disengage from specifics – and they are inclined to show rigid preferences for routines and familiar structures and to find change and transition difficult. Children with ASD may have moderate or severe learning difficulties, but around one-third have an IQ within the normal range for their ages (the term Asperger's Syndrome is often used for these children). Use of language and social understanding are particular problems for children with ASD. They are facilitated by clear and high expectations, visual cues as to what will happen, structure and routine and explicit information about what they should do and why things are happening; developing social skills and peer understanding (see Beaney and Kershaw 2003; Gray 2002; Howlin *et al.* 1998; Humphrey 2008). Traditionally, it was thought that children with ASD would not be able to play symbolically or participate in imaginative activities, but the groundbreaking work of Sherratt and Peter (2002), among others, has shown that this is not actually the case as exemplified in Box 9.4.

Box 9.4 Drama and play with autistic children

Farhad tended to poke other children and behave unpredictably; he had several mannerisms such as flapping and stamping. He was mainly interested in mechanical objects, especially washing machines. He showed some limited symbolic under-standing, e.g. pushing a box along the table and saying 'brrm'. His teacher used a highly structured drama approach to develop his ability to take part with other children in role play – by putting him in charge of a 'machine' (cardboard box) and getting him to ask them for items of clothing to sort and put in the machine on 'washing day'. This led to increased social play for Farhad, who began to be included in more class-room activities where he could ask for and give objects.[2]

Speech and Language Impairments (SLI)

These are generally classified into three groups (Broomfield and Dodd 2004):

- *Receptive group*: children with problems understanding language – nearly always associated with some expressive difficulties as well.

- *Expressive group*: children whose main difficulties are in expressing themselves. Understanding is in advance of, or equal to expression.

- *Speech impairment group*: children who have difficulties in articulating words and sentences.

In Broomfield and Dodd's study, there was a great deal of overlap in the problems experienced by these children: in the receptive group, virtually all had problems with expressive language structure (i.e. grammar) and with the development of vocabulary; two-thirds had difficulties with speech production as well. In the expressive group, over half also had problems with articulating speech sounds. Typically, children with expressive SLI will sound rather younger than they actually are when they talk, and verbs are particularly accurate markers of the problems: they will drop off endings (he *run* down the road; yesterday I *walk* to school); ask questions in a simplified way (*you like football?* Instead of *do you like football?*

It is important to recognize that although for the purposes of diagnosis and statementing, children will only be considered to have SLI if they are deemed to have problems in these areas which *cannot* be attributed to other causes such as learning difficulties, sensory difficulties, emotional or environmental deprivation, nevertheless there are many children with other sets of problems who may actually also have specific speech and language difficulties. For example, it is now recognized that children with Down's syndrome (hence with a primary categorization of learning difficulty) share many characteristics with children who have SLI (Laws and Bishop 2004); that children may have dual problems of deafness and language disorder (Mason *et al.* 2010), and that specific difficulties with verbal language may interfere with what appear to be non-verbal tasks.

Box 9.5 How verbal difficulties may extend beyond the auditory system

Mary has been diagnosed with a specific language impairment. She has great difficulty remembering sequences of words. Her teacher thinks that using pictures will help, and certainly she finds it easier to work with visual presentations. However, when she is given a complex visual problem to work out, that requires recalling a sequence and making inferences, she does much worse than other children with a similar level of language skill. Mary is shown sets of pictures in turn of animals climbing a tree. Squirrel is above woodpecker, mouse is above squirrel, and owl is above mouse. Is owl above or below woodpecker? In this case, Mary has to rely on working memory and it seems likely that there is some contribution from the verbal system – in other words, although it appears to be a totally non-verbal reasoning task, it actually isn't. Mary does better, however, on a task that requires her to explicitly reason out an answer with permanent visual cues that relates to real world knowledge. She has to choose a card to show whether or not a rule is being obeyed. The rule is 'you have to wear a shiny coat if it is dark' and she is given an explanation of why this is. She has to choose between a picture of a fluorescent yellow coat or a dark navy coat. In order to check the rule she should choose the dark navy coat – because if night is on the back, this is a clear violation – and she does.[3]

Deafness and hearing impairment

Children with hearing impairments are a very diverse group, with somewhat different needs, depending on their levels of hearing and the kind of language input they have received early in their lives. Around half of deaf pupils have a moderate or mild loss; half have a severe or profound loss. The ability to hear speech is, however, not predictable from the level of hearing loss alone – much depends on other factors such as environmental noise, ability to lip read, familiarity with the incoming information, motivation and health. About one-third of these children have additional SENDs. Acceptance of sign language has revolutionized our understanding of the needs of deaf children. Deaf children who are exposed to fluent sign language from birth seem to develop completely age-appropriate language skills – i.e. the grammar and the semantic system of sign, which is very different to English. Acquisition of sign language is not only a linguistic process, it is a cultural inheritance, involving a shared history and norms of social interaction. On the other hand, children who have not received fluent language models in a form that they can perceive and understand from birth are likely to have severe delays in all aspects of language (whether signed or spoken).

The communication needs of the deaf or hearing impaired child are profoundly affected by the educational approach which is adopted in their school. Gregory (2005) describes the continuum of approaches, from the purely aural-oral which emphasizes the use of residual hearing to master speech and English as the primary language, to sign bilingual approaches, where deaf children are taught together in sign and learn English as a second language (Swanwick 2010). In the middle are hybrid approaches, where, for example, deaf children are taught alongside hearing children using the services of a sign interpreter, or where teachers use English but accompany it with some signing. This latter approach has been found to be highly ineffective, rather like trying to teach English through using French words with English grammar. The picture for deaf and hearing impaired children is changing very rapidly with the advent of cochlear implantation, a surgical intervention which provides an artificial inner ear. Children with implants, however, do not automatically and immediately process speech as a hearing child would do, and may need sensitive management and teaching to learn to listen effectively (Ching *et al.* 2009; Inscoe *et al.* 2009).

Box 9.6 How teacher talk helps children

Marla has a severe hearing impairment, though with her aids and lip reading she can pick up speech. Her classroom is adapted with a loop system, and she has classroom support with signing for part of the week, and the class teacher and many of the children can use signs. However, her teacher is concerned that Marla takes little part in class talk and even on a one-to-one basis, gives minimal answers. The teacher decides to look at her own style of talking to Marla, and tape records about 10 minutes of talk. She notices how many questions she is asking and how often they are 'closed' requiring only yes/no answers; that she is dominating the dialogue, allowing few pauses, and that she often accepts an answer that is not correct from Marla in order to keep the conversation going. She realizes that she has a real sense of discomfort during these interactions, trying but not succeeding to put Marla at her ease. So she decides to try a different style: she gives Marla time to think of answers; she starts with open questions (*wh-* type) and occasionally prompts her very naturally by starting a sentence and letting Marla complete it. She also tries to relax and make Marla feel that she is really interested in what she has to say. She accepts Marla's use of gesture and uses gesture herself. On listening to the second tape she is surprised by how different Marla seems and how much more she is able to contribute (Wood *et al.* 1986; Grove 2010).

What works – the inclusive classroom

There is increasing recognition that if we modify the way we teach pupils and adapt the classroom environment in certain fairly simple ways, we can address the learning needs of all pupils. For example, Martin (2005) argues that adopting generic strategies to support comprehension and expression is relevant to both pupils with English as an additional language and pupils with SLI. Tallal (2000), reviewing techniques for working with children with SLI, suggests that although pupils may occasionally need teaching specific skills in isolation, it is absolutely vital that they learn to apply these skills in the classroom if they are to use them effectively – and this means that teachers need to support them appropriately. The following generic principles, if implemented, will support the development of listening and speaking

– comprehension and expression – for all children in your class, including those who have SEND.

Box 9.7 Simple rules for promoting good communication in the classroom

- Clear simple language, avoid complex sentences and instructions.
- Visual clues to the meaning of language and to help with memory – gestures and pictures.
- Plenty of practical, active, concrete tasks to engage attention and interest.
- Demonstration and modelling of what you want children to do – don't just tell them.
- Opportunities to rehearse and recall instructions – use repetition and be consistent.
- Always be ready to respond to children's spontaneous learning and communication, build what they give you into your teaching.
- Explanation and enrichment of vocabulary and concepts. Plan beforehand what vocabulary is needed and how you will teach it.
- A clear structure and predictable ritual to lessons, with different aspects labelled in ways children can understand, e.g. sign/picture for whole group work; discussion, reading, work on your own, work with a partner.
- Acceptance of all appropriate forms of communication.
- Alternating tasks which demand attention and listening with physical activity and discussion.
- Emotional support from staff and peers.
- Quiet well-organized environments which are adapted to their physical and learning needs: furniture which is comfortable and the right height.
- Availability of drinking water, access to nutritious snacks during the day.

There are now a range of excellent practical resources to support teachers. The best, however, is to observe and record what actually happens when you change your teaching style – and the way in which children's language skills change with the task and the social context in which they are required to work (Peets 2009).

Some final reflections

The strategies outlined in this chapter are fundamental to the success of an inclusive policy which seeks to fulfil the rights of children to be educated in an appropriate neighbourhood school with their local friends, and to take advantage of a broad and rich curriculum (Bishton 2007). To break the existing link between low attainment and special needs, confidence, expectations, enabling environments and the skills and commitment of staff are what count, regardless of the impairments of the children (DCFS 2010; Sheehy et al. 2009). If teachers can be confident in a pedagogy which supports all learners and recognizes the interaction between context, communication and the learner, it will be easier to identify the children who need extra provision to meet their distinct personal needs. Beyond the classroom, if young people are to become confident, empowered citizens, they need more than access to a subject-based curriculum, they need to be able to participate fully in the culture of the school and every aspect of school life.

Acknowledgements

I would like to thank the members of the team who collaborated on the development of materials for speaking, listening and learning: Nick Peacey, Maggie Johnson, Ann Miles, Janeta Guarneri, Jan Pennington, Wendy Rinaldi, Melanie Peter, Claire Topping, Julie Dockrell, and Ann Middleton. The ideas in this chapter are largely based on the information and experience they generously provided. Thanks to Nick Peacey for comments on an earlier draft of the revisions.

Notes

1 School Action Plus derives from the SEN Code of Practice (2001) and is used when the school seeks external advice from support services to give detailed interventions to children whose progress has been limited.
2 Based on case studies in Sherratt and Peter (2002); the authors show how to develop elaborate social and imaginative drama through careful use of explicit demonstration and a developmentally based approach.
3 Based on Newton *et al.* (2010).

Bibliography

Baddeley, A. D., Gathercole, S.E. and Papagno, C. (1998) 'The phonological loop as a language learning device', *Psychological Review*, 105: 158–73.

Barton, L. (2003) 'Inclusive education and teacher education', inaugural professorial lecture, London: Institute of Education.

Beaney, J. and Kershaw, P. (2003) *Inclusion in the Primary Classroom: Support Materials for Children with ASD*, London: National Autistic Society.

Bercow, J. (2008) *Review of Services for Children and Young People (0-19) with Speech, Language and Communication Needs*. Available at: www.dcsf.gov.uk/bercowreview.

Bishop, D. (1997) *Uncommon Understanding: Development and Disorders of Language Comprehension in Children*, Hove: Psychology Press.

Bishton, H. (2007) *Children's Voices, Children's Rights: What Children Have to Say about Their Inclusive Schools*. National College for School Leadership. Available at: www.nationalcollege. org.uk.

Blank, M. and Franklin, E. (1980) 'Dialogue with preschoolers: a cognitively based system of assessment', *Applied Psycholinguistics*, 1: 127–50.

Botting, N. and Conti-Ramsden, G. (2008) 'The role of language, social cognition and social skill in the functional social outcomes of young adolescents with and without a history of SLI', *British Journal of Developmental Psychology*, 26: 281–300.

Broomfield, J. and Dodd, B. (2004) 'Incidence and characteristics of speech language disability', *International Journal of Language and Communication Disorders*, 39: 303–24.

Bryan, K. (2004) 'Preliminary study of the prevalence of speech and language difficulties in young offenders', *International Journal of Language and Communication Disorders*, 39: 391–400.

Ching, T. *et al.* (2009) 'Early language outcomes of children with cochlear implants: interim findings of the NAL study on longitudinal outcomes of children with hearing impairment', *Cochlear Implants International*, 10: 28–32.

Cummins, J. (1984) *Bilingualism and Special Education: Issues in Assessment and Pedagogy*, Clevedon: Multilingual Matters.

DCFS (2009) *Statistical First Release: Special Educational Needs in England*, January. Available at: www.dcsf.gov.uk/rsgateway/D[HB]SFR/.

DCFS (2010) *Breaking the Link Between Special Educational Needs and Low Achievement: Everyone's Business*. Available at: www.teachernet.gov.uk/publications.

Doherty-Sneddon, G. (2004) 'Don't look now I'm trying to think: children's eye gaze and cues to comprehension', *The Psychologist*, 17: 82.

Gathercole, S.E. and Pickering, S.J. (2001) 'Working memory deficits in children with special educational needs', *British Journal of Special Education*, 28: 89–97.

Gray, C. (2002) *My Social Stories Book*, London: Jessica Kingsley.

Gregory, S. (2005) 'Deafness', in A. Lewis and B. Norwich (eds) *Special Teaching For Special Children: Pedagogies for Inclusion*, Maidenhead: Open University Press, pp. 15–25.

Grove, N. (2010) *The Big Book of Storysharing™: At Home, in School*, London: Special Educational Needs Joint Initiative for Training.

Howlin, P., Baron-Cohen, S. and Hadwin, J. (1998) *Teaching Children with Autism to Mind-Read: A Practical Guide*, Chichester: Wiley.

Humphrey, N. (2008) 'Including pupils with autistic spectrum disorders in mainstream schools', *Support for Learning*, 23: 41–7.

Inscoe, J., Odell, A., Archbold, S. and Nikolopoulos, T. (2009) 'Expressive spoken language development in deaf children with cochlear implants who are beginning formal education', *Deafness and Education International*, 11: 39–55.

Johnson, M. and Gallow, R. (2007) *Helping Children Hang on to Your Every Word*, London: QED.

Johnson, M. and Player, C. (2009) *Active Listening for Active Learning: A Mainstream Resource to Promote Understanding, Participation and Personalized Learning in the Classroom*, London: QED.

Kelly, T. P. (2000) 'The clinical neuropsychology of attention in school-aged children', *Child Neuropsychology*, 6(1): 24–36.

Lamb, B. (2009) *Special Educational Needs and Parental Confidence*. Available at: www.dcsf.gov.uk/lambinquiry.

Laws, G. and Bishop, D. (2004) 'Verbal deficits in Down's syndrome and specific language impairment: a comparison', *International Journal of Language and Communication Disorders*, 39: 423–52.

Leonard, L. (1998) *Children with Specific Language Impairment*, Cambridge, MA: MIT Press.

Lewis, A. and Norwich, B. (eds) (2005) *Special Teaching for Special Children: Pedagogies for Inclusion*, Maidenhead: Open University Press.

Lindsay, G., Desforges, M., Dockrell, J., Law, J., Peacey, N., and Beecham, J. (2008) *Effective and Efficient Use of Resources in Services for Children and Young People with Speech, Language and Communication Needs*. Available at: www.dcsf.gov.uk/research/dat[HA]uploadfiles/DCSF-RW053.pdf.

Mackenzie, S. (2009) ' "If you could wave a magic wand . . ." Special Educational Needs in London: diversity, complexity and context', paper presented at the British Educational Research Association Annual Conference, University of Manchester, 2–5 September 2009.

Martin, D. (2005) 'English as an additional language and children with speech, language and communication needs,' in A. Lewis and B. Norwich (eds) *Special Teaching for Special Children: Pedagogies for Inclusion*, Maidenhead: Open University Press, pp. 96–109.

Mason, K., Rowley, K., Marshall, C., Atkinson, J., Woll, B. and Morgan, G. (2010) 'Identifying specific language impairment in deaf children acquiring British Sign Language: implications for theory and practice', *British Journal of Developmental Psychology*, 28: 33–49.

Mirenda, P. and Donnellan, A. (1986) 'Effects of adult interaction style on conversational behavior in students with severe communication problems', *Language, Speech, and Hearing Services in Schools*, 17: 126–41.

Nation, K. and Snowling, M. (2004) 'Beyond phonological skills: broader language skills contribute to the development of reading', *Journal of Research in Reading*, 27(4): 342–56.

Newton, E., Roberts, M. and Donlan, C. (2010) 'Deductive reasoning in children with SLI', *British Journal of Developmental Psychology*, 28: 71–87.

Parsons, S., Law, J. and Gascoigne, M. (2005) 'Teaching receptive vocabulary to children with a speech and language impairment: a curriculum based approach', *Child Language Teaching and Therapy*, 21: 39–59.

Peacey, L. (2009) *A Storytelling Project in Two Sets of Co-Located Mainstream and Special Schools in Country and City: Findings from an Action Research Project*, London: Special Educational Needs Joint Initiative for Training.

Peets, K. (2009) 'The effects of context on the classroom discourse skills of children with language impairment', *Language, Speech, and Hearing Services in Schools*, 40: 5–16.

Pennington, L., Goldbart, J. and Marshall, J. (2004) 'Interaction training for conversational partners of children with cerebral palsy: a systematic review', *International Journal of Language and Communication Disorders*, 39: 151–70.

Rogerson, J. and Dodd, B. (2005) 'Is there an effect of dysphonic teachers' voices on children's processing of spoken language?' *Journal of Voice*, 19(1): 47–60.

Rose, J. (2009) *Independent Review of the Primary Curriculum*. Available at: http://webarchive. nationalarchives.gov.uk/20091109092614/http://www.dcsf.gov.uk/primarycurriculum review/.

Sadler, J. (2005) 'Knowledge, attitudes and beliefs of mainstream teachers of children with a preschool diagnosis of specific language impairment', *Child Language Teaching and Therapy*, 21: 147–64.

Sheehy, K., Rix, J. with Collins, J., Hall, K., Nind, M. and Wearmouth, J. (2009) 'A systematic review of whole class, subject-based pedagogies with reported outcomes for the academic and social inclusion of pupils with special educational needs', in *Research Evidence in Education Library*, London: EPPI-Centre, Social Science Research Unit, Institute of Education, University of London.

Sherratt, D. and Peter, M. (2002) *Developing Play and Drama in Children with Autistic Spectrum Disorders*, London: David Fulton.

Shield, B.M. and Dockrell, J.E. (2004) 'External and internal noise surveys of London primary schools', *Journal of the Acoustical Society of America*, 115: 730–8.

Stiers, P., Vanderkelen, R., Vanneste, G., Coene, S., De Rammelaere, M. and Vandenbussche, E. (2002) 'Visual-perceptual impairment in a random sample of children with cerebral palsy', *Developmental Medicine and Child Neurology*, 44(6): 370–82.

Swanwick, R. (2010) 'Policy and practice in sign bilingual education: development, challenges and directions', *International Journal of Bilingual Education and Bilingualism*, 13: 147–58.

Tallal, P. (2000) 'Experimental studies of language learning impairments: from research to remediation', in D. Bishop and L. Leonard (eds) *Speech and Language Impairments in Children: Causes, Characteristics, Interventions and Outcome*, Hove: Psychology Press, pp. 131–56.

Van Daal, J., Verhoeven, L., van Leeuwe, J. and van Balkom, H. (2008) 'Working memory limitations in children with severe language impairment', *Journal of Communication Disorders*, 41: 85–107.

Vigil, B., Eyer, J. and Hardee, W. (2005) 'Relevant responding in pragmatic language impairment: the role of language variation in the information-soliciting utterance', *Child Language Teaching and Therapy*, 21: 1–22.

Wood, D.J., Wood, H.A., Griffiths, A.J. and Howarth, C.I. (1986) *Teaching and Talking with Deaf Children*, London and New York: Wiley.

Using Talk for Learning in Science and Mathematics

Elizabeth Briten, Sarah Jackson-Stevens and Nicola Treby

Introduction

The very nature of science and mathematics suggests that neither is a spectator sport, rather these are subjects which are all about 'doing', whether it be problem solving, investigating or testing hypotheses through experimentation. They are about building on prior knowledge to construct new ideas which may challenge previous notions of understanding, thus addressing misconceptions along the way. Both science and mathematics help us make sense of the world around us and scientific and mathematical thinking and talking permeate our everyday lives even if we are not aware of it (Ernest, in White and Bramall 2000). But how do we engage children in such processes and how can we enhance their knowledge and understanding in these areas? Mercer (2004) suggests that critical to promoting children's knowledge and development is the quality of the dialogue and the inter-actions that occur not only between teachers and children, but the children themselves.

Children's talk, therefore, is an essential feature of the classroom. In science and in mathematics, it helps to build understanding as dialogue is used within group investigations to describe, predict, explore and explain. This collaborative activity provokes brain development as children consider their own scientific and mathematical ideas alongside those of others. Alexander (2004) suggests that talk helps to physically shape the brain and expand its power by building cells and making new connections so improving the capacity for learning and memory. This *brain building* talk does not happen incidentally, the teacher has a critical role in ensuring that classroom talk is purposeful, focused and directed towards learning. It is also important that children are aware of the value of learning through talk and how it helps to develop understanding in science and mathematics.

This chapter explores the use of talk for learning in science and mathematics focusing upon the following:

- the notion of exploratory talk and its role in developing children's scientific and mathematical knowledge and understanding;
- the role of the teacher in planning for talk and eliciting children's prior knowledge through constructive dialogue;
- some of the strategies and approaches that can be used (such as guided group work) as well as the choice and management of resources in stimulating high quality talk in science and mathematics.

These key areas will be illuminated by references to case studies, based on classroom experience and the experience of student teachers working towards qualified teacher status.

Exploratory talk in science and mathematics

Barnes (in Mercer and Hodgkinson 2009) suggests exploratory talk is vital in the early stages of constructing new ideas and trying out new ways of thinking and understanding. In contrast to presentational talk (Barnes 1992) which focuses upon presenting thoughts in a more organised way, exploratory talk is concerned with speculative talk which explores ideas and information, enabling children to consider others' views and use new knowledge to consider further possibilities. This means that in order for children to emerge as successful mathematicians and scientists, opportunities need to be provided for children to construct and challenge their knowledge and understanding through active participation in group problem-solving tasks and investigations. Such activities necessitate the use of thinking skills and the ability to explain, reason and justify which in turn requires knowledge and understanding of appropriate subject-specific language.

Talk within scientific enquiry

The steps taken in a scientific enquiry from the initial elicitation of ideas, to active exploration and the presentation of results, can engage children in a range of dialogue genres that promote talk and improve reasoning skills. With direction from the teacher, children can develop a type of talk termed 'dialogic talk' which is of a high cognitive demand as it encourages children to think about their work and articulate their understanding of it. It is not concerned with right answers but *why* an answer may be right or wrong. In this context, it is important that children feel they can have an opinion and that it is worthy of being shared.

Elicitation talk

As part of the initial elicitation of science ideas that commonly occurs at the start of a topic or lesson, children can be encouraged to reveal their scientific reasoning, using talk to describe and explain the ideas and beliefs they hold. Here misconceptions become apparent to both the child and teacher as personal ideas are compared to the thinking of peers. A number of resources may be used to encourage this rich dialogue:

Concept cartoons devised by Keogh and Naylor (2000) encourage debate as children think through and reason aloud, perhaps challenging their own thinking as alternative scientific concepts are presented. The cartoons show varying situations in which children are discussing possible solutions to science problems. One of the most commonly known shows three children gathered around a snowman discussing the best way to keep him frozen. They offer suggestions such as wrapping him in a coat to keep him cold, wrapping him in a coat to keep him warm or leaving him without any covering. Children can then be encouraged to share their own views and opinions as they debate a solution.

Classification tasks involve sorting objects/ideas and require children to make decisions and justify thinking, possibly defending personal ideas as new ones are presented. Such tasks can include sorting materials into those that float/sink, with the inclusion of counter-intuitive examples, e.g. a large candle or small pin, ensuring that children begin to debate the notion of why objects float or sink.

Sorting cards can include pictures of differing explanations of scientific phenomenon. Again, these are a valuable inspiration for talk and the revelation of often erroneous ideas. Pictorial representations suggested by Davis (2002) include possible reasons for the known phases of the moon; is it due to the Earth's shadow, the position of the moon as it is lit by the light of the sun or due to another planet casting a shadow on the moon? Again, the ideas will present an opportunity for rich discussion and debate.

Observing unusual events might include a jar with layers of liquid of different densities, e.g. oil, water, treacle, etc. Although the concept of density might be too complex to comprehend, the range of possible explanations provoked will provide an excellent opportunity for talk.

Exploratory talk

As the scientific enquiry progresses, children become involved in the dialogue of decision-making as alternative views are considered and differing ideas about method and process are negotiated and selected. Individual understanding grows as children think through problems together. This exploratory talk is described by Mercer *et al.* (1999) as a situation in which:

- All information about ideas is shared.
- All group members are encouraged to contribute.
- Individual opinions and ideas are respected and considered.
- Reasoning is made clear.
- Challenges and alternatives are made explicit and negotiated.
- The group seeks agreement before taking a decision or acting.

Presenting enquiry work as a *problem to be solved* will promote valuable exploratory talk, whether the children are constructing a burglar alarm, finding the strongest magnet or designing a pitched musical instrument. Thinking begins as children predict possible outcomes, consider how to carry out enquiries and decide on methods for recording and presentation. The role of the teacher is critical here in directing the talk to ensure debate occurs and key ideas are explored.

Scaffolding talk – the role of the teacher

Within the enquiry process, the role of the teacher is to use questioning to probe and clarify thinking and encourage the children to articulate a depth of understanding. (See Chapter 7 for further ideas on questions to stimulate children's thinking.) Scaffolding talk helps children to make connections in thinking through highlighting links to other concepts or identifying similar situations or events. This helps understanding to be reinforced and consolidated. Children will also scaffold each other's understanding as they talk through ideas within a group.

Presentation talk

The conclusion of the enquiry process provides an opportunity for children to verbally reveal new scientific thinking. The communication of results encourages children to use talk to explain, evaluate, hypothesise and justify both their thinking and working method to an audience. Prompt questions provided by the teacher can support the audience in this process. If children are to articulate their ideas about scientific phenomena, they need access to the specialized vocabulary of science. While children can enjoy using complex terms, they will need time to fully develop correct meaning. In the early stages it is useful to allow children to use 'everyday' language alongside the correct scientific term as understanding grows and an increasing glossary of terms is collated. For example *see-through* becomes transparent, *soaked up* becomes absorbed, *water can't get through* becomes *impermeable*, and so on.

Making talk productive

Purpose

In order to try to avoid off-task talk, there must be a clear purpose to the activity which will motivate the children and give them something meaningful to talk about. This may be a problem to be solved, an issue to be debated or an investigation to undertake where the children *have to* talk to find the solution. Guidance can be provided by the teacher with *talk cards* that include questions that structure and sequence the dialogue. For example, during a friction investigation, possible statements could include:

- What causes you to slip on ice in winter? How could you stop yourself from slipping?
- Why did the car travel furthest on the smooth plastic surface?
- Can you think of different ways in which we design objects so they have more friction, e.g. bicycle tyres?

Group identity

Kutnick and Rogers, in Dawes (2004), highlight potential problems that can occur when children are required to work in a group setting. For some, the social demands may be too great with children unable to collaborate in a mutually supportive manner. Time is needed to develop group skills such as active listening and taking turns, before the value of co-operative learning can be realised. To overcome potential problems, it is necessary for the teacher to structure the groups, initially experimenting with different blends of gender, ability and friendship until constructive groups are established. (See Chapter 2 which discusses planning and organising groups for effective talk.)

Rules for group dialogue

It is important to have *ground rules* (Dawes 2008) for group work to ensure its success. To avoid the dominance of socially confident children, all should be given the opportunity to share their views within a supportive climate where each idea is listened to and respected. All children have the potential for creative thought but time must be allowed for this to occur. Individual ideas should be open to evaluation and challenge as decisions are made and solutions sought. Ideas can be jotted down as they emerge, so thoughts can be revisited. It must be stressed that criticism of others' ideas is a healthy part of debate but should also be supported by valid counter-argument.

Classroom ethos

As highlighted in Chapter 1, it is necessary to promote a classroom ethos where talk is valued and celebrated. As with all areas, the climate in which scientific talk can flourish is one of collaboration and mutual intellectual appreciation where all children feel able to contribute and challenge is seen as an intellectually valuable process. Children should enjoy the social nature of group enquiry work and should come to appreciate and value the shared practice of co-operative learning conducted in true scientific style where peer evaluation supports productive learning and promotes the re-structuring of misconceptions. The case study below indicates the process in action.

Misconceptions in science – a case study

Science is an area where misconceptions can be formed very easily. Much work has been done by Black *et al.* (2003) on 'Assessment for Learning', and this research has informed the practice of teachers worldwide; less well documented is the value of exploratory talk to improve learning, especially in the area of identifying and resolving misconceptions. This approach was considered very effective when used by an experienced teacher working with a group of Key Stage 2 children in the area of plant science. The case study below illustrates how dialogue can be managed to address children's misconceptions in science.

Case Study 1 Anya and her KS2 class

Anya, the class teacher, devised a lesson to help her class identify and correct children's misconceptions by using exploratory talk within the classroom. This was used during a lesson which gave children the opportunity to reflect on prior learning by discussing what plants needed to survive, the function of the leaf and the importance of the roots in helping the plant survive and grow. Anya kept the 'teacher talk time' to a minimum. Initially, the teacher used teacher-led discussion to elicit children's ideas. The questions were given to the children on question cards to help provide purpose for exploratory talk. The children were arranged in groups of four to discuss the questions posed. The questions given were:

1. What do plants need to survive? Explain how we can prove this.

2. What does the leaf do? Explain how we can prove this.

3. Why does a plant have roots? What would happen if a plant didn't have roots?

By the end of the lesson, the class had identified and resolved misconceptions, had worked effectively within their groups, and demonstrated consideration in listening to each other's ideas. Additionally, they had used their own observations of plants and each other's ideas to develop their understanding of how the different parts of the plant each have a role to play in helping the plant to grow. The children had produced diagrams (which could be assessed) to provide a visual record of their final answers to the questions posed. Some of the class then suggested filming each other, talking about the plants in a *Newsround* style presentation. Other children were keen to develop the work by engaging in a series of practical investigations which would put all of their knowledge about plant survival to the test. The children's responsibility was to plan for these events and this ensured that the homework set seamlessly linked to their learning in school. Anya had already prepared a first homework task whereby prompt questions were given to the parents, with suggested answers, so that at home all of the children had the opportunity not only to develop their exploratory talk but also to prepare for presentational talk.

The successful outcome of a lesson such as this, both in developing children's skills to use talk effectively and in furthering their subject knowledge, derived from the crucial role played by the teacher. The role of talk had been a key feature of her teaching and was made explicit to the class throughout. She had also ensured that this lesson was well supported in providing dialogic talk that led to the discussion and correction of misconceptions. She matched this with a flexibility to really support the children in their speaking and consequently in their thinking too.

As the lesson was introduced, the teacher 'normalised' the likelihood of children 'falling out' over differences of opinion. She modelled this process by presenting the children with examples of possible conflicts of opinion and included them in suggesting possible resolutions. Although Anya had previously addressed her expectations of how the class should talk to each other and interact, she regularly reinforced and shared her expectations for effective discussion. In doing so, she developed a classroom ethos where talk was valued by both teachers and children alike and considered an integral part of the learning process.

In addition to managing the learning environment and creating a positive ethos for talk, it was necessary for the teacher to consider grouping arrangements and for this activity, she had organised the children into mixed ability groups. One person within each group was given a laminated card of questions to ask when people disagreed over an answer to prompt further dialogue. It included the questions below, which were designed to scaffold (Bruner 2006) their learning and further aid exploratory talk.

- Can you tell me what you have seen/heard that has led to your answer?

- Can anyone give me one reason why they think this may be the correct answer?

- Can anyone give me one reason why they think this may be a mistake?

These questions could be asked to both children with opposing answers. Although prompt cards such as these are designed to support collaborative learning, Anya was required to intervene and explain why a theory was correct and help a child to understand where their misconception had arisen from. However, the purpose of these questions was to support the discussion and try to help the children work through their own ideas to co-construct meaning. In the process of this they were also developing the following scientific skills:

- analysing how they had come to believe a certain idea;

- being challenged on their viewpoint;

- justifying their answer with evidence.

The teacher also tried to pre-empt the common misconceptions that the children might have. These included:

- plants need feeding, when in fact they produce their own food (in the form of glucose);

- water enters the plant through the leaf, when in fact it runs off the leaf (due to the waxy cuticle) onto the ground and the water is then absorbed by the roots of the plant (via root hair cells);

- in terms of the roots, Anya was keen to identify opportunities to help students understand how they helped to anchor the plant in one location (although technically plants can still 'move' as they can grow towards the light).

During the lesson there were times when the teacher was aware that significant numbers of children were having difficulty with a question. In this situation she chose to switch to whole-class dialogue and led from the front by involving children in working through the questions on the prompt sheets given. In this way she was consistent in her method of really helping the children to understand the context of their learning. Additionally, this provided an excellent opportunity for her to model the kind of talk that she wanted to hear within the small groups and pre-empt any further misconceptions that might arise.

This case study highlights how exploratory talk can help to develop children's scientific knowledge, to provide purposeful contexts to resolve misconceptions and to support children to analyse and justify their scientific thinking. Underpinning the success of such a lesson were the sensitive and timely interventions made by the teacher and her crucial role in modelling the dialogue with the children. The children were aware that having differing viewpoints can be a constructive way of furthering knowledge in a collaborative context. It is evident that managing exploratory talk in classrooms can be challenging, but it is undoubtedly of great value; the rewards for staff and students alike are immense.

Talk in Mathematics

Following the recommendations of the Independent Review of Mathematics in the Early Years Setting and Primary Schools (Williams 2007), there has been a focus on the promotion of opportunities for high quality talk in the mathematics classroom. In response to this, a small group of student teachers on an ITT course recently took part in a programme, organized by the mathematics department, to develop their own skills in promoting children's mathematical understanding through talk-based teaching and learning approaches. Some of the strategies and approaches used are now addressed through the following case study.

Case study 2 High quality talk through planned guided group work activities

The students initially participated in a workshop session to explore different ways to develop opportunities for high quality talk through planned guided group work activities. This was followed by time spent in school trying out some their ideas with a small group of children. The students evaluated and assessed the children's learning at the end of each session and reflected upon the effectiveness of their teaching in relation to engaging children in meaningful mathematical talk through the planned activities; they also considered their role as the teacher.

Guided group work presents a positive context in which to develop children's mathematical understanding through talk-based learning. The students planned specific group activities which were designed to encourage children to work collaboratively, sharing ideas and skills in order to build upon different levels of prior knowledge. This could then be used to construct new ideas with a collective aim of solving a problem or exploring outcomes to a particular investigation. Opportunities for exploratory talk were at the heart of this approach. At the end of the first week it was noted that discussions were generally very disjointed and at times hard to follow. However, by giving the children time to sort through their ideas, by posing carefully considered questions and really listening to and valuing their responses, students observed children's emerging ability to develop their mathematical understanding and construct new knowledge and understanding among themselves. It was also possible for the student teachers to gather much richer assessment data this way which enabled them to record more accurately the way in which individuals were emerging as mathematical thinkers.

Robinson identifies four 'E's for developing effective classroom talk:

- environment that encourages and values talk;
- enriching experiences that inspire the spirit of enquiry;
- enabling learning through collaboration;
- evaluating the learning processes.

(Robinson 2011)

For the students, these acted as a foundation for the planning, teaching and assessment cycle giving them a focus for later reflections. At the end of their school experience they highlighted three key areas as significant in promoting high quality mathematical talk:

- the teacher's role in the development of appropriate mathematical vocabulary;
- effective questioning and response techniques;
- the use of resources to stimulate mathematical talk.

Each of these aspects will be explored within the context of the students' work as they draw attention to some fundamental features of planning for and the development of effective mathematical talk.

The teacher's role in the development of appropriate mathematical vocabulary

Developing speaking and listening skills in mathematics is more than simply learning the relevant terminology. However, in order for children to be able to participate in collaborative problem-solving or investigative tasks they need to be equipped with the necessary technical vocabulary. Children come to school with experiences of everyday language which relate to mathematical concepts such as 'measure' in the form of comparative language – bigger, smaller and 'shape and space' – often the 2D word for the 3D experience (for example, circle instead of sphere). This is a relevant starting point for the development of mathematical vocabulary as teachers may use informal, everyday language in mathematics lessons before or alongside technical mathematical vocabulary. An example of this is demonstrated in a student teacher's introduction to a mathematics lesson:

> My shape has 5 faces, 6 points or corners also known as vertices – one vertex many vertices – and 9 edges. Two of the faces are similar or we can say in mathematics, congruent and they are made up of triangles or are triangular in shape; the other three faces are all rectangular. What shape am I?

Here, the student had noted the importance of being more explicit in the use and explanation of key mathematical terms and consequently she adapted her original plans in the next guided group activity to highlight the links between everyday language and mathematical terminology so that the children could begin to use this more successfully in their own mathematical discussions.

Effective questioning and response techniques

Opportunities should arise for children to clarify, consolidate and extend their thinking and this generally occurs through the use of open questions. The role of the teacher is crucial here in ensuring effective questioning and response techniques which encourage children to reason, justify and move their understanding forward. For example, *Can you explain how you worked that out? But what if we change this variable? What do you already know that might help you?* This last question was used successfully in a context where children were working together to solve a number puzzle and stated to the teacher that they did not know if 1 was a prime number. The easy option might have been just to give them the answer but instead the teacher asked the group to explain what they understood to be a prime number. They answered this successfully, so she went on:

Teacher: And so does 1 fit the properties that you have just outlined?
Child A: Well, 1 is divisible by 1 and itself.
Child B: But 1 is itself so it only has one factor.
Child A: So are you saying that it is not a prime number?
Teacher: Well, what was the rule you gave me for correctly identifying a prime number?
Child C: It is a number that is only divisible by 1 and itself so it has only two factors.
Child B: So 1 can't be a prime number as it only has one!

On reflection, this event identified the need to give more consideration to the *reason* for asking questions in the first place as well as the *quality* of the questions that were asked as this would affect the quality of answer given. This later prompted greater awareness for the student teachers that learning through speaking and listening is most effective when questions were purposeful, responses were valued and followed up with prompts and probing questions which promoted further mathematical thinking and engagement.

The use of resources to stimulate mathematical talk

Planning opportunities for children to engage in mathematical discussion does not necessarily mean that talk among a group will be forthcoming. Resources have a key role to play here. However, it is not only the choice of those resources which is crucial, but the way in which they are used which is vital in stimulating mathematical discussion. The student teachers noted that if materials were placed in the middle of the table as a free for all, it only encouraged some children to dive in and take over while others sat back and excluded themselves from the collaborative thinking approach that the students were trying to encourage. One way to address this was highlighted through an activity which required the use of a set of problem-solving cards. The key to success in encouraging speaking and listening was that each group member was not allowed to show each other the clue cards but rather they could read them out aloud as many times as necessary thus providing a springboard for mathematical discussion through the initial sharing of unknown information. So, in addition to the choice of resource, it is worthwhile considering how these will be managed within guided group activities as a stimulus for high quality and effective mathematical talk.

Some final reflections

Dialogue in the classroom is a powerful learning tool, and talk presents opportunities for children to generate new understanding (Dawes 2004). It is only when we seek to explain ideas to others that our understanding is fully tested as we attempt to link ideas together and use vocabulary that adds structure to our speech. Through this process, higher order reasoning is developed. To fully exploit the potential of talk in mathematics and science, it is evident that an environment committed to dialogue must be created and celebrated and careful consideration given to the role of questioning to promote both thinking and learning.

Bibliography

Alexander, R. (2004) *Towards Dialogic Teaching: Rethinking Classroom Talk*, Cambridge: Dialogos.

Barnes, D. (1992) *From Communication to Curriculum*, 2nd edn, Portsmouth, NH: Boynton/Cook-Heinemann.

Black, P., Harrison, C., Lee, C., Marshall, B. and Wiliam, D. (2003) *Assessment for Learning*, Maidenhead: Open University Press.

Bruner, J. (2006) *In Search of Pedagogy; The Selected Works of Jerome S. Bruner*, London: Routledge.

Davies, R. (2002) 'Misconceptions about space?: It's on the cards', *Primary Science Review*, 72, March/April, Herts: ASE.

Dawes, L. (2004) 'Talk and learning in classroom science', *International Journal of Science Education*, 26(6): 677–95.

Dawes, L. (2008) *Our Ground Rules for Exploratory Talk* and *Ground Rules: Traffic Lights Activity Thinking Together,* University of Cambridge, resources for Teachers. Online. Available at: HTTP:http://thinkingtogether.educ.cam.ac.uk/resources/ (accessed 11 January 2011).

Keogh, B. and Naylor, S. (2000) *Concept Cartoons in Science Education,* Sandbach: Millgate House Publishers.

Mercer, N., Dawes, L., Wegerif, R. and Sams, C. (2004) 'Reasoning as a scientist: ways of helping children to use language to learn science', *British Educational Research Journal,* 30(2): 359–77.

Mercer, N. and Hodgkinson, S. (eds) (2009) *Exploring Talk in School,* London: Sage.

Mercer, N., Wegerif, R. and Dawes, L. (1999) 'Children's talk and the development of reasoning in the classroom', *British Educational Research Journal,* 25(1): 95–111.

Piaget, J. (1955) *The Construction of Reality in the Child,* London: Routledge & Kegan Paul.

Robinson, D. (2011) 'Teaching mental calculations', in V. Koshy and J. Murray (eds) *Unlocking Mathematics Teaching,* 2nd edn, Abingdon: Routledge.

White, J. and Bramall, S. (eds) (2000) *Why Teach Mathematics?* London: London University Institute of Education.

Williams, P. (2007) *Independent Review of Mathematics in the Early Years Setting and Primary Schools,* London: DfES.

Emphasising the 'C' in ICT: Speaking, Listening and Communication

Yota Dimitriadi, Pamela Hodson and Geeta Ludhra

Introduction

Joti, Harry, Isobel and Gurdeep, four Year 2 pupils, were filming a sequence of shots using a digital video camera to provide instructions for visitors to help them navigate around their school. Joti and Harry were being guided by Gurdeep on where to stand. Gurdeep stood back and evaluated the image she could see through her camera,

'Stand closer and look this way.'

'If you pan left and right slowly, you'll be able to see all of the playground,' suggested Isobel and they all agreed. As the filming started, Isobel counted in the presenters who introduced themselves, welcomed potential visitors to their school and gave clear explanations and instructions on routes around the school.

In this extended activity, ICT, in the form of digital video, offered the children opportunities to work in role, engage in real-time situations which promoted team-work and involved them in choosing an appropriate genre to address purpose and audience (Becta 2003a). Digital filmmaking is an example of the multimedia opportunities offered by the availability of more inexpensive and easy to use digital cameras, camcorders and video editing software. The integration of digital video is becoming increasingly popular not only as a teaching and learning resource, but its potential for the development of a range of social skills, including problem-solving (Theodosakis 2002), communication, negotiation (Becta 2003a) and self-perception (BFI 2002) has also been recognized. As filmmakers, children are encouraged to develop a voice in the creative process, to explore ideas and reflect upon their decisions and to work effectively as part of a group (Dimitriadi and Hodson 2004).

This chapter explores the opportunities that ICT offers for communication in the primary classroom and for innovations in teachers' practice. The term ICT is used to encompass technological media that can assist, enrich or replace current practices and support interaction and communication. In this context, computer-related activities will be considered, together with the use of other digital resources like cameras or programmable toys.

What follows is a discussion of how ICT can enrich speaking and listening activities and factors that need to be considered when organising ICT-related tasks with children. The terms communication and interaction will also be used to address inclusive uses of technology (see Nicola Grove's Chapter 9). This is particularly important as the terms 'speaking and listening' can point to verbal exchanges in which some children with special educational needs or disabilities may not be able to participate fully. It also allows us to view the contribution of ICT to receptive and expressive interactions in a more holistic way, something which will be relevant in the case of children with English as an additional language (EAL) which is explored in more depth in Chapter 8. In this context, 'speaking and listening' will include expressive and receptive communication skills which may be observed in verbal and non-verbal utterances. This approach is concomitant with the Speaking, Listening and Learning exemplification materials produced to support children with special educational needs.

Other key areas for consideration will be the kinds of speaking and listening that a range of ICT resources can promote and how these opportunities for communication can be effectively embedded in the curriculum. Specific packages will not be evaluated, but rather, families of programs and peripherals and their potential to support communication and group work will be discussed.

The current context

Chapter 1 identifies that the primary curriculum has been the subject of two major reviews: The Cambridge Review (Alexander *et al.* 2009) and the Rose Review (DCSF 2009). Dugdale (2009) notes that there is an interesting difference in how these reviews perceive the relationship between ICT and language and literacy. He identifies that in the Cambridge Review, ICT is considered an integral part of the oracy and literacy domain of learning whereas the Rose Review recommends that ICT should be a separate cross-curricular discipline. He argues that integrating ICT into literacy should bridge the unhelpful false divide between literacy and digital or media literacy. This chapter adopts an holistic view of ICT which clearly locates children's development in speaking and listening within the new technologies.

In addition, teachers are now being actively encouraged to adopt a more flexible approach to teaching literacy and using ICT effectively in the classroom can have positive effects in enabling teachers to re-evaluate how they teach English. Becta (2003a) identifies research (Henessey *et al.* 2003) whereby ICT allows for opportunities in which teacher direction is reduced and children's control and self-regulation are increased.

Promoting the involvement of all children and young people and especially the most vulnerable ones in society also comes as a direct outcome of government policy within the children's agenda delineated in 'Every Child Matters' (DfES 2003), something which can support the development of more empowering practices in terms of children's participation within the curriculum. New technologies, as cultural commodities, can facilitate children's active involvement in developing a voice about themselves and the world around them.

In terms of speaking and listening, ICT can enable children to enrich a range of social learning skills such as communication, negotiation, decision-making and problem-solving (Reid *et al.* 2002) in a meaningful context. These skills are consistent with the requirements of the primary ICT curriculum in which the children are expected to develop skills, knowledge and understanding of appropriate uses of technology, coined under the term 'ICT capability' (DfEE 1999: 99). The children's ICT explorations need to demonstrate 'a conceptual understanding of the ways in which information is organised, accessed, presented and communicated with these technologies' (Sharp *et al.* 2002: 2).

The four strands of the Programmes of Study for ICT in the National Curriculum for England (2000) highlight the importance of speaking and listening as they suggest that ICT activities need to be collaborative and investigative. When children are engaged in 'exchanging and sharing information', 'developing ideas and making things happen', 'finding things out' or 'reviewing, modifying and evaluating work as it progresses', they are expected to develop communicative skills by participating in group activities and justifying their individual choices. In the wider context that the breadth of study covers, the children are also encouraged to explore and talk about uses of ICT within and outside the school. The ICT curriculum emphasises the importance of children developing skills progressively to describe, present and evaluate their work by taking into consideration purpose, relevance and appropriateness for their audience.

Communication is a key area in the Foundation Stage as well. Young children are involved in exploring and describing the world and themselves to peers and adults (see Chapter 3 for further exemplification of a discussion of early years and children's development in communication). The opportunities for ICT are embedded within all six Early Learning Goals and can take the form of playful activities in which a range of resources can be used from metal detectors to programmable toys and digital cameras.

Supporting engagement and interaction

Interaction is embedded within all ICT applications. Talking word processors, symbol processing programs or personal aids such as voice-activated software provide users with opportunities to learn and exchange information by employing diverse ways of communication like their voice, pictures and symbols. Table 11.1 indicates how ICT can involve children in a range of speaking and listening contexts and activities. Organisations like NESTA Futurelab (http://www.nestafuturelab.org) support creative uses of new technologies and also evaluate current approaches and use of digital resources. The 'Teem' (Teachers Evaluating Educational Multimedia) website (http://www.teem.org.uk) offers evaluations of educational software and websites.

These new technologies have started shaping speaking, listening and writing activities offering 'more fluid and informal forms of communication which in turn will influence decisions about the speaking and listening curriculum', as Eve Bearne

TABLE 11.1 How ICT can involve children in a range of speaking and listening contexts and activities

COMMUNICATIVE FUNCTIONS	ACTIVITIES AND RESOURCES
Collaboration	Working together on game-format activities, researching topics on the web to produce presentations, working in groups to develop digital videos, music and other multimedia work
Communication	WWW, email, Talking Books, Voice-Activated Software, Symbol Processing Software, Presentation packages, Storyboarding programs, DeskTop Publishing software, digital cameras, art packages, video conferencing, talking word processors, PC Tablets
Evaluation	Analysing media work, selecting relevant and appropriate information from the web and justifying their choices
Reflection	Programmable toys, webquests, control technology, developing and interpreting graphs

argues (QCA, undated). However, she continues, 'It is important to be able to distinguish between shifts in practices brought about by digital technology and fundamental changes in forms of language'.

What is becoming more and more challenging is a change of discourse conventions that accompanies the use of communication technologies. For instance, mobile phones have become popular media in the lives of many young people who choose them as favourite ways of keeping in touch with their local social networks (Livingstone and Bober 2004). Emoticons or abbreviations, usual features in texting, are considered as purposeful and legitimate elements of interactions and are used to indicate ideas, actions and pauses, all integral attributes of dialogical exchanges.

These functional uses of new technologies can often blend boundaries between formal and informal communications and settings, creating some continuities between prior experiences and knowledge for the 'digital natives' as children are sometimes described in the literature (Prensky 2001; Facer 2003). At the same time, though, they can create some discontinuities when their use is not supported by careful consideration of how they can provide accessible and purposeful ways of extending all children's knowledge, skills and capabilities.

The importance of planning for diversity is also highlighted by the principles of the inclusion statement of the National Curriculum. The statement recognizes the importance of providing access for all pupils to overcome barriers to learning, which in terms of ICT will include software and hardware, but also points out the importance of adapting our teaching styles and setting suitable learning challenges to support all learners.

ICT enhancing current practices

ICT does not aim to replace successful speaking and listening activities that are better presented without the use of technology but to enhance current practices in new and innovative ways. For instance, the internet is a research and learning resource that can support active participation as well as synchronous or asynchronous discussion of ideas. Consider the use of emailing which allows users to communicate with people from all over the world or the use of video-conferencing applications that can provide children with a vast range of audiences for speaking and listening activities. However, some internet uses, such as online chats, may need careful consideration due to their unmediated nature (Abbott 2002). Exposure to risks and unsuitable online materials is one of the current concerns regarding internet uses for schools. Becta with the DfES and Ultralab (2003) have produced a teaching pack with suggested activities and an interactive site hosted aimed for Key Stage 2 pupils to support awareness about safe internet uses.

The use of VLEs (Virtual Learning Environments), which provide activities in password-protected areas on the web, is becoming more and more popular in educational settings. Some primary schools use part of their e-learning credits to purchase access to content-rich online resources which include video clips, worksheets and interactive tasks for cross-curricular activities. In terms of speaking and listening, what the teacher needs to ensure is that these online activities are supported by opportunities for discussion among the children during the tasks as well as away from the screen. As Mercer and Wegerif (1998) suggest, the computer can play the role of prompting and sustaining children's use of 'exploratory talk' framing the discussion and directing it towards specific outcomes. What they define as 'exploratory talk' is a communicative process for reasoning through talk in the context of some specific joint activity. (See Chapter 9 for a discussion of the nature of exploratory talk.) Children working on a computer simulation, finding information on a webpage or an informational CD-ROM or developing a newspaper article together can discuss and negotiate the development of their thinking.

In this context, ICT becomes a concrete medium for the children to negotiate or describe ideas. In a Reception class, the children were learning about healthy eating. They had to use a drawing package to draw some 'healthy' food and then describe their drawing to the adult who was supporting them. The particular activity would have been more demanding on paper as it would have been more difficult for them to edit the pictures they drew. It also gave the adult assistant the opportunity to assess the children's IT skills (for instance, mouse control, hand–eye co-ordination) and discuss the use of colour, shape and the notions of 'background' and 'foreground' as they were developing their drawings. At the same time in the class next door the children were working in pairs taking pictures of each other after they had put their overcoats, hats and gloves on. The activity was based on sequencing. The pictures were then saved in their individual portfolios and formed part of their Profiles.

Case Study 1

A group of 18 higher ability Year 6 pupils were studying the poetic features and structures of the witches' chant, in William Shakespeare's tragedy *Macbeth*. Through their study of well-known poets, they were developing their oral performance skills. A simple piece of technology – the cassette recorder – provided a running record of the performances and development processes up to the finished, final product. The tape recorder allowed the children to hear themselves develop as confident performers over four stages of recording (mirroring the drafting and editing process in the written form).

> The tape recorder helped me listen to my voice and I realised that my voice wasn't projecting as well as others in my team. Me and my team worked really hard to get it right after draft one. Draft four was a lot better – I actually sounded quite scary.
>
> (Rupinder, aged 10)

The use of the cassette recorder offered the children a valuable auditory opportunity to focus on speaking and listening skills as two distinct, yet closely related skills. Speaking and listening skills need to be explicitly taught, rehearsed and modelled by the class teacher, especially in a bilingual environment where the models at home are often in their mother tongue.

Classic poetry like Shakespeare can be made accessible and brought to life for bilingual learners if they are provided with multi-sensory opportunities to 'feel' the rhythm and pattern of such classic poems and rehearse them by heart (like a favourite piece of music).

Most of the children in the class were advanced bilingual learners and confident speakers of their mother tongue. They were fluent users of English, yet slightly reserved about performing orally in a dramatic Shakespearian style. Opportunities were given for children to learn through personal reflection and constructive criticism. Through this activity, they were enabled to critically evaluate their own vocal performance skills within a small group.

The children became both the audience and critics for their own work – the simple tape recorder made this possible. The different groups in the class worked together as a team to put together a complete performance. Positive criticism was accepted and discussed where disagreements arose.

Draft one of the oral performance was recorded and the children were provided with short 'time-out' discussion opportunities to discuss and evaluate ways forward. The discussions focused around areas like:

- the use of simple vocal and sound effects;

- the variation of pitch at different lines;

- voice projection skills/volume;

- 'best fit' parts for the line/s.

Some children were given different speaking parts after listening to draft one. Children discussed whose voices should be used together in the performance of particular lines, the use of volume and greater emphasis on certain words for effect (close links with musical elements of texture and timbre).

The children were actively engaged in developing vital language skills in a process of:

- oral performance;
- listening and reflecting;
- evaluating;
- organising different roles;
- discussing, exploring and investigating different approaches.

Without the use of cassette recorder technology, such enrichment, depth and reflection would not have been possible.

> My team knew what we had to do to make it better. Draft 1 wasn't very good at all, we did not create witchy voices or use expression well. You could hardly hear some of our voices. By draft 4 we performed the voices and rhyme patterns spot on. I think we performed well because in our discussions we chose lines that we were confident with.
>
> (Lloyd, aged 11)

Storyboarding software also allows children to choose from a bank of resources (settings, props, characters, voice-overs) and retell traditional stories or discuss social issues such as bullying or friendship as part of the PSHCE curriculum.

Case Study 2

A Year 4 class was organised into small groups and each group was given the task to develop a narrative using a commercial storyboarding program. They were given instructions to create a story for a group of younger children with the teacher emphasising the word 'audience'. They were also asked to develop their story in five slides. They had already created a storyboard in their class and had moved in the ICT suite to put their stories on the computer. A group of boys, including two with literacy difficulties, who were usually quiet during literacy activities, and one boy with ASD (Autistic Spectrum Disorder) were working around the screen to develop their story about Alan the Alien.

Ali: Alan should go there . . . just next to the spaceship! Look! This is where we drew him last week.

Tom:	No! He should stay there (pointing to the tree in the setting). He has already arrived on Earth and he is hiding behind the tree so the guards can't find him!
Dennis:	Just wait a minute! Let's see what Lee wants. What do you want, Lee?
Lee:	Alan goes there (he points to the spaceship).
Dennis:	Do you mean next to the spaceship?
Lee:	Yes! He is walking to the tree, but he must walk from the spaceship to the tree.
Dennis:	I think he is right. Then our audience will know that he has arrived from space.
Tom:	. . . but we only have 5 slides! Lee? Can't Alan go behind the tree and we can say that he has just arrived from space?
Lee:	I want to say it.
Ali:	Yeah! We can say that he has just landed. (Ali pretends he is holding a spaceship that is about to land and makes the sound of the spaceship engine.)
Dennis:	Yeah! Let's do that!

While from an initial look it may seem that Dennis dominates the group, it is obvious that he tries to support them and reach a consensus. He is aware of Lee not participating in the decision-making process and brings him in. By becoming the central person in the group he allows others to express their points of view and move on with their story. The multimedia set-up of the program supports the engagement of the group in developing their narrative. The discussion focuses on the position of a character on the screen, which may seem like a low-level cognitive activity. However, it entails creative skills as the children negotiate how they can use the features of the program to influence their story.

Drama activities can also be supported by ICT. The British Film Institute (*bfi*) encourages the use of video extracts (*bfi* 2001) in language and literacy while tapes can be used for the children to listen to stories or music and describe emotions, characters and settings.

Programmable toys such as Roamers, Pixies or Bee-Bobs can also be used to initiate collaborative tasks and imaginative scenarios.

Case Study 3

Children in a Year 2 class worked in ability groups to develop a cross-curricular activity themed 'A day in the life of a mini beast'. The children dressed up their Roamers and Bee-Bobs as their chosen mini beast, drew settings on A1 sheets of paper (the sky over a field full of flowers, a forest in spring) and programmed the toys to follow the journey of the mini beast. When they were ready, they presented their stories to the rest of the class. As they were getting ready for their presentations the teacher asked each group to prepare two questions to ask their classmates about the mini beasts' journeys. Throughout the activity the children had to work collaboratively to negotiate ideas and develop their stories. They had to decide as a group on the route that the mini beast would take, program the toys, edit and refine their decisions as they moved on. The teacher made sure that the children had clear rules for group work and the adults in the class had clear ideas of how to support the children. She went around listening to and helping individual groups when they needed some guidance. Before she moved on to the next group, she made sure that the children gained some understanding of how to move on with the task independently.

Technology also offers the possibility to simulate social situations that can be potentially dangerous or demanding for some children. Learning about road safety or social interaction can be presented in a video extract and discussed with the children in the safety of the classroom environment. The local community can also provide the stimulus and context for children's collaboration using ICT.

Case Study 4

A class of 33 Year 6 mixed ability pupils were studying the ICT unit 'Graphical Modelling'. They used 'paint' software to present a graphic floor plan layout of a new local library. The children worked in carefully chosen pairs with a bilingual teaching assistant supporting the lesson. The duration of the lesson in the ICT suite was one hour. The children were presented with an open-ended task with the learning objective: 'Design a new local library.'

Prior to the ICT session, the children were given around 30 minutes to draft designs on their own, after which these ideas were shared as a whole class. This ensured that the initial brainstorming and thinking process had been explored before working on the computer. Children often waste valuable ICT lesson time because their 'self-thinking' process has not been explored individually. As a result, active collaborative talk does not take place as the pairs are trying to formulate ideas for the task rather than discussing and comparing ideas. Preparation talk time is extremely valuable for generating the pace and quality of talk needed in the ICT suite. It also allows the less able and early bilingual children to feel more confident in sharing their ideas.

The children actively compared their draft paper plans in the ICT suite with their buddies. The pairs were required to collaboratively discuss and compare their designs, identifying the best design features of each plan. In order for this collaborative and exploratory talk to be effective, clear speaking and listening rules had already been established as part of the normal classroom routine one of which was: 'To offer positive criticism.'

In order to develop critical speaking skills, the children were provided with speaking frame structures:

I like the way you included . . . because . . .
But I think . . . in mine is better because . . .
Shall we consider using . . . from yours and . . . from mine?

These speaking structures ensured the talk was focused and helped to avoid possible disagreements of a negative nature. One ICT buddy pair worked particularly well where an able Gujarati-/ English-speaking child supported a less able Gujarati-speaking child. Key phrases and nouns were translated and explained by the more fluent child. It is vital that knowledge is not equated to thinking capacity as this leads to low expectations of early bilingual learners where often language is the only key barrier.

Through collaborative discussion the pairs created inspiring designs with a variety of interesting furniture features. The discussions were lively, yet the talk was clearly focused around the task; the use of ICT allowing the children to quickly make changes on the plan and explore alternative furniture layouts. One pair was asked by the teacher:

■ Why have you placed all the book shelves so close together?

■ How would visitors feel in that area?

■ What if you moved/re-organized certain shelves to other areas of the library?

■ What effect would this have?

Working 'in role' as designers provided the children with the elevated status of imagined real-life professionals. As a result, the talk generated was focused, constructive and the task provided opportunities for genuine collaboration.

Supporting teachers' practice in organising speaking and listening activities

ICT can support teachers in preparing whole-class activities that they can share on the interactive whiteboard which have become an integral part of the teaching and learning environment in many schools. A summary of research evidence by Becta (2003) emphasises that, compared to other ICT resources, interactive whiteboards present more opportunities for teachers and children to interact and discuss in the classroom.

A recent lesson with Year 3 children demonstrated how the teacher made effective use of the potential of the whiteboard software by incorporating the 'Hide and Reveal' feature. The teacher uploaded the painting 'Beach Scene' by Degas taken from the National Portrait Gallery (www.takeonepicture.com) on the whiteboard and began by disclosing a small segment of the painting. The children were asked to look at the image individually and hypothesise about what was going on and where the picture was set and then share their ideas within a group context, justifying their responses. The images of shivering children inspired the children to generate a narrative in which people were fleeing from a catastrophe such as a fire in the middle of the night. Different sections of the painting were then revealed on the whiteboard which required children to reshape their ideas and their interpretations of the image they were seeing. The gradual reveal of the images to the whole picture generated excitement and enthusiasm among the children and provided the focus for the discussion. The teacher's role was to support the children's language development by providing key words and phrases suggested by the picture. The activity provided opportunities for the children to do the following:

- interrogate their own understanding;
- generate ideas;
- explain and instruct;
- argue a personal point of view;
- reach a consensus.

ICT can be a very powerful means of influencing the kind of talk that goes on in the classroom, particularly the relationship between teacher and pupil talk. The Literacy Hour presented a very teacher-centred, didactic model of teaching where the teacher initiated discussion, children responded and received feedback on their answers. The interpretation of the word 'pace' often led to very short interchanges where sustained responses or initiatives from the children which detracted from the learning objectives were not encouraged. Work by Robin Alexander (2003) advocates an approach where children and teachers consider learning tasks in a more open and discursive way, an approach he calls 'dialogic teaching' (see Chapter 1).

When organising for ICT activities, the teachers can consider what opportunities they offer the pupils to develop effective dialogic relationships in the classroom. The dynamic relationships between the pupil and the technology need to be supported by the teacher who will be able to structure relevant activities and help pupils develop understanding and independence. This is particular important with some ICT applications. For instance, developing criteria in evaluating the content of websites and selecting relevant information are crucial skills that pupils need to develop in KS2.

Planning for communicative ICT activities

Research into speaking and listening (Cormack *et al.* 1998) emphasises the need for teachers to plan rigorously and provide structured opportunities for the effective teaching of talk. In so doing, it is vital to build on children's previous experience, both in terms of ICT and in speaking and listening. Figure 11.1 presents the stages that you can consider when organising an ICT activity.

Corden (2002) also discusses the importance of developing clearly structured teacher–pupil interaction in establishing successful computer-based talk. He summarizes findings from research literature on computers and group work that

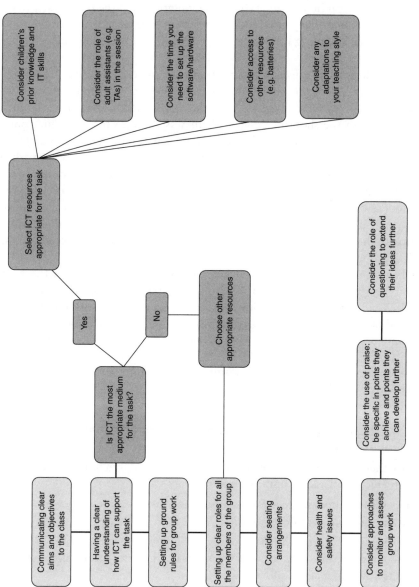

FIGURE 11.1 Organizing an ICT activity

were produced the early 1990s. These findings highlighted the importance of teacher interventions during the ICT activity. He comments that the task also needs to be based on clear aims, objectives and ground rules for group work, points that are still relevant in maintaining worthwhile ICT learning experiences. Furthermore, Ofsted (2002c) have identified that the most effective use of ICT is when there is a clear literacy focus (learning intention) and the ICT clearly matches the lesson objective. They also state that teachers have a tendency to 'spoon feed' children in terms of using ICT and do not allow them to develop independence in using ICT.

Another feature of effective group work and interaction using ICT involves setting up clear roles for the group. For instance, in the digital video project described at the opening of the chapter, the four children were clear about their contributions in the shooting: one of them was the director, the other one the camera person while the rest of the group were actors introducing the parts of the school. In another digital video project with a Year 6 class, the children worked in groups of 10: eight of them were involved in the shooting (director, camera person, two main characters and four extras) while the other two were evaluators following the film crew around and making notes on PC tablets of what went well and how they could improve the clip. When the group watched the clip, the evaluators fedback to them and as a group they decided whether there were scenes that they needed to film again.

When planning for an ICT activity, it is necessary to consider how the selected software can promote collaborative learning and provide appropriate contexts for speaking and listening. The following points are adapted from Wegerif's work (undated) and provide some starting points in making decisions about selecting a program:

- Does the software present meaningful challenges and problems for the children?
- Do these challenges provide a range of alternative choices for discussion?
- Does the software offer a clear purpose or task which is made evident to the group and kept in focus throughout?
- Are there on-screen prompts which remind the children to talk together, reach agreement and ask for opinions and reasons?
- Does it provide resources for discussion and opportunities to review decisions in the light of new information?
- Does it have features which encourage children to take turns, beat the clock or encourage competitive ways of working which detract from effective collaborative learning and exploratory talk?

Organising an ICT activity also involves considering the learning space and how this contributes to the development of the task. You will need to be aware of the school's policy of computer use along with health and safety issues related to the use of computers and other digital devices. You will need to take into account how assistive technology that some of the children need to use will be supported during the activity. You can involve the teaching assistants, who may be with you in the class, of how you would like them to help the children during the activity.

Table 11.2 suggests some final points that can be considered when planning for an ICT activity.

TABLE 11.2 Considerations for planning ICT

ICT CONSIDERATIONS	SPEAKING AND LISTENING CONSIDERATIONS
■ Will the children be able to work independently or will they need the support of an adult throughout? ■ What limitations for group work does the classroom/ICT suite present and how can you overcome them? ■ What is the children's prior knowledge of the activity and what are their IT skills? ■ Can the activity be differentiated for different abilities? Can it engage and motivate all children (taking into consideration cultural, gender differences)? ■ How are we going to monitor the development of the work? ■ What is the role of the Teaching Assistant or other adults who will be in the classroom?	■ What kind of talk does this activity facilitate? ■ What contexts will the children be working in (pairs/groups)? ■ How will the groups be organized? Who will choose? ■ Have children had the opportunity to work in groups before? ■ Are ground rules for group discussion and interaction needed? ■ What shared metalanguage will be needed? ■ How are we going to measure success?

Some final reflections

The chapter has discussed how ICT can support a range of speaking and listening activities and has considered examples of classroom practice. The importance of addressing the pedagogical aims and appropriateness of technology as starting points for speaking and listening activities has been emphasised. Speaking and listening have been explored within the broader framework of communication which is particularly relevant within the current context where the primary curriculum and the role of ICT within oracy and literacy are being debated. One response suggests that 'a more holistic approach to teaching [is necessary] which integrates speaking and listening with the use of new technologies'. This chapter has identified successful areas of current practice and a clear rationale for developing ICT within language and literacy teaching.

Bibliography

Abbott, C. (2002) 'Making the Internet special,' in C. Abbott (ed.) *Special Educational Needs and the Internet*, London: RoutledgeFalmer.

Alexander, R. *et al.* (2009) *Children, their World, their Education: Final Report and Recommendations of the Cambridge Primary Review*, Abingdon: Routledge.

Bearne, E. (n.d.) 'Texts and technologies'. Available at: http://www.qca.org.uk/11782_11909.html.

Becta (2003a) *What the research says about digital video in teaching and learning*. Coventry: Becta. Available at: [http://www.becta.org.uk/research/research.cfm?section=1&id=546].

Becta (2003b) *Entitlement to ICT in Primary English*. Available at: http://www.ictadvice.org.uk/.

Birmingham, P. and Davies, C. (2001) 'Storyboarding Shakespeare: learners' interactions with storyboard software in the process of understanding difficult literacy texts', *Journal of Information Technology for Teacher Education*, 10(3): 241–53.

Corden, R. (2002) 'Learning through talk', in T. Grainger (ed.) (2004) *The RoutledgeFalmer Reader in Language and Literacy*, London: RoutledgeFalmer.

Cormack, P. and Wignall, P. (1998) *Classroom Discourse Project*. Available at: http://www.griffithedu.au/schools/cls/clearinghouse/1998_classroom/cal.pdf.

DCFS (2009) *Independent Review of the Primary Curriculum*. Available at: http://publications.education.gov.uk/eOrderingDownload/Primary_curriculum-report.pdf (accessed September 2010).

DfES (2003) *Every Child Matters Green Paper*. Available at: http://www.dfes.gov.uk/everychildmatters.

Dimitriadi, Y. and Hodson, P. (2004) *Digital Video and Bilingual Children with Special Educational Needs: Supporting Literacy Activities*. Available at: http://www.becta.org.uk/research/reports/digitalvideo/.

Dugdale, G. (2009) *NLT Response to the Final Report of the Cambridge Primary Review*, Literacy Trust. Available at: http://www.literacytrust.org.uk/policy/nlt_policy/803_cambridge_primary_review (accessed October 2010).

Hennessey, S. *et al.* (2003) *Pedagogic Strategies for Using ICT to Support Subject Teaching and Learning: An Analysis across 15 Case Studies*. University of Cambridge Faculty of Education, Research Report no. 03/1.

Higgins, S. and Moseley, D. (2002) 'Raising achievement in literacy through ICT', in M. Monteith (ed.) *Teaching Primary Literacy with ICT*, Maidenhead: Open University Press.

Livingstone, S. and Bober, M. (2004) *UK Children Go Online: Surveying the Experiences of Young People and their Parents*, London: Department of Media and Communications, The London School of Economics and Political Science.

Marsh, J. and Singleton, C. (2009) 'Literacy and technology: questions of relationship', *Journal of Research in Reading*, 32(1): 1–5.

Mercer, N. and Wegerif, R. (1998) 'Is "exploratory talk" productive talk?' in K. Littleton and P. Light (eds), *Learning with Computers: Analysing Productive Interaction*. New York: Routledge.

Prensky, M. (2001) *On the Horizon*. Lincoln: NCB University Press, vol. 9, no. 5.

Reid, M. *et al.* (2002) *Evaluation of the Becta Digital Video Pilot Project*, Coventry: Becta.

Rudd, A. and Tyldesley, A. (2006) *Literacy and ICT in the Primary School: A Creative Approach to English*, London: David Fulton.

Theodosakis, N. (2002) *How Digital Filmmaking Develops Higher-Order Thinking Skills*. VSTE. Available at: http://www.vste.org.uk.

UKLA (2005) *Response to QCA's English 21 Initiative*. Available at: http://www.ukla.org/site/publications/papers/7.php.

Virtual Teacher Centre (2003) *ICT and the English Curriculum*. Available at: http://vtc.ngfl.gov.uk/docserver.php?temid=84.

Index